Evil and International Relations

Also by Renée Jeffery

Hugo Grotius in International Thought (Palgrave, 2006).

Evil and International Relations
Human Suffering in an Age of Terror

Renée Jeffery

EVIL AND INTERNATIONAL RELATIONS
Copyright © Renée Jeffery, 2008.

First published in 2008 by
PALGRAVE MACMILLAN™
175 Fifth Avenue, New York, N.Y. 10010 and
Houndmills, Basingstoke, Hampshire, England RG21 6XS.
Companies and representatives throughout the world.

PALGRAVE MACMILLAN is the global academic imprint of the Palgrave Macmillan division of St. Martin's Press, LLC and of Palgrave Macmillan Ltd. Macmillan® is a registered trademark in the United States, United Kingdom and other countries. Palgrave is a registered trademark in the European Union and other countries.

ISBN-10: 1-4039-7734-8
ISBN-13: 978-1-4039-7734-2

Library of Congress Cataloging-in-Publication Data is available from the Library of Congress.

A catalogue record of the book is available from the British Library.

Design by Scribe Inc.

First edition: January 2008

10 9 8 7 6 5 4 3 2 1

Contents

Acknowledgments

In writing this book, I have incurred many debts. Financially, I am particularly grateful to the School of Social Sciences at La Trobe University, where I held my first lectureship, and in particular, the then head of school, David de Vaus, for providing me with a generous research and travel grant to uphold a number of research and conference commitments I had made before joining the Politics Program there. I am similarly grateful for the Faculty of Arts grant I received in the same year that allowed me to present aspects of this work at the World International Studies Conference in Istanbul in August 2005.

During my time at La Trobe, I also benefited greatly from the support offered by many of my colleagues, including Judith Brett, Gwenda Tavan, and Tom Weber. Parts of this work were presented at the La Trobe University Politics Research Seminar, which provided me with an excellent opportunity to gain much-needed feedback on the central arguments of the work. In particular, I would like to thank Dennis Altmann, Judith Brett, and Tony Jarvis for their insightful comments and for their conversations on the subject that followed. Parts of Chapters 1 and 2 were also presented as "Confronting Evil in International Relations: Responding Ethically to Problems of Moral Agency" at the World International Studies Conference in Istanbul, August 24–27, 2005. On that and other occasions, I have greatly appreciated comments, questions, and constructive criticisms from Kirsten Ainley, Chris Brown, Stephanie Carvin, Ian Hall, Kimberly Hutchings, Tony Lang, and Nick Rengger. I would particularly like to thank Tony Lang for wading through the manuscript of this work on more than one occasion and for providing his customary polite and encouraging, yet testing, commentary. Of course, it goes without saying that the mistakes that undoubtedly appear in the work are mine alone.

In many ways, this book grew out of a number of articles that I published on the subject of evil in international, religious, and social thought in 2005. The first, coauthored with Nicholas Rengger—"Screwtape's

Return? Debating Gordon Graham's *Evil and Christian Ethics*," *Conversations in Religion and Theology* 3 (2005): 24–37—followed a hearty discussion of Graham's work, attended by the author himself, in St. Andrews in 2004. I would particularly like to thank Gordon Graham for engaging in such a lively discussion of his work, and for the comments and criticisms he made of our assessment of it both privately and on the pages of *Conversations in Religion and Theology*. Some of the general themes covered in this work were also addressed in an article also written with Nicholas Rengger for a special issue of the *SAIS Review of International Affairs*: "Moral Evil and International Relations: Old Concepts, New Challenges?" in "Villains and Villainy," special issue, *SAIS Review of International Affairs* 25 (2005): 3–16. Finally, I have also previously addressed some of the works discussed in Chapter 5 of this work in "Beyond Banality? Ethical Responses to Evil in Post–September 11 International Relations," *International Affairs* 81, no. 4 (2005): 175–86.

As always, however, the person who deserves the greatest thanks from me is Ian Hall. As a colleague, friend, and partner, Ian has continued to be an unending source of support and encouragement throughout the production of this work. Our never-ending discussions of the central issues raised by the work challenged, extended, and inspired me, forcing me to reconsider key assumptions present in my argument and, ultimately, to write a better book. Thanks also to Ian, along with Eddy and Paddy, for doing their very best to keep me as calm as possible during the final months of finishing this book.

1

Understanding Evil

> It is one thing to identify evils and quite another to understand or explain what we are saying when we pronounce a thing "evil." Few of us have any hesitation in judging things evil, but most of us find it surprisingly difficult to explain what we are doing when we make and support such judgements.[1]

On July 7, 2005, the world watched in stunned horror as four bombs rocked central London. In the hours and days that followed, world leaders, politicians and other dignitaries roundly condemned the acts in what have now become familiar terms. In his initial statement from the G8 Summit at Gleneagles, British Prime Minister Tony Blair called the bombing "barbaric," concluding at the Labor Party Conference nine days later that the attacks were driven by an "evil ideology."[2] In his response, President of the United States, George W. Bush, also speaking from Gleneagles, vowed that "those who have such evil in their heart" will not succeed in achieving their aims, while the leader of the British Conservative Party, Michael Howard, spoke of the "evil acts" that had taken place, adding that "these evil people will not have their way."[3] In the condolence book opened by the British High Commission in Canberra, Australian Prime Minister John Howard wrote in similar terms that "Evil deeds will never cower a free people."[4] "Evil," it seems, was once again at the forefront of the international political agenda.

Of course, the London attacks were not an isolated incident but rather represented one in a long list of events that have, in recent years garnered the title of "evil." Foremost among these incidents stand the Rwandan genocide,[5] the massacre at Srebrenica,[6] and the Beslan school siege, which, for its abhorrent treatment of the children held captive, seemed to take on a particularly heinous character.[7] More obviously, however, the characterization of the London attacks as "evil" came in the aftermath of the September 11, 2001, attacks on the World Trade Center in New York, the Pentagon in Washington D.C., and "Flight 93," which crashed in Pennsylvania having failed to reach its intended target, acts that President Bush almost immediately branded as "evil." In his address to the nation on the evening of September 11, Bush declared, "Today our nation saw evil, the very worst of human nature."[8] Just three days after the catastrophic events he repeated this sentiment when he told mourners at the National Cathedral, "Our responsibility to history is already clear: to answer these attacks and rid the world of evil."[9] In the months and years that have followed, President Bush has referred to evil on literally hundreds of occasions, most famously identifying an "Axis of Evil" in his 2002 State of the Union address.[10] As recently as his 2007 State of the Union speech, Bush continued to warn the American people that "the evil that inspired and rejoiced in 9/11 is still at work in the world," and added that among his government's "good purposes" is the duty "to guard America against all evil."[11]

Although President Bush may be credited with inspiring the latest resurgence of interest in "evil," the designation of adversaries, both individual and state, along with their actions, as "evil" has not been his exclusive preserve. Rather, a range of actors in the international sphere have been drawn to the term in recent years. Echoing widespread public sentiment, in 2000 the Report of the Panel on United Nations Peace Operations, the Brahimi Report, described the genocide perpetrated in Rwanda as an "obvious evil" the international community had failed to oppose.[12] More prominently, in his address to the General Assembly on Terrorism on October 1, 2001, the United Nations secretary general, Kofi Annan, followed President Bush's lead when he described the "terrorist attacks against the United States" as "acts of terrible evil which shocked the conscience of the entire world."[13] Similarly, on the first anniversary of the 9/11 attacks, the President of the General Assembly argued, "In our fight we must see terrorism for what it is—a global evil filled with hatred and extremism, an evil which threatens the common values and principles, as well as the diversity, of the entire civilised world."[14] Sometimes questionably, "evil" discourse has also been extended at the UN to include racism,[15] nuclear weapons,[16] rape in war,[17] HIV/AIDS,[18] cybercrime,[19] and even money laundering.[20] In the world of international criminal law, "evil" has even been used of late to add moral impetus to technical legal arguments. Thus, in the case of the Serbian general Radislav Krstic at the International Criminal Tribunal for the Former Yugoslavia (ICTY), the Judgement of the Trial Chamber did not hesitate to describe the execution of Bosnian Muslim men by Krstic's forces at Srebrenica as "an unspeakable evil."[21]

That a range of international actors from world leaders to international judges and the United Nations itself are drawn to the term "evil," is testimony to both its continued potency and the importance of understanding precisely what "evil" actually entails in the international realm. Indeed, despite this most recent resurgence of interest in the concept of "evil," exactly what it means is not well understood. As Richard Bernstein notes, far from elucidating the concept, the "all too familiar popular rhetoric of 'evil'" that emerges at "critical moments" such as September 11, actually serves to obscure and block serious discussion of what the term means.[22] In none of the instances discussed above is the meaning of "evil" made explicit: the judge of the ICTY simply used the term to provide moral force for what continued as an exclusively legal argument about the criminality of Krstic's actions in international law; the Brahimi Report seems to simply equate evil with genocide; President Bush fluctuates between using "evil" as an adjective to describe the actions of individuals, states, or other groups, and as a noun that signifies a "*thing*, or a force, something that has a real existence" in the world;[23] and precisely what the "evil ideology," of which Prime Minister Blair has spoken, actually entails has never been made explicit.

In contemporary discourse, evil is thus a phenomenon more commonly characterized than defined, and more often couched in ambiguity than clarity. As the discussion above illustrates, statesmen and practitioners use the term in a manifold number of ways to describe individuals, states, groups, and even supernatural forces, along with a range of activities including terrorism, genocide, and crimes against humanity. Little consensus exists as to what "evil" entails, how it is manifested, and, following from this, what we ought to do about it. What is more, with few exceptions, in much of the academic study of international politics the meaning of "evil," despite its current popularity, remains extremely vague.[24] This work therefore aims, at its most fundamental level, to remedy that situation.

The End of Evil?

In response to both the frequency with which "evil" is used and the apparent ambiguity that surrounds its meaning in contemporary

discourse, many writers have, in recent years, called for scholars and public figures alike to cease using the term altogether. In general terms, "evil"
is criticized for "obscur[ing] the moral complexity and ambiguity"
of international affairs, for simplifying multifaceted decision-making
processes and for "prevent[ing] us from making sound rational and
moral deliberations and judgements."[25] To brand an individual or an
action as "evil" is too easy; resorting to the most extreme form of moral
condemnation not only amounts to an assertion of victory before
rational and considered debate has been had, but it automatically
places those opposed to evil in a morally ascendant position. As Richard
Bernstein argues, this actually "represents an *abuse* of evil" for, rather
than challenging established notions of morality and immorality, it is
"used to stifle *thinking*."[26] As we will see in Chapter 7, by suppressing
meaningful debate and circumventing conventional decision-making
processes, certain Western liberal democracies have enabled themselves
to pursue all manner of actions in response to "evil" while remaining
oblivious to the possible evil they themselves may commit in doing so.
For this reason, international lawyers such as Stephen Toope and Jutta
Brunnée maintain that "evil is too loose a term with which to guide policy on the use of force in international relations."[27] Unsurprisingly, they
call for a reassertion of international law as the instrument according to
which atrocious acts are identified and responses to them justified.[28]

For a second group of thinkers, Inga Clendinnen among them, the
term "evil" ought to be abandoned on the grounds that it is "of no use
whatsoever when it comes to teasing out why people act as they do."[29]
Focusing on the atrocities of the Holocaust, Clendinnen has criticized the
representation of the Final Solution in terms of an "amorality beyond all
categories of evil" offered by writers such as Saul Friedländer, for failing
to help us understand what motivated its perpetrators.[30] Clendinnen is
not alone in this sentiment, Thomas W. Simon writes—with regard to
the specific evil of genocide—that philosophers, and presumably other
thinkers, "should discard the notion of evil since it seldom advances and
often hinders an understanding of genocide."[31] Simon even goes so far as
to make the somewhat exaggerated claim that "the commonplace appeal
to the idea of evil" is the "real villain" when attempting to discuss incidents such as genocide.[32] However, the continued popularity of "evil,"
particularly when used with reference to genocide, seems to indicate that
the term retains some meaning when used in these contexts to refer to the
most extreme humanitarian atrocities. That is, the fact that such acts

remain described as evil, rather than mere "crimes," "crimes against humanity," or "genocide," under international law seems to suggest that "evil" does have some utility in describing the very worst acts that confront the contemporary world.

The third and most significant reason often proffered for the abandonment of the idea of evil refers to the problem of its religious connotations. As Peter Dews explains, although Western thinkers are often drawn to describe events such as those that took place at Auschwitz or on September 11 as "evil," they are, at the same time, generally uncomfortable with the term's religious connotations. "In the disenchanted and predominantly secularized West," he writes, "the religious assumptions—however implicit—that gave the notion of evil its place in our thinking about the world, as the violation of a divinely sanctioned order, are no longer shared by the majority of people."[33] Indeed, for many contemporary thinkers, the theological underpinnings of evil are simply unpalatable. As Gil Bailie writes, "the very word *evil* seems to stick in the throat of most of our rationalist commentators. Like the even more suspect word *sin*, it seems to [harken] back to a benighted age of superstition."[34] This sense of unease is echoed more generally in the academic study of international relations, a field of study marked by what Scott Thomas has described as an "ideological reticence" to consider religious or theologically-derived thought.[35] Despite the pervasiveness of religion in international affairs, International Relations as a field remains reluctant to acknowledge the impact of religious ideas not simply on the world but on the concepts we use to understand it.[36] However, as I have argued at greater length elsewhere and as others, including Thomas, have made patently clear, the marginalization of religion from international political thought is an inherently anachronistic exercise.[37] Not only does religion remain an important element of the social world, but religious ideas have directed and continue to inform many concepts central to the way in which the world is understood. Taking Thomas's assessment one step further however, it seems that what has actually gripped the field is not simply a failure to consider religion in general, but a particular reluctance to address the specific place of Judeo-Christian thought within it. Thus, while works considering the role of Islam and other non-Western religions proliferate in contemporary scholarship, the consideration of Christian and Jewish theology, despite its central role in the history of Western political thought, is often deemed to reside outside the bounds of acceptable scholarship.

The "problem of evil" in international relations thus poses a particularly pointed problem for contemporary scholarship. Although it often sports a secular façade, evil is a concept that stands on fundamentally religious foundations. Yet, despite its theological underpinnings, in practical terms the "problem of evil" is one that affects believers and non-believers alike. As Richard Bernstein writes in his recent contribution, *The Abuse of Evil*: "It would be a serious mistake to think that the "problem of evil" is exclusively a religious problem. Secular thinkers have raised similar questions. They too want to know how to make sense of a world in which evil seems to be so intractable."[38] Evil is, indeed, a problem in both the secular and religious worlds and, in the Western tradition at least, its secular and religious variants share many facets of a common history, a predominantly Judeo-Christian one.

Writers at opposite extremes of the religious/secular divide approach the inherent dilemma of "evil" from understandably contradictory perspectives. Presenting a wholly secular view of "evil," John Kekes's *Facing Evil* argues that resorting to a Christian, or for that matter any other religious understanding of evil is "one way of succumbing to false hope."[39] For Kekes, a far more satisfactory treatment of evil conceives it as a problem that:

> arises for contemporary Western heirs of the Enlightenment, people whose sensibility is formed, negatively, by the rejection of all forms of supernaturalism and, positively, by the combined beliefs that whatever exists or happens is natural, that the best approach to understanding their causes is scientific, that while human beings are part of the natural world, we still have some control over our lives, and that one chief purpose for exercising the control we have is to make good lives for ourselves.[40]

The "secular problem of evil" can thus be summed up in the observation that "our aspirations to live good lives are vulnerable to evil." For Kekes, notions of evil must therefore be situated within an understanding of "tragedy," for it is tragedy that "compels us to face evil by forcefully reminding us that these conditions exist."[41] Christianity, along with Hegelian and Socratic ideals and most non-Christian religions, he argues, brings with it false hope by failing to confront evil head-on.[42]

At the other end of the spectrum, Reinhold Niebuhr argued in his 1939 Gifford Lectures that "only within terms of the Christian faith can man not only understand the reality of the evil in himself, but escape the error of attributing that evil to any one but himself."[43] More recently, John Haldane's *An Intelligent Person's Guide to Religion* proclaimed, "while the atheist can either deny the existence of evil or merely record the fact of it, only the theist can provide an explanation and an answer to it."[44] This is a view with which Gordon Graham, author of *Evil and Christian Ethics*, certainly concurs. Graham presents an overtly theistic account of evil that is, at least in part, written in direct response to Kekes's claim that a Christian understanding of evil brings with it a false sense of hope. As Graham writes in the preface to the work, he aims not simply to deny Kekes's claim or to present a different point of view, but to "*refute* it."[45] Indeed, for Graham, Kekes's notion of "our modern sensibility," with its related humanism and naturalism, is unable to deal satisfactorily with the fact that the problem of evil poses a significant challenge to moral endeavor.[46] Contrary to Kekes's humanist explanation, Graham argues, "without God, and theologically interpreted conceptions of good and evil (some of them pre-modern), what we call moral endeavour is fruitless."[47] For Graham, it is therefore not simply the case that the concept of evil makes no sense outside a general Christian framework, but that it cannot be made intelligible outside the context of the specific theological persuasion to which he adheres, a theology complete with angels, war in heaven, and the "crafts and assaults of the Devil."

However, a number of significant problems are associated with both wholly secular and overtly theistic accounts of evil in international relations. In the first instance, it appears a somewhat anachronistic conceit to suggest that a concept bearing so rich a history in theological thought can be presented in absolutely secular terms. Indeed, it is one thing to make the undoubtedly correct observation that the problem of evil is not exclusively a theological problem but one that confronts the secular world with equal force, and quite another to deny, or at the very least marginalize, its lengthy intellectual history in religious thought. At the same time however, although Graham's understanding of "evil" appeals to certain sectors of the international public, it does not resonate more generally in international thought about evil and is thus, although perhaps unfairly, readily dismissed as peculiar and arcane. As we will see as this work unfolds, among the most prominent features of the intellectual history of "evil" is indeed an ongoing tension between the religious and secular elements of its conceptualization.

Approaching "Evil" in International Thought

With these issues in mind, this work seeks to ascertain what is meant by "evil" when it is used to describe entities and events in the international realm, in both historical and contemporary Western secular and religious thought.[48] In doing so, it undertakes two main tasks. First, it traces the history of the idea of evil from the ancient Babylonians to the present. Although it does not claim to constitute a comprehensive account of the concept's intellectual heritage, it does seek to provide an overview of its development that, along the way, highlights particular themes that have remained significant to its conceptualization: ongoing tension between theistic and secular understandings of evil, disagreement over the nature and sources of evil, and debates about human responsibility for evil actions. As such, the focus of the work is on the major players, representatives, if you like, of the major themes, shifts, and tensions that have marked the history of the idea of evil. In the premodern period the focus is thus on Augustine to the detriment of Irenaeus, in the modern period the focus is on Rousseau and Kant, but not Hegel or Marx and, in the twentieth century, Arendt is discussed at length while Freud, Adorno, and Ricoeur are only mentioned in passing.[49]

The second half of the work investigates two of the most prominent instances in twentieth and twenty-first century history in which the term "evil" has been employed to refer to humanitarian atrocities; the Holocaust, and the terrorist attacks of September 11 and following. This is not to say that other evils have not occurred in the twentieth century or that other events have not been described as "evil." The bombing of Hiroshima and Nagasaki, atrocities committed during the Vietnam War—epitomized by the My Lai massacre—the Cambodian genocide, waves of famine that have swept sub-Saharan Africa since the 1970s, and the genocides and ethnic cleansings of the 1990s—in particular the Rwandan genocide and massacre at Srebrenica—all warrant being labeled "evil" on account of the abject undeserved suffering they have inflicted upon their victims. Rather, the two instances chosen represent the dominant historical moments in which "evil" has risen to the forefront of international political thought in the twentieth and twenty-first centuries and, as such, provide fertile ground for considering precisely what the meaning of the term "evil" actually is.

Discussing evil in this manner is, however, a surprisingly contentious enterprise. While a willingness to address the problems of evil and suffering in the world is generally met with applause, doing so in a strictly intellectual manner is not. Indeed, in many facets of theological and philosophical scholarship, discussions of evil and the suffering it brings are divided into two distinct, yet related, problems; the first "empirical" problem is "encountered in the 'real' world of blood, sweat and tears," while the second "theoretical" problem is "considered from the relatively more comfortable perspective of the ivory tower."[50] In this vein, proponents of the first empirical approach criticize works such as C. S. Lewis's *The Problem of Pain,* thought to belong to the second approach, for failing to provide comfort to those who are actually suffering.[51] For example, in his popular work *Where Is God When It Hurts?* Philip Yancey argues against the intellectualization of suffering that "most of our problems with pain are not mental gymnastics."[52] Similarly, Jennifer Geddes divides the study of evil into its theoretical and empirical forms. The "theoretical approach," she writes, "explores important questions about the ways in which we think, judge and understand the world around us" but at times it becomes "so abstract" that it appears "to have very little to do with the real suffering of those who are the victims of evil."[53] When considered in theoretical terms, evil therefore "becomes a problem for thought, rather than a problem of lived experience."[54] Alternatively, while the empirical study of evil "draws our attention to particular evils that occur in the world around us, it sometimes does so with an underdeveloped understanding of what it means to call something evil."[55] Geddes attempts to overcome these problems by "bringing together the concrete and the theoretical" by addressing "some of the conceptual and theoretical issues associated with evil in the context of particular, historical, empirical situations."[56]

Diverging slightly from Geddes, this work begins from the premise that it is unnecessary to distinguish between practical and intellectual considerations of evil; plainly, the problem of evil in the world is both a practical and an intellectual one. That this is the case is demonstrated most forcefully by the wealth of theoretical accounts of evil and human suffering composed by survivors of the Holocaust and their descendants. Such scholarship, as we will see in Chapter 2, is not driven by pure intellectual curiosity, but by the survivors' need to understand, comprehend, and give meaning to their own experiences of extreme suffering. In philosophical and historical terms, the distinction between ideas about evil and the "real world" of evil is something of an anomaly. Events in the "real world" are gone; they are not "out there" waiting to be "discovered" in the past, we have no direct access to them, and thus no means of studying them as events. What we do have are ideas about past events that, having been preserved, continue to exist in the present.[57] For this reason, when we claim to study historical events, however recent the history, what we are actually concerned with are *ideas about events*. This is, admittedly, a radically ideational approach to the philosophy of history but one that allows us to consider ideas about evil and suffering that have emerged in both the context of "real life" incidents and intellectual challenges. It is also an approach to the history of ideas that is compatible with the claim that the language used to represent events and the events themselves are mutually constitutive.

Contrary to more popular understandings of its function, language is not simply "*about* objects and experiences" but is itself "*constitutive* of objects and experience."[58] Language therefore "not only describes events but is itself 'a part of events, shaping their meaning and helping to shape the political roles officials and the general public play. In this sense, language, events, and self-conceptions are part of the same transaction, mutually determining one another's meanings.'"[59] This is, of course, a distinctly Gadamerian position. As Shapiro writes, "for hermeneuticists," such as Hans Georg Gadamer, language is "treated as an expression of human existence rather than a symbolic structure that is external to existence and is to be used to represent or stand in place of things."[60] Language is thus, as Gadamer wrote, "the fundamental mode of operation of our being-in-the-world and the all-embracing form of the constitution of the world."[61] It is not, he argues, "simply an instrument, a tool," but is constitutive of all knowledge, both of ourselves and of the world.[62]

There are two main implications of this that are of importance for this work. The first follows the previous discussion of the relationship between intellectual and "real" understandings of evil and contends that the language of evil and actual instances of evil are mutually constitutive. The second implication of Gadamer's hermeneutical approach is that we must recognize that, as a mutually constitutive element of evil itself, the particular way in which the language of evil is used in any given situation stands at the center of the negotiation of its meaning. That is, simply saying that a particular event was described as "evil" does not tell us what "evil" actually means. In large part this is due to the fact that very often language does not have a stable meaning. As Fred Weinstein writes:

> [Language] does not have the fixity or stability of meaning implied by the dictionary definitions of the words that comprise it. The crucial feature of

language is that meaning is not fixed—it is emergent—tied to specific situations and constantly changing. The meaning of language is really no more stable than the particular situations it may be used to describe.[63]

As we will see as this work unfolds, the term "evil" certainly does not display any sort of permanence or fixity of meaning; it is, and has been, used to signify and describe a wide range of disparate actors, actions, and events. What this means is that in order to ascertain what "evil" actually means, we must engage in an interpretive exercise that considers both actual instances of evil and the language and ideas used to describe them that together give them meaning.

With this in mind, Chapter 2 identifies the attempt to make otherwise meaningless suffering comprehensible as the common feature that has traditionally united almost all understandings of evil. It doing so, it provides a brief outline of a range of different notions of evil before exploring the two most prominent obstacles that generally stand in the way of attempts to arrive at a solid understanding of the term—the sense of mystery that surrounds the most heinous humanitarian atrocities, and concerns about whether or not instances of extreme suffering can ever be fully comprehended or made intelligible. In doing so, the chapter argues that although the very nature of evil often has indelibly mysterious elements, we can, nevertheless, go some way in attempting to understand it. This understanding is to be found, it is argued, in the relationships between pain and suffering and, in particular, suffering and evil that have traditionally marked the concept. Chapter 3 then introduces the so-called "problem of evil," the theological problem of how to reconcile the existence of evil, understood in terms of suffering, with the supposed existence of an all-knowing, all-powerful, all-good God. This chapter charts various historical attempts to answer the question "why do I suffer?" by reference not only to the concept of evil, but to the assumed nature of God, the figure of Satan, and the notion that malevolent forces are at play in the cosmos.

Deviating slightly from conventional treatments of the exclusively theological problem, Chapter 4 follows the work of Susan Neiman and argues that the modern "problem of evil" is better conceived as two distinct, yet interrelated problems: the traditional theological or cosmological problem introduced in Chapter 3 and the more secular problem of why human beings knowingly commit evil acts. Focusing on the discussion of evil in eighteenth-century thought, this chapter therefore outlines the move from theological to moral, or philosophical, explanations of evil that took place in the aftermath of the Lisbon earthquake and the advances of the Enlightenment. With this, the dominant modern understanding of evil, conceived exclusively in terms of the human moral agent, is introduced.

In Chapter 5 the focus turns to understandings of evil that emerged in response to the atrocities of the Holocaust. In particular, the chapter examines the continuing shift that took place in thought about evil to the "moral" problem introduced in Chapter 4, and catalogs the range of problems derived from the direct association of evil with human moral agency that emerged beginning with the Nuremberg Trial. Chapter 6 continues in this vein and focuses, in particular, on Hannah Arendt's understandings of evil in *The Origins of Totalitarianism* and *Eichmann in Jerusalem* and on the implications of her "banality of evil" thesis for subsequent thought. Considered together, Chapters 5 and 6 bring into serious question the modern, agent-centered understanding of evil that dominated political and social thought from the late eighteenth century onwards.

Finally, Chapter 7 turns to the use of "evil" in contemporary international scholarship and rhetoric. Focusing on the speeches of George W. Bush and the so-called "war on evil," it seeks to uncover the foundations of the U.S. president's understanding of evil. In particular, it catalogs the range of different ways in which Bush uses the term in public discourse and seeks to account for its popularity among large sectors of the American public. The chapter concludes that, at the beginning of the twenty-first century, what the world has been witnessing is not simply a return to older, premodern, religious understandings of evil, but a shift away from its traditional association with the meaning of human suffering. Thus, evil has at once ceased to be the means by which the otherwise meaningless suffering that regularly blights the human population is comprehended and given some sort of meaning, and become a sort of moral touchstone, a form of absolute condemnation that seeks to justify the foreign policy objectives of states, such as the United States, and to a lesser extent, Britain. Here, it is argued, lies the greatest problem of evil.

2

The Meaning of Suffering

I've spoken with death
and so
I know
the futility of things we learn
a discovery I made at the cost
of a suffering so intense
I keep on wondering
whether it was worth it.[1]

The concept of "evil" is marked by an intriguing paradox. On the one hand, it is a source of human fascination, its appeal commonly derived from the fact that it is associated with the "forbidden . . . the exotic, the surreal, and the extraordinary."[2] That is, evil is couched in mystery. Understood in this sense, it is often connected to witchcraft, defilement, and even physical deformity, and appeals to what Simone Weil described as our sense of "imaginary evil," the "romantic and varied" evil of myths and fairytales.[3] On the other hand however, what Weil terms "real evil," is "gloomy, monotonous, barren, boring."[4] It is evil that we are quick to identify—as the plethora of evils identified in Chapter 1 would seem to suggest—but reluctant to confront in its stark reality. The paradox at play here is, of course, the fact that in many instances "imaginary evil" and "real evil" are actually one and the same; that is, the line separating reality from fantasy is an extremely blurry one. As Raimond Gaita explains, many "real" events commonly conceived as evil, particularly those, that inspire extreme moral condemnation, such as the Holocaust, exhibit mysterious elements.[5] Thus, despite their very real, material nature and origins in human conduct, the very worst atrocities seem to include intangible, metaphysical features. Similarly, when Robert Manne characterizes the Holocaust as "a central event in human history," he argues that it was "a deed so evil that the centuries would not wash its mystery away," thereby drawing together a very "real" evil with the sense of mystery in which it is encased.[6] To address the problem of evil in this manner is, as Charlotte Delbo writes, *"expliquer l'inexplicable,"* "to explain the inexplicable."[7]

Given the sense of mystery that surrounds it and the manifold number of ways in which it is used, it is not surprising that evil is cited in W. B. Gallie's famous work, *Philosophy and Historical Understanding,* as an "essentially contested concept."[8] Evil is, as Frederick Sontag notes, "difficult, even elusive, to define simply, for [it] comes in so many forms."[9] In English, the word "evil" has Teutonic origins and is etymologically related to the "concepts of *too much, exceeding due measure,* [and] *over limits.*"[10] As David Pocock explains, when understood in this way, a connection can be identified between the root of "evil" and the sense of unruliness that often accompanies the designation of an act or actor as "evil."[11] That is, "evil" behavior is understood to reside outside the bounds of what is socially acceptable, to go beyond the limits of ordinary, rule-governed human interaction. However, in common usage "evil" often takes on a much simpler meaning and denotes the "antithesis of good in all of its principal senses."[12] In this sense, it may be said to exist in both weak and strong forms. In its weaker form, "evil" is conceived in terms of imperfection, the primordial defilement of that which is good or, more simply, as the corruption of good.[13] In its stronger sense however, "evil" is often equated with ultimate depravity, monstrousness, or demonic qualities. Thus, when an individual such as Hitler, an event such as the Holocaust, or an action such as the torture of a child is described as "evil," an extreme moral judgement is being made; that is, the individual, event, or action being described as "evil" is deemed to be "beyond bad." As David Pocock writes, to be "evil" in the strong sense of the word is to be barely human, to exist on the margins of human society.[14]

However, as David Parkin notes in the introduction to his anthropological study of evil, what unites the wide range of disparate understandings of "evil" is the fact that "suffering is *never* lacking" from its conceptualization. Suffering may, he continues, "be culturally defined," but is always present in some form or another.[15] That is, the idea of evil, in its range of secular and theistic forms has traditionally sought to make sense of human suffering, to make otherwise meaningless suffering intelligible. As we will see in Chapter 7, among the most serious problems associated with the contemporary use of the term evil is the extent to which it has become dissociated from the concept of suffering. With this in mind, this chapter explores the theoretical association of human suffering with the concept of evil. It argues that although the experience of suffering is central to our understanding of evil, suffering does not by itself create the problem of evil. Rather, the "problem of evil" emerges when we attempt to explain the meaning of what would otherwise be conceived as "meaningless suffering."

Confronting Suffering

Suffering, it seems, is in superabundant supply in international politics. A quick look at the evening news makes it patently clear that conflict, violence, poverty, and other forms of abuse and deprivation are everyday occurrences in the international realm. Yet although these types of events are the standard fodder for the study of international relations, the suffering associated with them has not been widely addressed. Indeed, despite a proliferation of works addressing subjects as distressing as the widespread and systematic abuse of human rights, genocide, crimes against humanity, torture, and, more recently, terrorism, philosophically oriented treatments of suffering are in short supply. There are a number of possible reasons for this.

The first reason is that questions of intelligibility and a perhaps misguided sense of "Holocaust piety" motivate some of our reluctance to confront the reality of suffering. So appalling were the atrocities committed, and so great their magnitude, that the evil of the Holocaust has, in many spheres, been rendered "unintelligible." As Susan Neiman writes, "like no other event in human history," the evil committed in the Nazi concentration camps "defies human capacities for understanding."[16] There are two main variants of this view in contemporary thought. The first, which Gillian Rose has termed "Holocaust piety," refuses to confront the atrocities of the Holocaust on the grounds that doing so will inevitably diminish the reality of the suffering experienced by its victims. In short, to attempt to make sense of the Holocaust would be an "impious" and disrespectful violation of those who experienced its horrors first hand.[17] The second variant of this view is more moderate in its sentiments and simply questions the extent to which absolute comprehension of the Holocaust can ever be achieved. In large part, it is derived from the testimonies of several prominent Holocaust survivors including Primo Levi, Jean Améry, and Jorge Semprun, who have all questioned their own ability to comprehend their experiences in the concentration camps. As Richard Bernstein notes, all three of these prominent figures have confessed that a disparity exists "between what they actually experienced and their persistent attempts to describe and understand it."[18] The argument would seem to follow that if survivors cannot fully comprehend their own experience, there is next to no chance that the rest of us will do any better.

Although highlighted with some force in the discourse about evil that followed it, arguments about the intelligibility of evil were not new phenomena of post-Holocaust thought. In her recent work, *Evil in Modern Thought*, Susan Neiman characterizes thought about evil from the Enlightenment to the present as being dominated by two contending views about its intelligibility. The first of these views, she writes, stretches from Jean-Jacques Rousseau to Hannah Arendt and "insists that morality demands that we make evil intelligible."[19] As Rousseau remarked, "to deny the existence of evil is a most convenient way of excusing the author of that evil."[20] Indeed, as Neiman writes elsewhere, "it was because of his solution to the problem of evil that Kant designated Rousseau as 'Newton of the mind.'"[21] The other view of evil, the view that stretches from Voltaire to Améry, "insists that morality demands that we" do not attempt to make it appear intelligible.[22] In this vein, Theodore Adorno famously wrote that "to write poetry after Auschwitz is barbaric,"[23] his "Meditations on Metaphysics" suggested on several occasions that "the very attempt to comprehend the evil of the Holocaust was close to an act of obscenity, a betrayal of the magnitude and horror of the victim's suffering."[24] Interestingly however, some years later, Adorno revised this claim and said: "I have no wish to soften the saying that to write lyric poetry after Auschwitz is barbaric ... but ... it is now virtually in art alone that suffering can still find its own voice, consolation, without immediately being betrayed by it."[25]

The division about which Neiman writes mirrors closely Primo Levi's description in *If This Is a Man* of Holocaust survivors as belonging to one of two categories. In Levi's assessment, one category of Holocaust survivors is comprised of those who refuse to discuss their experiences. These survivors, he wrote, would either "like to forget but do not succeed in doing so and are tormented by nightmares," or actually have forgotten, "have dismissed everything, and have begun again to live, starting from zero." Members of this category generally ended up "in the camps through bad lack, and not because of a political commitment." As such, although their "suffering was traumatic," it was generally "devoid of meaning." As we will see later in this chapter, this notion of meaningless suffering is central to understanding not just the "evil" of the Holocaust but its more general manifestations in international relations. The second category of Holocaust survivors, Levi wrote, are the "ex-political prisoners, or those who possessed at least a measure of political preparation, or religious conviction, or a strong moral consciousness. For these survivors, remembering is a duty."[26] However, the extent to which it is possible to do this in an accurate or comprehensive fashion is another matter entirely.

Indeed, Elie Wiesel has, on several occasions, sought to question the ability of the non-survivor to comprehend the evil of the Holocaust. "The truth of Auschwitz," he wrote, "remains hidden in its ashes. Only those who lived it in their flesh and in their minds can possibly transform their experience into knowledge." "Others," he concluded, "despite their best intentions, can never do so."[27] As Levi's discussion seems to suggest however, even many of those "who lived [the Holocaust] in their flesh and in their minds" recognize that it is not possible to quantify or even adequately express what they experienced. It seems that Wiesel shared this sentiment when he argued:

> Only those men and women who lived through the experience know what it was, and others—to my great distress—will ever know. Even if you were to see all the documentaries, listen to all the testimonies, visit all the camp sites and museums, read all the memoirs (and only the memoirs are important), you would still not enter the gates of that eternal night. Hence, here lies the tragedy in the survivor's mission. He must tell a tale that cannot be told, he must tell a story that cannot be communicated. We have no tools, we have no vehicles, we have no methodology. We don't even know where to begin. In this respect, to a certain degree, ironically the enemy's goal has been met. Because he pushed the crime to the limits and because we cannot reach those limits with our language, the full story of his crimes cannot be told.[28]

Crucially, however, this does not necessarily mean that we ought to cease thinking about the Holocaust. Indeed, contrary to the views expressed above, many Holocaust survivors maintain that despite the limitations inherent in doing so, we must at least attempt to understand what happened. Addressing this issue, although not as a concentration camp survivor herself, Hannah Arendt wrote:

> Comprehension does not mean denying the outrageous, deducing the unprecedented from precedents, or explaining phenomena by such analogies

and generalities that the impact of reality and the shock of experience are no longer felt. It means, rather, examining and bearing consciously the burden which our century has placed on us—neither denying its existence nor submitting meekly to its weight. Comprehension, in short, means the unpremeditated, attentive, facing up to, and resisting reality—whatever it may be.[29]

Indeed, there are good historiographical reasons for arguing that the Holocaust, along with other instances of evil, can, in fact, be comprehended, if within certain limits. As Inga Clendinnen writes, the claim that the Holocaust cannot be comprehended poses "a particular threat to historians," for to declare certain parts of the human record as "off-limits" is to bring the entire historical enterprise into question.[30]

Alternatively, in her 1977 work *On Photography*, Susan Sontag suggested that our widespread inability to respond to the reality of human suffering can be attributed to the fact that "our capacity to respond to our experiences with emotional freshness and ethical pertinence is being sapped by the relentless diffusion of vulgar and appalling images" in contemporary society.[31] That is, we are so bombarded with images of evil and human suffering that we have become increasingly apathetic towards them. In attempting to explain this phenomenon in her later work *Regarding the Pain of Others*, Sontag draws on Virginia Woolf's 1938 work *Three Guineas*.[32] In doing so Sontag recounts a thought experiment that Woolf proposes to present to a King's Counsel:

> Imagine then a spread of loose photographs extracted from an envelope that arrived in the morning post. They show the mangled bodies of adults and children. They show how war evacuates, shatters, breaks apart, levels the built world. "A bomb has torn open the side," Woolf writes of the house in one of the pictures. To be sure, a cityscape is not made of flesh. Still, sheared-off buildings are almost as eloquent as bodies in the street. (Kabul, Sarajevo, East Mostar, Grozny, sixteen acres of lower Manhattan after September 11, 2001, the refugee camp in Jenin . . .) Look, the photographs say, *this* is what it's like. This is what war *does*. And *that*, that is what it does too. War tears, rends. War rips open, eviscerates. War scorches, war dismembers. War *ruins*.[33]

"Not to be pained by these pictures," Sontag argues, "not to recoil from them" would be, for Woolf, "the reactions of a moral monster."[34] And yet, we are no more pained by such images than we recognize ourselves to be "moral monsters." These are images the news-watching public views on a daily basis, images that have become part and parcel of everyday life. Thus, as Woolf herself concluded, it is not so much that we are all "moral monsters," but rather that we lack imagination in responding to such images.[35] Our imaginations, it seems, are suffering from what might be called "empathy fatigue." Thus, while we continue to exhibit some sort of "prurient interest" in "depictions of tormented, mutilated bodies," we do so in a detached, almost abstract sense. The very "*sense* of reality . . . is eroded," this despite the fact that such images are not artistic creations but news footage of the day's events.[36]

However, echoing the sense of mystery that surrounds the concept of evil in her discussion of cruelty, Judith Shklar happens upon another reason for our general reluctance to confront the reality of suffering. For Shklar, "cruelty is different" from other vices such as hypocrisy, betrayal, disloyalty, and snobbery. [37] Its difference, however, is not simply that "we are too squeamish" to properly confront cruelty but that it is "baffling." "Cruelty is baffling," Shklar notes, "because we can live neither with nor without it."[38] The same can be said to hold for suffering. Suffering is not simply baffling and confusing but, at its extreme, stretches our powers of comprehension to their very limit. Suffering, at its worst, can seem simply incomprehensible and it is here that the concept of "evil" finds its primary utility.

Conceiving Suffering

Despite its centrality to human existence and, some would argue, the very meaning of life itself,[39] precisely what it is to suffer is not well understood in general discourse. As Jamie Mayerfeld notes, the term "suffering" is generally used in two main ways. In the first "objectivist" sense, it is basically "synonymous with calamity or misfortune" and can, in certain circumstances, designate "the experience of objective calamities, *without* referring to the psychological state of the people concerned."[40] For example, when we say that someone suffered a particular fate we do not necessarily consider the actual impact it had on the person; we assume that they "suffered" even though they may not have.

Conversely, the second sense in which it is commonly used, "suffering" refers precisely to the psychological state of a person and designates feeling bad. Perhaps the most prominent proponents of this notion are those thinkers, including Epicurus, Jeremy Bentham, John Stuart Mill, and Henry Sidgwick, commonly known as utilitarians who each conceived of suffering, albeit in slightly different ways, as "objective disvalue." Indeed, all three viewed suffering as "the paramount evil," although, in Mayerfeld's view, "they went too far in claiming it is the *only* evil."[41] Thus, although they are often assumed to be synonymous, the precise relationships between pain and suffering, and suffering and evil, are not always clear.

Pain and Suffering

Suffering is most commonly associated with pain of the mental, physical, or spiritual varieties. In C. S. Lewis's estimation, pain is "any experience, whether physical or mental which [a person] dislikes."[42] It is an unpleasant sensation caused, in its most common physical form, by the stimulation of nerve endings in a way that is disagreeable to the person experiencing it. However, although this is broadly correct, it is immediately apparent that this definition is untenably broad and could include a range of things not ordinarily understood to constitute pain; for instance, although not painful as such, sneezing or being tickled are considered disagreeable sensations for some individuals. Lewis agrees and adds that with the designation of an experience as "pain" comes an inferred claim about the intensity of the dislike a person experiences. It therefore seems that we might want to distinguish between pain and the less intense experience of physical discomfort. Although it is not possible to identify exactly where the line between pain and discomfort lies—not least of all because it lies in different places for different individuals in different contexts—it suffices to say that pain is distinct from mere physical discomfort, at least in its level of intensity.[43] Of course, it also goes without saying that this relationship between pain and discomfort is not restricted simply to physical experiences but also applies to mental, emotional, and spiritual varieties of pain.

Just as it is not possible to identify a direct correlation between discomfort and pain, it is similarly not possible to identify a direct correlation between pain and suffering, even though they are, of course, intimately related. As Mayerfeld notes, "pain and suffering . . . appear synonymous" because the "intensification of pain commonly entails the intensification of suffering."[44] Indeed, we recall that for writers such as Bentham and Mill, pain could be directly equated with suffering that in turn essentially defined "evil." However, there are two main reasons why it is not the case that the intensification of pain *necessarily* entails the intensification of suffering. The first is derived from recognition of the fact that "a person's degree of suffering does not always correspond directly to the intensity of his or her pain."[45] That is, there are circumstances in which the increased intensity of pain inflicted on an individual will not add significantly to their suffering. For example, situations exist in which the suffering of an individual is so great that further physical assault will make little difference to his or her situation. The second reason why pain and suffering cannot be directly equated with one another is that not all pain results in suffering.

The question of whether or not "pain logically entails suffering" is one that R. M. Hare investigated in his 1969 essay, "Pain and Evil." In Hare's view, it is possible to identify three different categories of pain.[46] In the first sense, pain refers to a "bare sensation" and carries with it no indication that it is a negative experience. On the contrary, pain in this sense may be a source of enjoyment or, in a more limited sense, may not be disliked. For example, pain associated with acupuncture or some sexual practices may constitute an enjoyable sensation for some individuals. In the second sense Hare discusses, pain is understood to constitute a sensation that is disliked and can vary greatly in intensity from a mild toothache, for example, to a severed limb. As discussed above, this does not imply that *all* dislike *is* pain but that pain coupled with dislike is understood to constitute a different sort of pain from that which is not disliked. Finally, the third category Hare identifies associates pain with a range of other experiences such as "distress" and, as I am most concerned with here, "suffering."[47]

It is immediately apparent from Hare's schematization that not all pain constitutes suffering. There are two main reasons for this. The first is derived from the recognition that pain in the first and second senses does not automatically lead to "suffering pain" in the third sense. In particular, pain that is a source of enjoyment very often does not result in suffering. However, many would argue that this is simply a matter of intensity, "that it is logically impossible for a man who is experiencing intense pain not to be suffering, because suffering just *is* intense pain."[48] As Hare argues, however, this contention is "clearly wrong" for it precludes the possibility that some individuals—he gives the example of a performer lying on a bed of nails—despite experiencing intense pain, do not suffer. Adi Ophir agrees with Hare in part, writing, "not all continuous pain necessarily causes suffering." However, he continues to argue, contrary to Hare, that even for the circus performer, as for the brave warrior, "there is a threshold beyond which the intensifying pain will cause suffering. Beyond this threshold, in performance as in war," he writes, "suffering begins."[49]

Secondly, pain and suffering do not necessarily exist in direct and exclusive relationship with one another because pain is not the only cause of suffering. Rather, pain, of both the physical and psychological varieties, stands alongside a raft of other things such as mental anguish, despair, and, as both Amartya Sen and Martha Nussbaum argue, deprivation, as possible causes of suffering.[50] Indeed, the inability to feed oneself or one's children, or a lack of adequate sanitation, heath care or education, can all be reasonably conceived as sources of suffering that do not necessarily entail pain of any sort. However, just as it is the case that not all pain leads inevitably to suffering, deprivation similarly does not always cause suffering.[51]

It is worth noting at this juncture that although not all pain necessarily causes suffering and not all suffering is the result of pain, pain remains one of a number of sensations that can cause suffering. As mentioned earlier, pain beyond a certain threshold, pain that is no longer tolerable, can be a source of suffering. In this sense, suffering is the function of an excessive sensation. However, it is not simply the case that a "surplus" of pain tips the scale toward the experience of suffering. Rather, pain becomes associated with suffering when it is either too excessive and/or the person experiencing it is unable to make it stop. Thus, an individual suffers when they cannot "disengage" from the cause of the suffering, either because it is inescapable (for example, where the continuation of their suffering rests entirely in the hands of another individual) or because they must choose "not to disengage in order to prevent more suffering."[52] As Emmanuel Levinas wrote in this vein: "physical suffering in all its degrees entails the impossibility of detaching oneself from the instance of existence. It is the very irremissibility of being. The content of suffering merges with the impossibility of detaching oneself from suffering. . . . In suffering there is an absence of all refuge."[53] What is central to understanding the relationship between pain, deprivation, and other experiences, and suffering, is therefore the meaning it is accorded by the individual experiencing it. Whether sensations are liked or disliked, bearable or unbearable, or can be associated with another experience such as distress or suffering, is a matter of personal interpretation. Thus, as David Kraemer writes along these lines, "suffering is a problem of meaning—of making sense of one's condition."[54] Indeed, what one person enjoys may be a source of profound distress for another. However, the claim that suffering is defined in terms of the personal meaning an individual attaches to it raises the problem of the "magnitude gap," the phenomenon by which the experiencing of suffering is almost always greater for the person experiencing it than for those causing or witnessing it.[55]

Judith Shklar touches upon elements of this problem when she argues not only that we should "put cruelty first" among the vices of humanity, but that we should think, first and foremost, not of the leader who inflicts cruelty, but of the victims. That is, we should interpret cruelty from the standpoint of its victims, rather than that of its perpetrators; instead of viewing an act of cruelty as a wrong that someone has committed, thereby focusing on the perpetrator, it ought to be viewed in terms of what the victim suffered. However, Shklar recognizes that it is "not only undignified to idealize political victims, it is also very dangerous."[56] The danger of identifying too strongly with the victims of cruelty, she writes, is that in doing so we forget that "the victims of political torture are often no better than their tormentors. They are only waiting to change places with the latter."[57] However, Shklar resolves this conundrum by arguing that if we "put cruelty first," then it makes absolutely no difference whether "the victim of torture is a decent man or a villain." What matters is that "no one deserves to be subjected to the appalling instruments of cruelty."[58] However, in putting cruelty first and viewing the victim simply as a victim of cruelty, she warns that we must remain aware of both the fact that "anyone can be a victim" and that not all victims are "equally innocent."[59] These arguments would also seem to hold for the experience of suffering. Putting suffering first and thinking about the victims of suffering does not necessarily mean that we must forgo all other judgements about that person.

A second important factor in considering the limitations of focusing an analysis of suffering on the meaning it holds for the individual experiencing it is that although suffering "can be represented, identified with, interpreted and understood," it can never be experienced by an other.[60] That is, we "can never appropriate an other's suffering" but must rather attempt to interpret its meaning by observing the bodily responses and utterances of the individual who is suffering.[61] Thus, although it is possible for an individual who is "not 'really' suffering" to "produce utterances of suffering,"[62] the ability of the outsider to make a definitive judgement about that individual's suffering is critically limited. On the flip side of this, it is also the case that individuals are known to hide their suffering in certain circumstances, thereby making it extremely difficult for an outsider to interpret or understand their experience.

What this discussion would seem to suggest is that "suffering" is an extremely slippery concept. Suffering is, necessarily, an experience confined to the individual; the individual determines whether or not they are suffering, represents that suffering to others, and in doing so, gives their suffering meaning. At the same time, however, we also know that individuals are notoriously unreliable when it comes to self-representation and can often exaggerate their negative experiences. As such, those outside the individual retain some ability to judge the circumstances of the suffering individual. For the purposes of this work however, the sheer magnitude of the sufferings being discussed make this problem less central than it might have been had the subject matter been less extreme. The suffering of the victims of the Holocaust, the genocides of the late twentieth century, and the terrorist attacks of the early twenty-first century, is beyond dispute. What is less clear is what meaning the pain and suffering endured by victims of these atrocities has held for them. It is here that we can see more clearly the relationship between pain and suffering that we have been grappling with thus far.

Although the intensification of pain beyond an individual's "pain threshold" and the inability to disengage from a painful experience can both be conceived as causes of suffering, suffering may be more accurately equated with meaningless or incomprehensible pain. As Erich Loewy writes, "pain can become suffering when it is seen to serve no purpose and, in that sense, to have no meaning."[63] Thus, pain willingly endured for a greater purpose, for example, that caused by cosmetic surgery, body-piercing, or tattooing, is not commonly viewed as suffering. Pain that is beyond that which we can endure or that serves no purpose, but from which we have no means of escape, is meaningless for the person experiencing it. It is the essence of suffering.

The Meaning of Suffering

Just as the relationship between pain and suffering centers around the negotiation of meaning or, more accurately, the meaninglessness of certain painful experiences, so too the relationship between suffering and evil also pivots about notions of meaning. In recognition of this, Adi Ophir engages in what he terms a "hermeneutics of suffering," thereby distinguishing it, in his mind at least, from theological "theodicy" type explanations of suffering, to be discussed in Chapter 3.[64] However, if hermeneutics is understood in general terms as "the theory or philosophy of the interpretation of meaning," it seems a somewhat peculiar conceit to suggest that those meanings cannot be theologically derived.[65]

In both general secular and theological discourse suffering is accorded a wide range of meanings. These meanings do not seek to provide a definitional account of what suffering means in objective terms but rather to imbue particular types of instances of suffering with meaning. That is, they attempt to afford the experience of suffering meaning by reference to another concept during or after the event. For example, in Jewish theology it is possible to identify up to eight different meanings of suffering—retributive suffering, disciplinary suffering, revelational suffering, probational suffering, suffering as illusory or transitory, mysterious suffering, eschatological suffering, and meaningless suffering—although, as we will see, many of these are not exclusively theological in orientation.[66] Rather than delve too far into each of these, I will focus on the four meanings of suffering most common in general secular and Judeo-Christian theological discourse.

In the first instance, suffering is associated with punishment. In the Old Testament, for example, accounts of suffering are often explained as punishment from God for a range of misdemeanors. In Genesis 3, God curses Adam and Eve with "painful toil" and pain in childbirth for eating from the tree of the knowledge of good and evil and in Numbers 12, punishes Aaron for speaking against Moses by afflicting Aaron's wife Miriam with leprosy. As we will see in Chapter 5, more recently and controversially, some Orthodox Jewish and Christian theologians have argued that the immense suffering of the Holocaust represents an instance of "divinely inflicted punishment," either for reformed Judaism's abandonment of the ways of the Torah or, as some Christians argue, for failing to recognize that Jesus Christ was the Messiah.[67] Of course, a range of serious theological and ethical problems are associated with these views. Many rightly argue that they represent a repulsive justification for what remains the most significant humanitarian atrocity of the modern era, if not all human history. Despite their controversial status however, such arguments illustrate well the punitive meaning accorded real instances of extreme suffering.

In a similar frame, in secular society the suffering incurred by individuals as a result of just punishment for crimes committed is understood to serve a range of specific purposes: to reform the individual, to protect society, and to deter others from committing similar acts.[68] However, in both the theological and secular cases, suffering endured as punishment can only be meaningful *if* it is deserved. This means that both punishment itself must be warranted *and* the form of punishment inflicted must be appropriate to the crime committed. That is, the punishment for a crime must conform to ordinary, reasonable expectations about punishment, those expectations that, in the ordinary course of events, make the punishment meaningful. However, the question of desert is a particularly tricky one; how do we know precisely *what* someone deserves for committing a particular crime? What particular punishment is befitting of the crime committed? As R. A. Dudd and D. Garland write, "some writers appeal to the supposedly shared intuition that the guilty 'deserve to suffer.'"[69] What they ought to suffer, the penalty for their guilt, and the extent of their suffering is something determined by the society in which they find themselves and, as such, conforms to that society's reasonable expectations. For example, in almost all societies an individual who is found to have committed armed robbery can reasonably expect to serve a lengthy prison sentence. This amounts to a reasonable, and hence meaningful, punishment for the crime committed. However, this is in direct contradiction to Jeremy Bentham's claim that "all punishment is mischief: all punishment in itself is evil."[70] Indeed, for classical utilitarians such as Bentham, "punishment is morally problematic because it involves the infliction of pain or suffering." Thus, the only punishments that can be justified are those that produce "sufficient pleasures" or "prevent sufficient pains" to outweigh their very "evil" nature.[71] However, the majority of people do not accept the claim that all punishment is evil; justly deserved punishment that is befitting of the crime committed is not commonly viewed as evil in any sense of the word. At the same time however, this is not to say that punishment cannot be evil if it does not conform to the two criteria identified above. For example, the imposition of the death penalty for the fairly minor misdemeanor of overstaying a parking meter would be incomprehensible to all but the most sadistic of the population. As we will see shortly, it is this notion of incomprehensibility or meaninglessness that connects the experience of suffering to the concept of evil. Thus, enforcing the death penalty for parking violations could be conceived as evil along these lines.

What often accompanies understandings of suffering associated with meaningful and justly deserved punishment, is the related notion of redemption; the idea that suffering endured as just recompense for an act allows the perpetrator to be redeemed. For Marilyn McCord Adams, redemptive suffering is a key component of the Christian solution to the "problem of evil."[72] Thus, for Christians it is the suffering of Christ that provides his followers with redemption from their sinful natures and the re-establishment of a right relationship with God. As Simone Weil wrote, redemptive suffering must "have a social origin."[73] That is, for suffering to hold meaning as a redemptive experience, it must be coupled with a sense that, once completed, the individual will be considered redeemed by those around them or, in a religious sense, by God. As Weil continued in this vein: "Redemptive suffering is the shadow of the pure good we desire."[74] It is suffering endured in anticipation of the restoration of good.

The third common meaning of suffering sees it bound up in the meaning of life itself. According to Pope John Paul II, suffering is even more than this: it is an aspect of life *"essential to the nature of man."*[75] Suffering is, in this sense, "an inescapable part of any kind of physical existence"[76] that cannot be "subtracted from life without destroying its meaning."[77] Whether suffering is essential to the meaning of life is a particularly thorny question that pivots on what the meaning of life is itself thought to be. Unsurprisingly, it is beyond the scope of this (or possibly any) work to attempt to answer that eternal question. Rather, what can be claimed with some confidence at this juncture is that suffering is part and parcel of ordinary human life. Taking this idea somewhat further, the renowned pessimist, Arthur Schopenhauer argued in his essay, "On the Suffering of the World," that suffering is a normal mode of being in the world. Given its abundance and the human inability to avoid it completely, Schopenhauer argued that unless suffering is "the immediate and direct purpose of our life . . . then our existence is the most ill-adapted to its purpose in the world: for it is absurd to suppose that the endless affliction of which the world is everywhere full, and which arises out of the need and distress pertaining essentially to life, should be purposeless and purely accidental."[78] Presenting a slightly more positive outlook, the psychoanalyst Carl Jung makes the alternative claim that the meaning of suffering as part of everyday life is associated with personal development and growth.[79] That is, it helps us to understand our limitations and address them accordingly.

As we will see in Chapter 5, in Judeo-Christian theological terms, the suffering of the Jewish people is sometimes understood in this sense as "a manifestation of this people's covenantal destiny."[80] The Biblical passage often used to justify the claim that suffering is part and parcel of the meaning of life as a Jew in ancient Hebrew times is Genesis 15:13–14, which reads: "Then the LORD said to [Abram], 'Know for certain that your descendants will be strangers in a country not their own, and they will be enslaved and mistreated for four hundred years.'" Further to this, and as made particularly apparent in the Old Testament book of Amos, the meaning of Jewish suffering is often said to be intimately linked to their "chosenness" as "God's people," an idea I will discuss further in Chapter 5.

Finally, in the fourth common sense in which it is conceived, suffering is understood as a trial endured in anticipation of a promised reward. In this sense, suffering may be willingly chosen or it may be an unchosen experience imposed upon the individual. In the former sense, an individual may choose to suffer what they perceive as "a necessary evil to achieve something vital," or they may choose to suffer their current affliction in order to prevent worse suffering in the future.[81] In Christian theology, suffering is often conceived as something the believer must endure in order to receive the reward of eternal life. As Romans 5:2–4 reads: "And we rejoice in the hope of the glory of God. Not only so, but we also rejoice in our sufferings, because we know that suffering produces perseverance; perseverance, character; and character, hope." Similarly, in Romans 8:17, Paul tells his followers that they must share in the sufferings of Christ in order to share in his glory. In this, the believer is implored to conceive his or her own suffering in terms of what Adi Ophir terms "a cosmic exchange relation"; that is, in exchange for believing in the suffering Jesus, the believer "gets a promise of compensation for [their] suffering, which will come when Jesus returns."[82] Of course, it is also possible to cite numerous secular examples of this type of suffering, the most obvious of which is childbirth—the endurance of suffering brings with it the reward of a new baby.

Meaningless Suffering

Despite the force with which some of these meanings have been presented in both theological and secular thought, not all suffering can be attributed to one of these four purposes, or, indeed, the first seven meanings that Sanders identified above. For example, many Holocaust survivors find it impossible to accord their experiences any meaning whatsoever. For them, the "meanings" described above bear little, if any, relation to what they experienced themselves. There is absolutely no sense in which the Holocaust can be conceived as meaningful punishment on account of the fact that its victims had not committed any sort of crime deserving of the horrors inflicted upon them. Similarly, it cannot be rendered meaningful as a means of redemption (from what? by whom?), part of the meaning of life, or as something endured in pursuit of a reward (what reward?).[83] However, this is not to suggest that all such survivors do not want to understand the suffering they endured during the Holocaust. On the contrary, as Teria Shantall's study of Holocaust survivors reveals, "the factor of greatest importance in the vivid memory recall among survivors is their struggle and desire for meaning."[84] Survivors, as R. J. Braham writes, often exhibit a need to "impose meaning on their suffering, so that the memories of the past with all their pain are bearable."[85] However, as the previous discussion of the comprehensibility and intelligibility of evil acts indicates, this is not a simple matter.[86]

Among the most prominent proponents of the idea that suffering can be, and indeed, often is, "meaningless" was Friedrich Nietzsche. For Nietzsche, "the aspect of suffering that actually causes outrage is not suffering itself but the meaninglessness of suffering."[87] As part of the final tract of *On the Genealogy of Morals* reads: "Man, the boldest animal and the one most accustomed to pain, does *not* repudiate suffering as such; he *desires* it, he even seeks it out, provided that he has been shown a *meaning* for it, a *reason* for suffering. The meaninglessness of suffering, and *not* suffering as such, has been the curse which has hung over mankind up until now."[88] Thus, Nietzsche posed in stark terms what is often the most troubling aspect of suffering, the fact that we cannot always find an answer to the question, "why do I suffer?"

However, perhaps the most interesting discussion of the meaning(lessness) of suffering is found in Emmanuel Levinas's essay "Useless Suffering." A Jew of Lithuanian heritage and a French citizen at the outbreak of World War II, Levinas fought on the side of France and, after being captured by the Germans, spent some years interned in a German prisoner of war camp. Suffering, Levinas argued, is intrinsically useless; it is "for nothing."[89] Indeed, what he termed "pure suffering" is suffering "which is intrinsically meaningless" and is "without exit"; that is, it is both meaningless and inescapable.[90] In this sense, Levinas's understanding of meaningless suffering accords well with the conceptualization of meaningless pain discussed above. However, when Levinas discussed the uselessness of suffering, he was not simply referring to intolerable, inescapable pain. Rather, writing at the end of what he viewed as "a century of nameless sufferings," Levinas was most concerned with the meaning of the "other's" suffering. For Levinas, the *suffering of the Other* is radically different from "suffering *in me*."[91] This radical difference is located in the meaning ascribed to my own suffering and the other's suffering. My own suffering, Levinas wrote, is "my own adventure of suffering" and is one that, despite being constitutionally or congenitally "useless," "can take on a meaning."[92] That is, the individual can impose meaning, whether consciously or otherwise, on the suffering they are experiencing. The suffering of the other cannot, however, have any meaning imposed upon it. For Levinas this provides the driving force behind his ethical account of our responsibility to respond to the useless suffering of others, an idea I will return to in the Conclusion of this book. Although we will also return to Levinas in Chapter 5 to discuss his account of the "end of theodicy," it is worth noting that for him the "paradigm of gratuitous suffering, where evil appears in its diabolical horror" was Auschwitz, the place where most of his family was killed.[93]

Conclusion

The concept of evil, in its various forms, has long been associated with human suffering. However, just as the relationship between pain and suffering is not one of direct correlation, so too the relationship between suffering and evil is not as direct as it first appears. For many thinkers, suffering is conceived as an intrinsic evil.[94] That is, the very existence of suffering is itself evil for it is evidence of an imperfect world. For example, Adi Ophir argues that "suffering is an evil by its mere occurrence."[95] However, there are two main problems immediately associated with understandings of evil that are directly equated with suffering. First, although it is certainly the case that some suffering is evil, "evil" is not generally used in this sense. For example, we do not designate as "evil" the suffering of an individual's life ruined by the effects of mental illness. We say that it is unfortunate, a "tragedy" even, and we certainly acknowledge the undoubted suffering of the person experiencing it, but we do not generally say that their suffering is "evil." "Evil," it seems, is reserved for a different type of experience. Thus, the second problem with the direct equation of suffering with evil is related to the utility of the term "evil" and flows from the first. If suffering is synonymous with evil and evil is synonymous with suffering, then why use the term evil at all? Why not just say that an individual suffered? Or that a person inflicted suffering on another? Again, it seems that "evil" designates a particular type of experience, action, or event that somehow stands beyond or outside the realm of ordinary everyday suffering.

The argument implicit in my discussion here is a contentious one. The general claim that not all suffering is "evil" contradicts the vast majority of attempts to conceptualize evil in explicit relation to suffering. However, the claim that all suffering is evil is an argument more often asserted than demonstrated. For example, Jamie Mayerfeld writes:

> What I claim is that suffering is intrinsically evil for the individual who experiences it—evil in itself. I'm afraid I have no argument for this claim. This doesn't strike me as a great embarrassment, since few moral claims appear to me more certain. Rather than argue for this claim, I shall simply assert it, and hope that enough of my readers agree.[96]

Similarly, C. S. Lewis, taking a logical step back to the concept of pain, argues that it is "unmistakable evil." "Every man," he writes, "knows that something is wrong when he is being hurt."[97] Again, no explanation is provided for the relationship between pain and evil, it is simply asserted. For the reasons provided above, these unexamined associations are problematic ones; they do not accord well with the manner in which the term "evil" is used in contemporary discourse, and they limit the utility of designating individuals and actions as "evil" to the point of obsolescence.

What seems a more reasonable assertion, and one that can be demonstrated with reference to the sense in which the term "evil" is actually used in contemporary discourse, is that while evil almost always entails suffering, not all suffering can be considered evil. That is, we only attach the additional, more extreme designator of "evil" to certain types of suffering, in particular, suffering that is meaningless. Suffering that is meaningless may be brought about by a natural disaster or at the hands of another human being and, crucially, is not for another purpose such as justly deserved punishment or redemption. Suffering is meaningless and hence "evil" when we cannot find an answer to the question, "why do I suffer?" As Clifford Geertz writes, "the so-called problem of evil is a matter of formulating in world-view terms the actual nature of the destructive forces within the self and outside of it, of interpreting murder, crop failure, sickness, earthquakes, poverty, and oppression in such a way that it is possible to come to some sort of terms with them."[98] As he continues elsewhere, the problem of evil is "in essence the same sort of problem of or about bafflement and the problem of or about suffering."[99]

As we will see in the following chapters, the concept of evil has traditionally attempted to make sense of otherwise meaningless suffering in both theological and philosophical terms. It has generally been concerned with the "transposition of the primordial experience of suffering into the theistic problem of evil,"[100] although, as the preceding discussion makes clear, this problem is not exclusively theistic in orientation. What follows from this is that the existence of suffering in the world does not by itself create the problem of evil. Rather, suffering, whether caused by pain, deprivation, despair, or something else, only becomes what is known as the "problem of evil" when it is attached to another narrative, one that seeks to render meaningful the experience of otherwise meaningless suffering. Nowhere has this been more apparent than with regard to theological manifestations of the "problem of evil," which is the subject matter of the following chapter.

3

The Problem of Evil

For what is that which we call evil but the absence of good?[1]

Despite being conceived in secular terms in much contemporary thought, the "problem of evil" has traditionally been a theological one concerned with the question of how to reconcile the existence of suffering, and hence evil, in the world, with the characterization of the Judeo-Christian God as benevolent, omniscient, and omnipotent. Formally articulated by Epicurus (341–270 BCE) and originally quoted in the work of Lactantius (c. 260–340 CE), the "problem of evil" is traditionally presented as follows:

> God either wishes to take away evils, and is unable; or He is able, and is unwilling; or He is neither willing nor able, or He is both willing and able. If He is willing and is unable, He is feeble, which is not in accordance with the character of God; if He is able and willing, He is envious, which is equally at variance with God; if He is neither willing nor able, He is both envious and feeble and, therefore not God; if He is both willing and able, which alone is suitable to God, from what source then are evils? Or why does He not remove them?[2]

Presented syllogistically, the problem is this:

> God is benevolent.
> God is omnipotent (which should be taken to include omniscience).
> There is evil in the world.

> If the first two propositions are true, the third cannot be.

Now the third is true as a matter of observable fact.
From this it follows that one (or both) of the first two premises must
be false.
But if either is false, there is no God as Judeo-Christianity portrays Him.3

Of course, "evidence" of the existence of evil is the "observable fact" that
there is suffering in the world. However, what makes the existence of suffering the "problem of evil" in this context is the juxtaposition of "*particular* narratives of events of pain, dereliction, anguish, oppression,
torture, humiliation, degradation, injustice, hunger, godforsakeness, and
so on" with the "Christian community's narratives" about the character
of God.[4] That is, the problem of evil arises from the juxtaposition of the
existence of suffering in the world with specific assumptions about God's
benevolent, omnipotent and omniscient character. As Marilyn McCord
Adams explains, however, even this is not a straightforward equation for
there is no "explicit logical contradiction between" the seemingly incompatible claims that, on the one hand "God is benevolent" and "God is
omnipotent," and on the other that "There is evil in the world."[5] Rather,
the contradiction arises because of the way in which the first two premises are commonly construed. That is, a contradiction emerges because
benevolence and omnipotence are commonly interpreted to incorporate
the following additional claims:

A perfectly good being would always eliminate evil so far as it could;
An omniscient being would know all about evils; and,
There are *no limits* to what an omnipotent being can do.[6]

Thus, the primordial experience of suffering is only conceived as a "problem," the "problem of evil," when its meaning is sought in relation to an
all-good, all-knowing, and all-powerful God who is both capable of pre-
venting it and ought to do so.
    What also becomes clear at this juncture is the fact that there is not
one "problem of evil" at play here but rather two problems; the logical
and the evidential problems of evil. The logical problem of evil is fundamentally concerned with the internal logic or consistency of theistic
explanations of evil. That is, it is "the problem of clarifying and reconciling a number of beliefs" that constitute the "essential parts of most theological positions."[7] It is, in short, the most common version of the
"traditional" problem associated with reconciling the character of God

with the existence of evil discussed above. On the other hand, the evidential problem of evil poses a different problem to theists with its claim that "the facts of evil constitute *evidence* against the hypothesis that the world was created, and is governed, by an omnipotent, omniscient, perfectly good God."[8] Among the most prominent proponents of this view in late twentieth century aetheology is William Rowe, who expressed the problem as follows:

1. There exist instances of intense suffering which an omnipotent, omniscient being could have prevented without thereby losing some greater good or permitting some evil equally bad or worse.
2. An omniscient, wholly good being would prevent the occurrence of any intense suffering it could, unless it could not do so without thereby losing some greater good or permitting some evil equally bad or worse.
3. There does not exist an omnipotent, omniscient, wholly good being.[9]

As such, Rowe's argument from evil "asserts that the evidence of God is *incompatible*" with the type of evil described in the first premise.[10] Thus the existence of evil, understood in terms of suffering, brings the very existence of God into serious question.

However, leaving the finer points of these arguments aside for now it suffices to say that these two problems have, in various ways, exercised the minds of theologians and philosophers alike for many centuries. In order to get a better sense of this, this chapter therefore traces the development of the "problem of evil" from the Babylonian theodicy to the works of Thomas Aquinas. In doing so it illustrates the manner in which various thinkers, throughout an extensive period of history, sought to provide meaning for what could otherwise be conceived as instances of meaningless suffering by reference to the character of God and the nature of the created order. However, foreshadowing a distinction that took hold in modern thought about evil, to be discussed in Chapter 4, it also highlights the emergence of an important division in the conceptualization of the problem of evil in the work of Augustine of Hippo: that which distinguished between the theological problem of why a good God allows suffering, and the moral problem of why human beings choose to commit evil acts.

Theodicy

Traditionally, theological problems of evil, in their logical and evidential forms, have been the focus of that area of scholarship known as theodicy (combining the Greek *theos*, God, with *dike*, righteousness),[11] a term coined by Gottfried Wilhelm von Leibniz at the beginning of the eighteenth century to describe attempts to reconcile the goodness, and indeed existence of God, with the existence of evil.[12] Before discussing its finer points in more detail however, it is worth noting that what is often termed "theoretical theodicy" is not without its detractors. For some, the "putative solution" to the problem of evil proposed by theoretical theodicy "does not solve the problem at all, but instead avoids confronting the real difficulties" posed by the existence of evil in the world.[13] Others, echoing the criticisms leveled at the theoretical treatment of evil more generally, "condemn it as an inappropriate response to human suffering."[14] Indeed, claims that theodicy overlooks or even "sanatizes" the reality of human suffering abound.[15] Even the Archbishop of Canterbury, Rowan Williams, has suggested that "perhaps it is time for philosophers of religion to look away from theodicy—not to appeal blandly to the mysterious purposes of God, not to appeal to any putative justification at all, but to put the question of how we remain faithful to human ways of seeing suffering, even and especially when we are thinking from a religious perspective."[16] However, what is really at stake here is the very point of theodicy itself. Is the point of engaging in theoretical theodicy to understand the phenomenon of evil, or is it to remove the problem of evil altogether? If it is the former, then the criticisms leveled above are somewhat overstated for what is actually at stake is the way in which suffering is understood. This, as we will see, is not necessarily incompatible with Williams's call to "remain faithful to human ways of seeing suffering." On the other hand, "solving" the problem of evil, in the sense of eradicating evil from its worldly existence would seem to be a futile exercise. If we accept the existence of evil and that it is fundamentally eradicable, our problem is how to understand its place in our world view. That is, the problem is, in traditional theological terms, one of how to *reconcile* the existence of evil with our understanding of the divine order, an exercise that does not entail overcoming evil in the world but ultimately seeks to provide otherwise meaningless suffering with some sort of meaning.

Perhaps the oldest known theodicy is the *Babylonian Theodicy*.[17] A short and fragmentary poem possibly composed as early as 1400 BCE,

the work is posed as a dialogue between two friends, one who has suffered the evil of a social injustice, and the other "who tries to reconcile"
the facts of the case "with established views on the justice of the divine
ordering of the universe."[18] The particular suffering the anonymous
author laments is what he has endured at the hands of a rich man who
has ruined him. He writes:

> People extol the word of a strong man who is trained in murder,
> But bring down the powerless who has done no wrong.
> They confirm the wicked whose crime is [...]
> Yet suppress the honest man who heeds the will of his god.
> They fill the sto[re house] of the oppressor with gold,
> But empty the larder of the beggar of its provisions.[19]

The author cannot understand the suffering he is experiencing for in his
view, he is an "honest man who heeds the will of his god." For him, as was
common at the time, suffering was seen as a consequence of angering the
gods, something believed he had not done. In response to his anguish, the
author's friend attempts to comfort him:

> Narru, king of the gods, who created mankind,
> And majestic Zulummar, who dug out their clay,
> And mistress Mami, the queen who fashioned them,
> Gave perverse speech to the human race.
> With lies, and not truth, they endowed them forever.
> Solemnly they speak favour of a rich man;
> "He is a king," they say. "Riches go at his side."
> But they harm the poor as though he were a thief;
> They lavish slander upon him and plot his murder,
> Making him suffer every evil like a criminal because he has no protection.
> Terrifyingly they bring him to his end, and extinguish him like a flame.[20]

However, his words of comfort are to no avail and the author concludes
that all he can possibly do in the face of suffering is continue to worship
the gods and trust that they will do what is in the best interests of their
believers. He wrote:

> May the god who has thrown me off give help!
> May the goddess who has [abandoned me] show mercy!
> For the shepherd Shamash gu[ides] the peoples like a god.[21]

Here already we see the emergence of the central theme of the broadly conceived "problem of evil," the attempt to explain otherwise meaningless suffering by reference to a deity or, in this case, deities. This theme, as we will see, has been repeated throughout the almost three and a half thousand years of thought about the problem of evil that have followed. Although the field of theodicy has developed in many diverging directions since its inception and is not an exclusively Judeo-Christian pursuit,[22] a great deal of energy is spent explaining the existence of suffering in the books of the Old Testament.

The Problem of Evil in Early Hebrew Thought

It is important to note at the outset that the ancient Hebrews did not have a great fascination with the idea of "evil." In Biblical terms, the discussion of "evil" is concentrated in the Greek, Christian writings of the New Testament and, as we will see shortly, though sharing its common heritage, is distinctly different from the Hebrew idea. In Hebrew, the word most often translated as "evil" is *ra*. From the root "to spoil," *ra* primarily denoted "worthlessness or uselessness, and by extension it came to mean bad, ugly, or even sad."[23] In the works of the Old Testament, the word "evil" is a term of moral judgement generally confined to the actions of the Israelites. "Evil" first appears in the Genesis story as Eve is tempted by the serpent to eat the fruit of the tree of the knowledge of good and evil. As the serpent tells Eve, "For God knows when you eat of it your eyes will be opened, and you will be like God, knowing good and evil" (Genesis 3:5). That is, to eat the fruit would allow Adam and Eve to gain moral judgement independent from that of God.

More commonly however, "evil" appears in the Old Testament to describe the behavior of the Israelites. For example, the book of Judges tells of the Israelites' time in the Promised Land after the death of Joshua and, in many ways, reads as an account of their continual acts of apostasy. The author of the account repeatedly writes that "the Israelites did evil in the eyes of the Lord," usually by worshipping the Baals (Jdg 2:11).[24] Crucially, until the age of the prophets, Judaism had "no idea of evil as a force or principle opposed to God."[25] Rather, "evil" was simply conceived as an action as opposed to an entity, an action that brought ruin to that which was good.

However, perhaps the most famous treatment of suffering in the Western tradition to date is found in the Old Testament book of Job. As Joseph Kelly writes, Job is not only "the ancient world's most significant theodicy" but deals with the "mystery of innocent suffering" by challenging what had been the traditional approach to the problem.[26] Prior to Job, conventional approaches to the problem of evil argued that people suffer because they have committed evil acts. The logical corollary of this was the further claim that "innocent people simply do not suffer."[27] In the particular case of Job however, this argument did not seem right. Job, as the story goes, was an exceptionally righteous man. He was "blameless and upright; he feared God and shunned evil" (Job 1:1). However, with God's permission, Satan strips Job of his livelihood, his wealth, his children, and his health, leaving him covered in festering boils and destitute outside the city walls.[28] Struck by such calamity, Job's friends assume that "he has done something to deserve this suffering" but Job maintains his innocence and even "calls on God to acknowledge this."[29] Job's friends pressure him to confess his sins but their arguments are to no avail, even Elihu's claims about the redemptive nature of suffering fall on deaf ears. Job maintains that only God can explain his apparently meaningless suffering. God obliges Job, speaking to him out of a storm, and asks him:

> Where were you when I laid the earth's foundations?
> Tell me, if you understand.
> Who marked off its dimensions? Surely you know!
> Who stretched a measuring line across it?
> On what were its footings set, or who laid its cornerstone—while the morning stars sang together and all the angels shouted for joy?
> (Job 38:1–7)

God continues in this vein for three chapters before Job responds by acknowledging: "Surely I spoke of things I did not understand, things too wonderful for me to know" (42:3).

Several lessons can be drawn from the story of Job, the most significant of which is that "we cannot argue for the invariable connexion of sin and suffering, or of righteousness and prosperity."[30] Rather, it is the case that in many instances "the wicked prosper, while the righteous are doomed to pain."[31] The other major lesson to be drawn from Job's experience is that God, his universe and the governance of creation is more complex than we can possibly comprehend. That is, the answer to the problem of how to reconcile suffering, and hence evil, with the existence of God as He is characterized in the Judeo-Christian tradition, is simply beyond human comprehension.[32] This would seem to suggest that suffering may have meaning, even if we cannot ascertain for ourselves precisely what it is. Despite the lessons of Job however, the idea that suffering was the direct result of individuals' evil actions remained until well into the eighteenth century when the destruction of the Lisbon earthquake brought an end to that pattern of thought. Indeed, as Joseph Kelly writes, "Job's theodicy presented too decisive a break with the past to win instant acceptance" and, as such, "the traditional view persisted" for some time.[33]

By the second century BCE, Jewish literature was experiencing a significant surge in the emergence of apocalyptic works that brought with them renewed popularity in the combat myths that the ancient Jewish sects had used to explain the existence of good and evil in the world. Members of these sectarian and apocalyptic movements "saw themselves as engaged in spiritual battles fought out at both cosmic and earthly levels,"[34] spiritual battles fought between the contending forces of good and evil. Thus, writings such as those known as the Dead Sea Scrolls provided "apocalyptic interpretations of prophetic texts such as Isaiah and Hosea, expounded by a 'Teacher of Righteousness'" who, it was thought, would "prevail in the final battle over armies of the Angel of Darkness" at what was thought to be the rapidly approaching end of time.[35] The Dead Sea Scrolls, discovered in 1947, speak of the Qumran people, a Jewish sect that established a community on the northwest shore of the Dead Sea and remained there until their destruction in the Roman-Jewish War of 66–70 CE. As their most famous work, *War of the Sons of Light against the Sons of Darkness* claimed, "God had given them the Prince of Light to support them against the wiles of the Adversary (*satan* in Hebrew) whose name was Mastema."[36] Significantly, as an extremely pious group of believers, the Qumran people went so far as to demonize other Jews they believed did not keep the Law of God to a sufficient degree. Unsurprisingly, as Kelly notes, "this shocking development found no support among other Jewish groups."[37] Although defeated by the "Sons of Darkness," that is, the Romans, who also destroyed the Jerusalem Temple, apocalyptic literature remained influential until the second defeat of the Jews at the hands of the Romans in 135 CE. In the intervening period however, with the priesthood associated with the Temple destroyed, the rabbis began to emerge as the central force driving Jewish thought and practice. Fearing that Judaism was being transformed along wholly dualist lines and wishing to preserve the unity of God in the Jewish faith, many rabbis came to accept Job's conclusion that human beings cannot possibly comprehend how the existence of evil can be reconciled with the all-good character of God.[38]

The Personification of Evil

Significantly, it was the merging of these Hebrew ideas that brought about the advent of early Christian notions of "evil" that appear in the New Testament and are personified in the figure of Satan. This marks an important transition for in much of the Old Testament Satan appears not as the epitome of "evil" nor as God's great adversary but as an instrument of his will. For example, in the books of Numbers and, as we saw in the previous section, Job, Satan appears as a servant of God sent to test his subject's faithfulness. As Elaine Pagels explains, the "Hebrew term *satan* describes an adversarial role" and, crucially, is "not the name of a particular character." Rather, satans (in the plural) were conceived as "angels sent by God for the specific purpose of blocking or obstructing human activity."[39] The root *śtn* from which *satan* is derived "means 'one who opposes, obstructs, or acts as adversary.'"[40] Indeed, "Satan" only appears once in the Old Testament, in 1 Chronicles 21:1 in which he tempts David to take a census of his military forces. Interestingly however, the account of the same events in 2 Samuel 24 claims that it was God himself who tempted David. This ultimately leads the 1 Chronicles 21:1 passage to often be interpreted not as Satan interfering in the affairs of the Israelites for his own purposes but as a messenger of God sent to test David.

It was thus, in reality, only with the New Testament that the picture of Satan as the personification of evil and, by extension, God's great adversary began to emerge.[41] Indeed, the notion of a battle being waged between God and Satan, good and evil, is particularly apparent in the Gospels of Matthew, Mark, and Luke. In the first instance, this idea is introduced in the Gospel accounts of the forty days Jesus spent in the desert being tempted by Satan at the beginning of his ministry. In this, "Satan" is introduced as a specific character for the first time. More significant however, is the posing of a battle between good and evil in the Gospels, particularly as it appears in Mark's account. As Pagels writes, in recounting the life and ministry of Jesus, Mark was struck by a necessity to explain its apparent failure. "If Jesus had been sent as God's anointed king," he questioned, "how could the movement he initiated have failed so miserably?" After all, his ministry had not ended in the defeat of Rome, as had been expected of the Messiah, but his own crucifixion. In attempting to answer this question, Pagels writes, Mark places the events surrounding Jesus's life and death not simply within the context of the struggle against Rome but in the context of an ongoing battle between good and evil in the universe.[42] What is more, in this historical context, a context in which a number of Jewish sects were all vying for supremacy, the Jewish opponents of Jesus's movement became associated in Christian texts with "evil" and Satan. Thus, members of Jesus's sect explained their battle not only by arguing that "forces of evil act *through certain people*," in this case the opposing Jewish sects, but by using the figure of Satan to "characterize one's actual enemies as the embodiment of transcendent forces."[43] With this, their struggle was provided with a sense of greater cosmic legitimacy and, in many ways, echoed the Jewish apocalyptic literature of the time.[44]

At first glance, early Christian thought thus appears to present a thoroughly dualist understanding of good and evil. Good is from God, evil from Satan, and the two are locked in a perpetual battle with one another. However, this is not quite the case for in Christian thought, God retains ultimate control over Satan; that is, God and Satan are not viewed as equal and rival gods but rather Satan remains subordinate to God. For this reason, Christianity is often thought of as a "semi-dualist" religion.

Forces of Good and Evil

More thorough-going dualist accounts of "good" and "evil" are found in the Zoroastrian and Manichaean faiths. Famously, the tenth century BCE Iranian figure Zoroaster sought to resolve the question of how to reconcile the existence of good and evil in the world by denying "the unity and omnipotence of God in order to preserve his perfect goodness." In what Jeffrey Burton Russell has described as "a radical innovation in the history of religion," Zoroaster, also known as Zarathustra, posited the existence of two rival gods or "primal spirits . . . the better and the bad."[45] The better, known as Ahura Mazdah or Ohrmazd, represents "goodness and light" and is locked in perpetual battle with Angra Mainyu or Ahriman, who represents "darkness and evil" and was the "first real

Devil in world religion."[46] As Russell explains, Zoroaster argued that it is "only by engaging and defeating Ahriman" that Ohrmazd could become both "infinite and eternal."[47] Zoroastrianism is thus an "essentially militant" religion whose human followers are implored to fight evil, the "common enemy of Ahura Mazdah" with all their "being, body, mind, and spirit."[48] The similarities apparent between Zoroastrianism and the apocalyptic Jewish writings discussed earlier can be attributed to the fact that Persia ruled the Jews from Cyrus the Great's defeat of Babylon in 539 BCE until the conquest of Alexander the Great in 331 BCE.

In the early centuries after Christ however, one of the most significant challenges to Christianity was that of Gnosticism. Derived from Zoroastrianism, Platonism, and Mithraism, Gnosticism particularly sought to challenge the Hebrew underpinnings of Christian faith. Based on the Greek notion of "gnosis," meaning spiritual knowledge derived by intuition, the Gnostics maintained that the "Hebrew Bible contained a lot of nonsense, like a talking snake (Genesis 3) or a talking donkey (Numbers 33)" and argued that the existence of a spiritual God who created a physical world was impossible. Gnosticism therefore called for Christians to "reject the God of the Hebrew bible" and was "united tenuously by the belief that Christ saved humans not by the redemptive death of his irrelevant physical body but by the knowledge which he brought to them."[49] Although by the fourth century it had reached "an intellectual dead end," Gnosticism championed a "radical dualist theodicy" that, as we will see shortly, exerted a significant influence on a number of later approaches to the problem of evil.[50]

However, Gnosticism came under fire with the writings of the "first great Latin theologian," Tertullian, a member of the ascetic Montanist sect.[51] Although he maintained the dualist notion prevalent in Jewish thought that "a disciplined moral life was part of the campaign against the Devil, whereas an immoral, worldly life was service to Satan," his "refutation of Gnostic dualism was direct and compelling."[52] If God is an all-powerful being, Tertullian reasoned, then the existence of a god powerful enough to rival him was impossible. Thus, Tertullian argued that evil was not from an independent power rival to God but originated from the sins of both humans and angels.[53] Presenting a fairly pointed version of the traditional problem of evil directed toward Sinope and the Cynic Diogenes, Tertullian wrote:

Now for all the questions raised by you dogs as you growl against the God of truth: and dogs, say the apostle, are cast out (of the city of God). Here are the bones of wranglings you gnaw at. If God is good, you ask, and has knowledge of the future, and also has power to avert evil, why did he suffer the man, deceived by the devil, to fall away from obedience to the law, and so to die? For the man was the image and likeness of God, or even God's substance, since from it the man's soul took its origin. So if, being good, he had wished a thing not to happen, and if, having foreknowledge, he had been aware that it would happen, and if he had had power and strength to prevent it from happening, that thing never would have happened which under these three conditions of divine majesty it was impossible should happen. But, you conclude, as that did happen, the very opposite is proved, that God must be assumed to be neither good nor prescient nor omnipotent: because inasmuch as nothing of that sort could have happened if God had possessed these attributes of goodness and prescience and omnipotence, it follows that it did happen because God is devoid of these qualities.[54]

However, rather than accept this reasoning, Tertullian set about proving that God does indeed, "possess these characteristics on which doubt is cast, goodness . . . prescience and omnipotence."[55] Having done so he concluded that human beings have "free power" over the choices they make and, as such, blame for the ills that befall humankind should be "imputed to [human individuals] and not to God."[56] In doing so, Tertullian helped to form the basis of what later became known as the "free will defense," the claim that evil is the result of human beings misusing the free will granted them by God.

As Jeffrey Burton Russell writes however, during the third and fourth centuries, the fear and insecurity precipitated by the decline of the Roman Empire led to resurgent interest in dualist theodicies.[57] Amongst its most prominent proponents was the early Christian apologist Lactantius (c. 245–325).[58] Lactantius was primarily concerned with the question of "why the just suffered as much in life as the unjust."[59] He asked: "Why does the true God permit these things to exist instead of removing or deleting the evil?"[60] His answer was two-fold. First, he argued that "evil is logically necessary" because "good cannot be understood without evil, nor evil without good." Secondly, he argued that evil exists because "God makes it to be so." He wrote:

We could not perceive virtue unless the opposite vice also existed, nor could we accomplish virtue unless we were tempted to its opposite; God willed this distinction and distance between good and evil so that we might be able to grasp the nature of good by contrasting it with the nature of evil. . . . To exclude evil is to eliminate virtue.[61]

However, Lactantius was unable to uphold this monist view of God and reverted to a dualistic one, writing that: "before he made anything else, God made two sources of things, each source opposed to the other and each struggling against the other. These two sources are the two spirits, the just spirit and the corrupt spirit, and one of them is like the right hand of God while the other is like his left."[62] Although he later realized his error and attempted to correct this view, his efforts only managed to further confuse the issue and Lactantius remains characterized as being at least semi-dualist in his theology.[63]

Drawing on the fundamental tenets of Zoroastrianism, along with elements of Gnosticism and Christianity, Manichaeism, the brainchild of the third century Babylonian figure Mani (215–276 CE), also posited the existence of two rival forces of good and evil that are "utterly and irreconcilably opposed to one another" and exist in a state of perpetual conflict.[64] In particular, Manichaeism adopted the Zoroastrian association of evil with matter. As Neil Forsyth writes, although Mani primarily wrote in Syriac, he used the Greek word *hyle*, the word for "matter," to denote evil, and by doing so perpetuated the idea that evil is an entity that exists independently of all others.[65] Significantly however, in doing so he infused the Greek term *hyle*, used to denote visible matter, with the Iranian notion that matter is "evil," thereby conceiving invisible forces of evil as actually existing. For this reason, Alexander of Lycopolis felt it necessary to explain in his fourth-century treatise *Of the Manichaeans*, a work written in opposition to Manichaeism, how Mani's understanding of *hyle* was distinct from that of both Plato and Aristotle:

[Mani] laid down two principles, God and Matter. God he called good, and matter he affirmed to be evil. But God excelled more in good than matter in evil. But he called matter not that which Plato calls it, which becomes everything when it has received quality and figure, whence he terms it all-embracing—the mother and nurse of all things; nor what Aristotle calls an element, with which form and privation have to do, but something besides these. For the motion which in individual things is incomposite, this he calls matter. On the side of God are ranged powers, like handmaids, all good; and likewise, on the side of matter are range other powers, all evil. Moreover, the bright shining, the light, and the superior, all these are with God; while the obscure, and the darkness, and the inferior are all with matter. God, too, has desires, but they are all good; and matter, likewise, which are all evil.[66]

Contrary to the conventional Greek understanding of the term as "the basic substance of reality," in the works of Mani *hyle* therefore took on an entirely different meaning derived from the "Gnostic revision of Iranian dualism."[67] This, of course, was because Mani conceived "evil" as a malevolent force that exists independently in the world; that is, it is something that exists outside its association with notions of the "good" and its interactions with human beings. Thus, for Manichaean dualists, the "problem of evil" was not really a problem at all. Suffering did not, by their account, impinge upon the goodness of God but was rather the manifestation of an evil force operating in the world.

Evil as the Privation of Good

Perhaps the most famous Manichaean of all was also its most prominent critic, Augustine of Hippo, born in Thagaste in Numidia Proconsularis, now Algeria, in 354 CE. Indeed, despite devoting himself to the Manichaean sect for some nine years, it is in Augustine's works that some of the most important criticisms of the dualist good/evil scheme are to be found. "Evil," it is well known, was among Augustine's primary fascinations, leading him first to the Manichaean faith and then on to Christianity. As it is also well known, Augustine was also preoccupied with sex, his famous plea to God to "let me be chaste, but not yet" revealing his inner turmoil about the subject. Manichaeism thus appealed to both of his primary fascinations; first with its claim that "matter is evil," and second, with its pronouncement that as a natural entity the "body is evil" and, further to this, that "sex is sinful" because it ultimately produces more material beings.[68] Although it appears in a large number of his one hundred seventeen works, it is in two that trace his "pilgrimage from Manichaeism to the Christian faith," his popular *Confessions* and less well known *On the Free Choice of the Will* that many of his most important discussions of evil are found.[69] Augustine began writing *On Free Choice of the Will* only two years after his conversion and completed it seven or eight years later, by which "time he had become an ordained priest of the Church at Hippo Regius."[70] The work takes the form of a dialogue between himself and a friend named Evodius. It begins with a question from Evodius: "Tell me, please, whether God is not the cause of evil." Augustine replies: "But if you know or believe that God is good (and it is not right to believe otherwise), God does not do evil."[71] In doing so, Augustine began to present what is commonly viewed as the classic Christian theodicy.

However, it is in the first of these works, the *Confessions*, that Augustine explains how his interest in the problem of evil came about. The story he tells is a famous one in which he and some friends as adolescents had stolen some pears. What concerned Augustine about this act was not the sheer wastefulness of it—they ate some of the fruit and gave the rest to the farmer's pigs—but the fact that they had stolen the pears simply for the sake of stealing.[72] This in turn led Augustine to ask why human beings knowingly do things that are clearly wrong. His initial answer to this question was Manichaean; humans knowingly commit wrongful acts because they are marked by an internal tension between good and evil. Although this explanation remained satisfactory in his mind for some time, he later became unconvinced by aspects of Manichaean thought and so turned his efforts to providing a sustained critique of it.

Augustine's central complaints with the Manichaeans were as follows. First, as Peter Brown notes, was the fact that Manichaeanism was "essentially a static religion," Augustine writing that he could "not make progress in it."[73] At least in part, this seemed to Augustine to be a function of the extent to which the Manichaeans "dwell[e]d upon the evils" rather than the good aspects of nature.[74] However, given Augustine's own decidedly pessimistic view of the possibility of human progress,[75] this seems like a rather strange reason for abandoning his faith. The second and related reason for Augustine's disillusionment with Manichaeanism is discussed in some detail in his *Confessions*. Specifically, Augustine describes the disappointment he felt when, having been filled with the anticipation of hearing one of the most prominent Manichaean priests, Faustus, speak in Carthage, he realized that despite his "charming manner and pleasant address . . . [Faustus] said just what the others used to say, but in a much more agreeable style."[76] In particular, Augustine was disappointed to discover not only that Faustus could not account for the Manichaean exclusion of a number of important scientific discoveries in their world view, but that he was "quite uninformed about the subjects in which [he] had expected him to be an expert."[77] Most seriously of all however, was the recognition than Manichaean dualism was fundamentally heretical for presupposing the existence of a power equal to God, denying the omnipotence of God, and for weakening the "logic of human responsibility to the point of enervation."[78] Thus, Augustine came to realize that he had spent nine years of his life being "led astray" and, in his position as an auditor in the church, leading others astray.[79]

Augustine's conversion to Christianity was not affected immediately after his resignation from Manichaeanism but occurred some time later in Milan after he had been regularly attending the church at which Saint Ambrose preached.[80] It was thus in the context of his Christian faith that Augustine returned to the problem of evil. Aside from refuting the heretical duality that the Manichaean's proposed however, Augustine came to realize that one of the fundamental faults in the Manichaean understanding of evil was a function of its methodology, a methodology that sought to enquire as to the "origin of evil, without first asking what evil" actually is.[81] This faulty methodology, he reasoned, had led the Manichaeans "only to the reception of foolish fancies" and not, as it were, to a proper understanding of evil.[82] Thus, Augustine reversed this method in his own works, enquiring first into the nature of evil and only then considering its origins. For, as Augustine reasoned, it is not possible to accurately ascertain what the sources of evil might be without first coming to some understanding of what it is.

The Nature of Evil

In order to comprehend Augustine's understanding of evil and, by extension, his response to the "problem of evil," it is necessary to first come to grips with what he conceived as "good." Here Augustine relied on the work of the third-century critic of Gnosticism and founder of neo-Platonism, Plotinus (204–270 CE).[83] For Plotinus, "good" "is that on which all else depends, towards which all Existences aspire as to their source and their need" and, as such, is equated with being.[84] In a similar vein, Augustine also equated good with being, although he emphasised the position of God in this claim more strongly than Plotinus did. According to Augustine, God is the highest, most perfect and unchangeable good.[85] He is, in a Platonic sense, identified with "eternal Form, through which 'every temporal thing can receive its form.'"[86] In accordance with this, Augustine argued that "all things that exist . . . seeing that the Creator of them is supremely good, are themselves good."[87] As Geivett highlights with some force in his work *Evil and the Evidence for God*, "this belief in the existence and omnibenevolence of God as Creator is *the cornerstone of Augustine's theodicy*."[88] As will be seen shortly, he certainly does not overstate this claim.

For Augustine, evil is thus "a name for nothing other than the absence of good,"[89] *privatio boni* (the privation of good), an idea previously spoken of by Clement of Alexandria (c. 150–210). Augustine explained the privation theory of evil in his *Enchiridion on Faith, Hope, and Love* by reference to an analogy:

> For what is that which we call evil but the absence of good? In the bodies of animals, diseases and wounds mean nothing but the absence of health; for when a cure is effected, that does not mean that the evils which were present—namely, the diseases and wounds—go away from the body and dwell elsewhere: they altogether cease to exist; for the wound or disease is not a substance, but a defect in the fleshly substance—the flesh itself being a substance, and therefore something good, of which those evils—that is, privations of the good which we call health—are accidents. Just in the same way, what are called vices in the soul are nothing but privations of natural good.[90]

This conception of "evil as ontological privation" is essentially Platonic[91] and appears in a similar form in Plotinus's *Six Enneades*. As Plotinus argued, if good is equated with being, then it stands to reason that "Evil cannot have a place among Beings or in the Beyond-Being," for these are both good.[92] Rather, Plotinus suggested, "If Evil exists at all," it must be situated "in the realm of Non-Being."[93] Evil is therefore defined in terms of what Plotinus termed "absolute lack." He wrote: "What falls in some degree short of the Good is not Evil; considered in its own kind it might even be perfect, but where there is utter dearth, there we have Essential Evil, void of all share in Good."[94] As evil is the absolute lack of good, Plotinus reasoned that "we," as manifestations of being, and hence good, "cannot be, ourselves, the source of Evil."[95] Rather, he argued, "Evil was before we came to be" and, further distancing its source from human beings, added, "The Evil which holds men down binds them against their will."[96]

However, this does not sound much like the passive evil described above as the lack of good. Indeed, as John Hick notes, Plotinus utilized a dual notion of evil here. In the first instance it is conceived as "negative and passive" and appears in instances where he "is using it to support the thesis that the universe, as the emanation of Perfect Goodness, contains no independent power of evil."[97] Thus, evil in this sense forms part of an aesthetic whole, an idea that, as we shall see, was particularly attractive to Augustine. However, in the second instance, evil is conceived "as positive and active," that is, "liable to actively attack and infect all that it touches," and it is this version Plotinus used when he wanted to "explain the felt potency of evil in human experience."[98] As will be seen shortly, this part of Plotinus's conception of evil is distinctly antithetical to Augustine's understanding.

Thus, adapting Plotinus's "passive" conception of evil and discarding his active alternative, Augustine argued that evil "has no nature of its own."[99] If evil is "no substance at all" then it cannot be an entity that exists independently of that upon which it acts as the Manichaeans believed. Adding to this argument, Augustine also argued that as all creation is good, evil cannot possibly be of any substance for, if it was, it would be good.[100] Thus, contrary to the Manichaeans, Augustine reconceived the relationship between *hyle*, matter, and evil to reflect his contention that matter is not evil:

> For neither is that material, which the ancients called Hyle, to be called an evil. I do not say that which Manichaeus with most senseless vanity, not knowing what he says, denominates Hyle, namely, the former of corporeal beings; whence it is rightly said to him, that he introduces another god. For nobody can form and create corporeal beings but God alone; for neither are they created unless there subsist within them measure, form and order which I think that now even they themselves confess to be good things, and things that cannot be except from God. But by Hyle I mean a certain material absolutely formless and without quality, whence whose qualities that we perceive are formed, as the ancients said.[101]

If evil is understood not as an independent existent entity but as the privation of good, then it also stands to reason that it cannot exist apart from the good. Rather, evil must be parasitic on the good.

However, Augustine's reasoning thus far left the critical question of how it is possible that God's "good" creation is susceptible to evil for, as the argument stood, it remained possible to assert that God is responsible for human suffering. Although he had managed to answer the question of what evil is, he was not, as yet, able to explain why a good God allows suffering or why humans choose to do what is morally evil, the question raised by the pear-stealing incident of his youth. Thus, Augustine sought to preserve the goodness of God's creation by arguing that individuals "are not, like their Creator, supremely and unchangeably good" but that "their good may be diminished and increased."[102] In particular, the good of the individual may be diminished as the result of his or her susceptibility to corruption, an argument Augustine directed toward the Manichaeans in *Against the Fundamental Epistle of Manichaeus*:

> Different evils may, indeed, be called different names; but that which is the evil of all things in which any evil is perceptible is corruption. So the corruption of an educated mind is ignorance; the corruption of a prudent mind is imprudence; the corruption of a just mind, injustice . . . Again, in a living body, the corruption of health is pain and disease.[103]

Of course, in arguing that evil is corruption and nothing is by nature "corrupt," Augustine once again refuted the Manichaean claim that evil exists as an independent entity in constant conflict with good. Along with privation therefore, this notion of corruption established evil as a nonentity fundamentally dependent on the good that sustains it.

Although this understanding of evil as the absence of good resembled the passive notion of evil articulated by Plotinus, Augustine recognized the inherent limitations of neo-Platonism in one further critical aspect. Despite being able to address questions of the nature of evil so readily rejected by the Manichaeans, neo-Platonism could not, having conceived what evil is, account for its origins.[104] By extension, it was therefore also unable to account for the roles that both humans and God play in its perpetration.

The Origins of Evil

If evil is not from God, the creator of all that is good, then where does it originate? Augustine attributed the origins of evil to "the wrong choices of free rational beings."[105] Evil, understood as the privation of good, is thus caused by "the defection of the will of a being who is mutably good from the Good which is immutable."[106] It is the turning away of the will from the good that is, in its most fundamental form, sin. As Augustine explained in *Freedom of the Will*:

The will which turns from the unchangeable and common good and turns to its own private good or to anything exterior or inferior, sins. It turns to its private good, when it wills to be governed by its own authority; to what is exterior, when it is eager to know what belongs to others and not to itself; to inferior things, when it loves bodily pleasures. In these ways a man becomes proud, inquisitive, licentious, and is taken captive by another kind of life which, when compared with the righteous life we have just described, is really death.[107]

Against the Manichaean notion that sin is a manifestation of the "two souls" with which they believed individuals are endowed, Augustine argued that "Sin is only from the will" and, as such, "takes place only by exercise of will."[108] Sin, and by extension evil, is thus not the result of any form of external force or form, but rests wholly with the will and decisions of the individual agent. For this reason, responsibility for sin, and hence evil, also rests exclusively with the individual.

However, John Hick argues that the location of sin and evil in the will of the individual agent is "radically incoherent" with the supposed benevolent character of God. Why, he asks, would a good God create beings that are susceptible to sin?[109] Surely by doing so, he suggests, God remains responsible for evil. For Augustine however, the answer to Hick's question is a relatively simple one. Susceptibility to sin, he argued, is part and parcel of humans being endowed with free will. Free will is, in turn, essential if individuals are to willingly choose repentance and enter into a right relationship with God that ensures their salvation. At the same time, others argue that surely, by giving human beings a free will that inevitably leads them to sin, God can still be held responsible for creating evil, if only implicitly. However, Augustine anticipates this criticism and makes "a subtle distinction between the *having* of human free will and the *exercise* of human free will." The possession of free will, as Geivett writes, "obtains through divine agency," while the exercise of free will is exclusively a function of human agency.[110] The mere giving and having of free will does not bring about sin, what does is the misuse of that free will.

Indeed, it is in his doctrine of "original sin"—a doctrine often attributed to Augustine but that actually "had powerful precedents in the North African Christian thought he inherited," particularly that of Cyprian and Tertullian[111]—that this becomes particularly apparent. God, Augustine argued, "created Adam and Eve to be perfect," that is, to be wholly without sin. What this meant, however, was that their sin, eating from the tree of the knowledge of good and evil, carried "weight that no subsequent sin could." Adam and Eve were the only human beings in creation who, "relying on their free will alone," could have chosen not to sin. But of course they did; by sinning they fell away from the good and, in doing so, they brought "evil," understood in the privative sense, into the world.[112] Thus, Augustine argued not that evil caused sin, as many before him, including the Manichaeans had, but rather that "sin caused evil."[113] He thereby attempted to absolve God of all complicity in the sins of human beings by laying responsibility for evil wholly at the feet of human agents.

Augustine to Aquinas and Beyond

Augustine's understanding of evil remains amongst the most prominent responses to the theological problem of evil to date. In particular, until the middle of the eighteenth century Augustinian ideas enjoyed alternate periods of resurgence with Manichaean dualism. Although Augustine roundly refuted the notion that a power to rival God existed in the universe, a number of different sects and faiths persisted in this view. In particular, both the "Paulicians of seventh-century Armenia, [and] the Bogomils in the Balkans of the tenth century . . . had implicitly or explicitly within their teachings the idea that there were two Creators, one of good and one of evil."[114] In the twelfth and thirteenth centuries, the Albigensians, or Cathars of the Languedoc region of southern France even went so far as to claim that while God ruled the spiritual world, the material world was created by the Demierge and, being composed of matter, was inherently evil. By extension, they also argued along these lines that Jesus could not be "the son of God because he had a body, which was evil, and God could not be evil."[115] In 1209, Pope Innocent III persuaded King Philip Augustus of France to launch a crusade, known as the Albigensian Crusade, to stamp out the Cathar's heresy. More than twenty thousand ordinary men, women, and children were "put to the sword" by the Army of God while several hundred Cathar knights, Perfects, and leaders were burned at the stake.[116] Despite these horrors, more moderate forms of dualism continued to challenge Augustine's view from time to time.

The first major revival of Augustinian ideas about evil came later in the thirteenth century with the works of Saint Thomas Aquinas

(1225–1274). Although the nature of evil is discussed at some length in his less well-known work, *Quaestiones disputatae de malo*, published sometime around 1270, it is in his most famous work the *Summa Theologiae* that a fairly standard presentation of the "problem of evil" appears:

> It seems that God does not exist; because if one of two contraries be infinite, the other would be altogether destroyed. But the word "God" means that He is infinite goodness. If, therefore, God existed, there would be no evil discoverable; but there is evil in the world. Therefore God goes not exist.[117]

However, rather than respond to this objection by explaining the nature and origins of evil, as Augustine had done before him, Aquinas turned instead to demonstrate the existence and goodness of God. It is thus in this context that Aquinas's famous argument that the "existence of God can be proved in five ways" appeared.[118] Considered together, Aquinas's proof of God's existence rested on the observation that things exist in the world that do not cause their own existence. So, his reasoning went, they must logically have been created by another and, for the first things that came into existence, that *other* that caused their existence must have been God. Having established God's existence, Aquinas preempted his own answer to the question of God's goodness by quoting Augustine's *Enchiridion*: "'Since God is the highest good, He would not allow any evil to exist in His works, unless His omnipotence and goodness were such as to bring good even out of evil.'"[119] This, he argued, "is part of the infinite goodness of God, that He should allow evil to exist, and out of it produce good."[120] By establishing the existence and goodness of God at the outset, Aquinas ensured that the existence of evil could not bring either into question. Following Augustine's privation thesis then, Aquinas argued that "evil is the absence of the good."[121] Interestingly however, he also argued that although "evil . . . has a cause by way of an agent," that cause is not direct, but is accidental. That is, evil is not sought deliberately but occurs by accident.

However, it is in *De Malo* that Aquinas included a thorough examination of the nature and causes of evil. It is important to note that the Latin term *malum*, often translated as "evil" in English, was actually a wide-ranging term that included a broad range of ideas united by a sense of being "undesirable in general." Thus, *malum* could be translated as "damage," "harm," "hurt," "injury," "misfortune," and "misdeed," along with "evil" used to describe large scale natural disasters and morally reprehensible behavior.[122] In general, however, Aquinas conceived evil as existing "wherever goodness is lacking."[123] The first article of the first of sixteen questions addressed in the work thus examines whether or not evil can be considered an entity. On the one hand, Aquinas writes, it can be argued that: "Everything created thing is an entity. But evil is something created, as Is. 45:6–7 says: 'I am the Lord, who causes peace and creates evil.' Therefore, evil is an entity."[124] On the other hand however, Augustine argues, "in *The City of God* that evil is not a nature, but that the lack of good took on this ascription."[125] To resolve this dilemma, Aquinas argued that "we speak of evil in two ways." In one way, we understand evil as "the subject that is evil, and this subject is an entity." In the other way, however, we "understand evil itself, and evil so understood is the very privation of a particular good, not an entity."[126] Thus, he concluded his answer by stating that "evil is not an entity, but the subject that evil befalls is, since evil is only the privation of a particular good."[127] Evil is thus "in things" although only "as a privation and not as an entity."[128] Thus again, Aquinas presents a developed and ultimately more sophisticated understanding of Augustine's conception of evil.

The second major revival of Augustinian theology came with the Reformation in the sixteenth century, its central figures John Calvin and Martin Luther both quoting "extensively from Augustine."[129] Despite their reliance on the Pauline as opposed to neo-Platonist elements of Augustinian theology however, neither Luther nor Calvin included in their works a "general theory of the nature of evil" to rival Augustine's privation thesis.[130] As John Hick suggests, this may have been due to the fact that there was not, at the time, any significant heretical discussion of evil to be combated.[131] As we will see in Chapter 4 however, by the middle of the eighteenth century this was no longer the case.

At the same time however, debates about Luther's interpretation of the Pauline epistles did spill over into wider debates about the problem of evil, particularly amongst the Jesuit and Dominican theologians of the sixteenth and seventeenth centuries. Central to Luther's famous "rejection of the efficacy of good works" in courting God's favor and ultimately attaining salvation, was the concept of divine predestination that, to some extent, amounted to a denial of complete human freedom.[132] In very broad terms, the doctrine of predestination maintained that individuals were predestined, from the beginning of time, to eternal salvation or damnation and thus, no amount of good works in this life could secure a place in heaven. Rather, salvation was a gift of God's grace that could not be earned. What this seemed to imply is that individuals did not possess complete freedom over their own wills but were, in a sense, moving along a predetermined path through life. Furthermore, it also seemed to imply that God was somehow complicit in the sin of humankind.

In the immediate term, Luther's pronouncement drew a range of responses, from Erasmus's work *On the Freedom of the Will*, the central arguments of which were refuted in Luther's *Bondage of the Will*, to an attempt by the Church to provide "a definitive answer to Luther at the Council of Trent."[133] As Kremer and Latzer note, this "more than a century of rancorous struggle over grace and freedom" fought between Catholics and members of the Reformed and Evangelical Protestant churches, "spilled over into battles among Catholics," the most important of which took place at the Congregationes de Auxiliis, held from January 2, 1598 to August 28, 1607.[134] Here, a group of cardinals were called together to resolve a dispute that had arisen with the publication in 1588 of the Jesuit Luis de Molina's "work on the agreement of free will with grace, and related matters, 'according to Several Articles in St. Thomas'" and its refutation by the Dominican theologian Domingo Bañez. Despite meeting for nine years, the congregation was unable to resolve the dispute.[135]

Thus, at the beginning of the seventeenth century, Catholic and, in particular, Jesuit thought about questions of free will and grace had become extremely complex. In the work of the Jesuit theologian Francisco Suarez, the *Disputationes Metaphysicae*, the impact of these debates upon discussions of the problem of evil became clear. As Alfred J. Freddoso explains, Suarez fundamentally agreed with "traditional writers that what is 'evil in itself' is either (a) the privation of some good that ought to belong to a given subject in view of its nature and powers or (b) the subject itself insofar as it suffers such a privation."[136] In a manner typical of his style of scholarship, Suarez divided the concept of evil into two distinct forms, natural evil, "a positive entity that deprives its subject of some natural good it ought to have according to the standard set by its own nature," and moral evil.[137] Moral evil was itself "divided into the evil of sin or fault *(malum culpae)* and the evil of punishment *(malum poenae)*"[138] as follows:

We can say succinctly and clearly that the evil of sin (*malum culpae*) is a disorder in a free action or omission—that is, a lack of due perfection as regards a free action—whereas the evil of punishment (*malum poenae*) is any other lack of a due good that is contracted or inflicted because of sin.[139]

Sin as punishment, in Suarez's view, could be "either a sin that is causally connected with other sins or some other type of suffering that God directly inflicts or at least permits."[140] However, in a similar manner to moral evil, Suarez conceived sin as the ultimate cause of natural evil as well:

> Even though, leaving aside divine providence, one could conceive of some natural evil in a rational creature which was not inflicted because of any fault and which would thus be neither a sin nor a punishment, nonetheless, we believe that in conformity with divine providence no lack of a due perfection can exist in a rational creature unless it is a sin or else takes its origin from sin. It is for this reason that Augustine, *In Genesim ad litteram*, chap. 1, says that every evil is either a sin or a punishment for sin.[141]

Thus, Suarez resolved the problem of free will and God's causal role in the perpetration of evil in two ways. First, he argued that "because of its depravity, the evil of sin cannot be intended or willed by God, but only permitted."[142] Thus, evil is the result of sinful actions, the misuse of free will that results in the free agent rejecting God's will.[143] At the same time however, "other kinds of evil," including natural evils, "can be directly willed and intended by God, as long as they do not include sin."[144] With this, Suarez attempted to uphold the good nature of God by placing responsibility for only some forms of evil with God and attributing the rest to the sinful human agent. For Kremer and Latzer, Suarez's solution to the problem of evil is a particularly dangerous one for it is essentially "an attempt to talk the razor-thin line between ascribing the causation of evil acts to God (and so violating divine goodness) and ascribing their causation to creatures (and so violating omnipotence)."[145] As we will see in Chapter 4, it was these debates between the Christian denominations and within Catholic theology that provided Pierre Bayle with much of the material for his highly influential discussion of the problem of evil at the end of the seventeenth century.

Conclusion

The question of how to reconcile the all-good character of God with the existence of evil in the world has long exercised the minds of some of the most important thinkers of the Western tradition. From the ancient Babylonians, Hebrews, and Zoroastrians, to the early Christians, Manichaeans, and, much later, Thomas Aquinas, perhaps none were so intrigued by the matter than Augustine, undoubtedly the most influential theorist of evil in history. As we have seen in this chapter, Augustine's understanding of the nature and causes of evil was formulated at a time when Christianity was facing significant challenges at the hands of the Gnostic-derived sects, including Manichaeanism. What Augustine's conceptualization of evil sought to achieve was thus not simply a clearer understanding of the phenomenon in general, but a more solid, and theologically defensible account of the nature and origins of evil in Christian thought. Thus, although several writers have argued in recent years that Augustine's discussion of evil cannot be accurately considered a "theodicy" as such, it is clear that his work, whether consciously or otherwise, fulfilled that role by achieving a theoretical reconciliation of the character of God with the existence of evil.[146]

For Augustine, the problem of evil was, at the same time, a profoundly personal and challenging intellectual problem. On the one hand, he was struck by a very personal need to understand why human beings commit evil acts, a need derived from his youthful pear-stealing escapade. On the other hand, he was also fascinated by the same theoretical "problem of evil," the problem of how to reconcile the existence of the Judeo-Christian God, characterized as benevolent, omnipotent, and omniscient, with the existence of evil, that gripped the minds of so many who came before and after him. Significantly, although Augustine acknowledged, at least implicitly, that two different "problems of evil" were at play in the world and needed to be answered, he did not allow them to become completely separate. Rather, he answered his own personal problem of evil by reference to the more general theological problem of evil. Human beings commit morally evil acts because their sinful human nature leads them to misuse the free will with which God has endowed them. Thus, although he did not acknowledge the existence of two separate problems of evil, by placing responsibility for evil squarely at the feet of the individual human agent, Augustine unconsciously began to pave the way for their formal separation, the subject matter of Chapter 4.

4

Moral Evil

The human being must make or have made *himself* into whatever he is or should become in a moral sense, good or evil.[1]

In many ways, the eighteenth century can be viewed as "the golden age of theodicies."[2] Indeed, it was during the eighteenth century that some of the most famous and important theodicies appeared and as a result, some of the most significant shifts in thinking about evil took place. In 1702, the Anglican thinker and later Archbishop of Dublin, William King (1650–1729), published an *Essay on the Origin of Evil* in Latin, an English translation of which appeared in 1731. As he wrote in the Preface to the work, already directing his argument at the Manichaean view:

> Both the usefulness and antiquity of that celebrated controversy, concerning evil, as well as the notorious absurdity of the *Manichean* method of accounting for it, have been so frequently and fully set forth, that there is no need of enlarging upon them, since all that ever seemed necessary to a complete conquest over those wild Hereticks, and their extravagant Hypothesis, was only some tolerable solution of the difficulties which drive them into it.[3]

The significance of King's work was three-fold. First, King introduced a three-part division of evil into contemporary discourse. Evil could, in his estimation, be divided into "imperfection" (understood as "the absence of those perfections or advantages which exist elsewhere, or in other beings"), "natural evil" ("pains and uneasiness, inconveniences and disappointment of appetites, arising from natural motions"), and "moral evil" ("vicious elections, that is, such as are hurtful to ourselves, or others").[4] As we will see shortly, this type of division, particularly that which sought to distinguish natural and moral evils, became a hallmark of eighteenth century accounts of evil. Secondly, and perhaps more importantly, King introduced the notion of "optimism" that marked many more prominent works on evil than his own. "Optimism," in its eighteenth-century form was, as Hick explains, "a variation of the Augustinian type of theodicy."[5] It maintained, on a fundamental level, that despite the existence of evil in the world, this was the "best of all possible worlds." As King explained, although it "is manifest that good be mixed with evil in this life, yet there is much more good in nature."[6] The created world, he argued, "might have been better perhaps in some particulars, but not without some new, and probably greater inconveniences, which must have spoiled the beauty either of the whole, or of some chief part."[7] Finally, the original Latin version of King's *Essay* provided the philosophical foundations for Alexander Pope's *Essay on Man*, to be discussed shortly.

Leaving the significant contribution of William King aside however, the most famous theodicist of the eighteenth century was undoubtedly Gottfried Wilhelm von Leibniz (1646–1716). As such, this chapter begins by outlining Leibniz's contribution to thought about the problem of evil before turning to the works of his critics and defenders, and finally, to the thought of Immanuel Kant. In doing so, the chapter follows the work of Susan Neiman and argues that what was most significant about the discussion of evil in the eighteenth century was that the two problems of evil, introduced in Chapter 3, became further and further divorced from one another until, in some areas of scholarship, two separate and independent problems could be identified. The first, as Neiman explains, was the "cosmological problem" described in Chapter 3, the problem of reconciling the existence of suffering with an all-good God. The second, however, was the moral problem of why rational beings choose to do moral evil and, in many ways, can be equated with Augustine's "personal" problem of evil.[8] Both derived from the question, "why do I suffer?" As we saw in Chapter 3, in the ancient and medieval worlds the second problem was answered by reference to the first, thereby rendering human actions with a theological explanation. However, by the late Enlightenment, writers came to consider the second question in isolation from the first; that is, the problem of human moral agency, to be discussed in detail in Chapter 5, could be addressed without reference to God. With this, the history of thought about the "problem of evil" saw, for the first time, a truly modern understanding of the nature and causes of evil. As such, this chapter is concerned with the rise and fall of theodicy and the accompanying emergence of wholly secular accounts of human moral evil that took place in the eighteenth century.

Theodicy

Despite his fame as the originator of the term "theodicy," it is widely accepted that Leibniz viewed the "problem of evil" as "an intellectual puzzle rather than a terrifying threat to all the meaning that he had found in life."[9] Indeed, as Geivett writes, "Leibniz's philosophical treatment of the problem of evil was occasioned by the peculiar circumstances in which he found himself."[10] In the late seventeenth and early eighteenth centuries, among the most influential thinkers in Western Europe was the French author of the *Dictionnaire historique et critique* [Historical and Critical Dictionary] (1697), Pierre Bayle (1647–1706). Although technically a dictionary comprised of numerous articles on figures both popular and obscure designed to counter the inaccuracies of Louis Moréri's (1643–1680) encyclopedia, Bayle's work included extensive footnotes in which he expounded his own views on the most prominent philosophical and theological issues of the time, including of course, the "problem of evil."[11] Indeed, although Bayle had included a lengthy examination of William King's discussion of the problem of evil in his *Résponse aux questions d'un provincial*, it is his dictionary that has had the greatest influence on thought about the subject.

At the time when Bayle was rising to some prominence for his writings on evil, Leibniz was employed as a tutor and librarian to the court of Brunswick-Luneburg at Hanover in which capacity he taught the Queen of Prussia. In fact, it was his student who encouraged him to publish his criticisms of Bayle's *Dictionary*. As he wrote in a letter to Thomas Burnet, explaining his reasons for writing *Theodicy*:

> The greater part of the work was composed piece by piece, at a time when the late Queen of Prussia and I were having discussions of these matters in connection with Bayle's Dictionary and other writings, which were being widely read. In our conversations I generally answered the objections raised by Bayle and contrived to show that they are not so powerful as certain people who are not well disposed to religion would have us believe. Her Majesty frequently commanded me to set down my answers in writing, so that one could think them through more carefully. After the death

of this great princess I gathered the pieces together, at the instigation of friends who had heard about them, and, with some additions, produced the book in question. It is a book of considerable size. As I have reflected upon this topic since my youth, I dare say that I have treated it thoroughly.[12]

Although Leibniz admired elements of Bayle's work, he was particularly critical of what he saw as a "sympathetic presentation of the Manichaean heresy" contained in it.[13] Indeed, for Bayle, Manichaeanism provided the most plausible account of evil because it included elements of "happiness and suffering, wickedness and virtue" in its worldview.[14] The Manichaean notion of a world ruled by forces of good and evil, he believed, helped to preserve "belief in God's benevolence" in the face of human suffering by arguing that God is locked in a perpetual battle against the forces of evil.[15] As Bayle wrote in the "Manichees" entry in his dictionary, "Their weakness did not consist, as at first it may seem, in their doctrine of two principles, one good, and the other bad; but in the particular explications they gave of it, and in the practical consequences they drew from it."[16] The result of Leibniz's attempt to re-establish an Augustinian understanding of evil in the face of Bayle's Manichaeanism was his only published book, *Theodicy*, which appeared in 1710.

In attempting to reconcile the goodness of God with the existence of evil in the world, Leibniz invoked a monist understanding of theodicy. In general terms, monism maintains that "the universe forms an ultimate harmonious unity [and] . . . that evil is only apparent and would be recognized as good if we could see it in its full cosmic context."[17] First attributed to Epicurus, this pattern of thought exists in both theistic and secular forms, finding its most prominent articulation in the works of Benedict de Spinoza (1632–1677). Referred to as the "virtuous atheist" by Bayle,[18] in adhering to a monist worldview "Spinoza saw reality as forming an infinite and perfect whole—perfect in the sense that everything within it follows by logical necessity from the eternal divine nature—and saw each finite thing as making its own proper contribution to this infinite perfection."[19] Within this perfect whole, evil—and for that matter, good—is not conceived as an objective reality (*entia realia*) but as a mental entity (*entia rationis*). As Spinoza explained:

> After men persuaded themselves, that everything which is created is created for their sake, they were bound to consider as the chief quality in everything that which is most useful to themselves, and to account those

things the best of all which have the most beneficial effect on mankind. Further they were bound to form abstract notions for the explanation of the nature of things, such as *goodness, badness, order, confusion, warmth, cold, beauty, deformity*, and so on; and from the belief that they are free agents arose the further notions of *praise* and *blame, sin* and *merit. . . .* We have now perceived, that all the explanations commonly given of nature are mere modes of imagining, and do not indicate the true nature of anything, but only the constitution of the imagination; and, although they have names, as though they were entities, existing externally to the imagination, I call them entities imaginary rather than real.[20]

Thus, Spinoza denied that "evil" could have any objective meaning. Rather, "knowledge of evil" was, in his view, "inadequate knowledge" and would not be conceived of at all "if the human mind possessed only adequate ideas."[21]

Echoing some, but critically not all of Spinoza's ideas about evil, Leibniz also wrote in a monist sense that "all the evils in the world contribute, in ways which generally we cannot now trace, to the character of the whole as the best of all possible universes."[22] However, where Spinoza made the stronger claim that the absolute perfection of the world was "a necessary expression of the eternal and infinite perfection of God or Nature," Leibniz argued that this was "the best practicable world."[23] Indeed, taking this argument to its logical extreme, Leibniz argued, "If the smallest evil that comes to pass in the world were missing in it, it would no longer be this world; which, nothing omitted and no allowance made, was found the best by the Creator who chose it."[24] As Susan Neiman explains, in making this argument that the creation is "the best of all possible worlds," Leibniz was, in part, referring to the Castilian King Alfonso X, a student of Ptolemaic astronomy who appeared in Bayle's work. Significantly, Bayle devoted some attention to Alphonso's blasphemous claim that "if he had been God's counsel at the time of creation, certain things would be in better order than they are."[25] For Alfonso, this was certainly not the "best of all possible worlds" and, as such, he "proved a perfect foil in Leibniz's polemic against Bayle."[26]

In part, the wide discrepancy between Alfonso's and Leibniz's views of the order of creation can be attributed to "the miserable state of thirteenth-century astronomy." Neiman writes in this vein that, "had the world been created as Ptolemy supposed, the Creator could indeed have used advice in design."[27] However, Leibniz's view of future understanding was far more optimistic:

And if we hold the same opinion as King Alfonso, we shall, I say, receive this answer: You have known the world only since the day before yesterday, you scarce see farther than your nose, and you carp at the world. Wait until you know more of the world and consider therein especially the parts which present a complete whole (as do organic bodies); and you will find therein a contrivance and a beauty transcending all imagination. Let us thence draw conclusions as to the wisdom and the goodness of the author of the world, even in things that we know not. We find in the universe some things which are not pleasing to us; but let us be aware that it is not made for us alone. It is nevertheless made for us if we are wise: it will serve us if we use it for our service; we shall be happy in it if we wish to be.[28]

What accompanied Leibniz's theodicy was a division of human misery into metaphysical, physical (natural), and moral categories of evil, a division that echoed King's earlier attempt at the categorization of evils. Metaphysical evil, Leibniz argued, "consists in mere imperfection"; that is, it was viewed as a function of creation's finitude.[29] Physical evil is conceived as suffering and, although Leibniz claimed that God "does not will [it] absolutely," he does "will it often as a penalty owing to guilt, and often also as a means to an end, that is, to prevent greater evils or to obtain greater good."[30] That is, physical evil was understood to be the "pain and suffering" humans experience as the penalty for committing moral evil, conceived as sin.[31] Thus, Leibniz argued, as Augustine had done before him, that human beings suffer because they sin, although he thought the connection "too self-evident to warrant serious question."[32] This, however, was all to change with the destructive force of one of the most spectacular events of the early modern period, the Lisbon earthquake.

The Lisbon Earthquake

Described as a "watershed event in European history," the Lisbon earthquake, which struck on All Saints' Day, November 1, 1755, inspired a distinct shift in conventional views about the relationship between evil and human suffering.[33] In particular, in the aftermath of the earthquake, the optimism that had marked much thought about evil in the first half of the eighteenth century and especially Leibniz's arguments seemed somewhat misplaced. Most famously, through the character of Dr. Pangloss, Voltaire's *Candide* ridiculed the idea that a world in which something as catastrophic as the Lisbon earthquake could happen was "the best of all possible worlds." "If this is the best of all possible worlds," Candide asked, "what are the others?"[34] In a similar vein, the renowned pessimist Arthur Schopenhauer wrote some time later: "Even if Leibniz's demonstration that this is the best of all *possible* worlds were correct, it would still not be a vindication of divine providence. For the Creator created not only the world, he also created the possibility itself: therefore he should have created the possibility of a better world than this one."[35] However, Voltaire's harshest criticisms of the Leibnizian view of evil are found in his poem, "The Lisbon Earthquake: An Inquiry into the Maxim, 'Whatever is, is right.'" The maxim included in the subtitle of the poem was the central thesis of Alexander Pope's *Essay on Man*, a work noted for its optimism.[36] Despite his later criticisms of Pope's work however, Voltaire made his "love and admiration" for "the illustrious Pope" clear in the preface to the poem, writing that he:

> acknowledges with all mankind that there is evil as well as good on the earth; he owns that no philosopher has ever been able to explain the nature of moral and physical evil; he asserts that Bayle, the greatest master of the art of reasoning that ever wrote, has only taught us to doubt, and that he combats himself; he owns that man's understanding is as weak as his life is miserable.[37]

However, Voltaire maintained that by arguing that, "whatever is, is right," and describing this as "the best of all possible worlds," Pope and Leibniz, respectively, failed to show sufficient compassion to the people of Lisbon:

> If when Lisbon, Moquinxa, Tetuan and other cities were swallowed up with a great number of their inhabitants in the month of November, 1755, philosophers had cried out to the wretches who with difficulty escaped from the ruins "all this is productive of general good; the heirs of those who have perished will increase their fortune; masons will earn money by rebuilding the houses, beasts will feed on the carcasses buried under the ruins; it is necessary effect of necessary causes; your particular misfortune is nothing, it contributes to universal good," such a harangue would have doubtless been cruel as the earthquake was fatal, and all that the author of the poem on the destruction of Lisbon has said amounts only to this.[38]

Although these are serious criticisms, it was Leibniz's claim that suffering was the result of sin that was particularly problematic in the thought that tried to make sense of the earthquake. It simply did not follow that the pious population of Lisbon had brought this calamity upon itself. Two important ideas thus emerged in response to the Lisbon earthquake. The first, as discussed briefly above, was the idea that although a connection could be retained between sin and suffering, it could only be conceived in general, indirect terms; that is, the suffering of humankind could be attributed to its general sinfulness. As Schopenhauer wrote in this vein, "generally speaking, it is the grievous *sin of the world* which gives rise to the manifold and great *suffering of the world*" not in accordance with "any physical-empirical connexion" but a metaphysical one.[39] The second idea that emerged from the Lisbon earthquake owes its foundations to both King and Leibniz and entails the distinction between natural and moral evils that appeared in a more fully articulated form with the works of Jean-Jacques Rousseau.

Evil in the Thought of Jean-Jacques Rousseau

Jean-Jacques Rousseau (1712–1778) engaged the problem of evil by responding, in the first instance to Leibniz's pronouncements about Alfonso X's blasphemy and, in the second, to Voltaire's "The Lisbon Earthquake." Unlike Leibniz, who had concluded that Alfonso would have understood creation better had he studied the modern sciences, Rousseau argued that "he would have done better not to study at all."[40] Thus, in his "Observations by Jean-Jacques Rousseau of Geneva: On the Answer made to his Discourse" he wrote that:

> One always believes one has said what the Sciences do, when one has said what they should do. Yet the two seem to me quite different: the study of the Universe should elevate man to his Creator, I know; but it only elevates human vanity. The Philosopher, flattering himself that he fathoms God's secrets, dares to liken his supposed wisdom to eternal wisdom: he approves, he blames, he corrects, he prescribes laws to nature and limits to the Divinity; and while he is busy with his vain systems, and take endless pains to arrange the machine of the world, the Plowman who sees the rain and the sun by turns fertilize his field admires, praises and blesses the hand from which he receives these graces, without troubling himself about how they come to him. He does not seek to justify his ignorance or his vices by his incredulity. He does not censure God's works, nor challenge his master in order to display his self-importance. Never will the impious remark of Alfonso X occur to one of the vulgar: that blasphemy was reserved for a learned mouth.[41]

However, as Neiman notes, it is in his letter to Voltaire of August 18, 1756 that a "more sustained set of remarks" about evil are found.[42] Rousseau's admiration of Voltaire is apparent from the first line of the letter that told of "my love for your writings," to the final paragraph in which he wrote that Voltaire is "the one among my contemporaries whose talents I most honour, and whose writings speak best to my heart."[43] These platitudes aside, among Rousseau's foremost tasks in this work was the defense of the optimism promulgated in the writings of Pope and Leibniz. As discussed earlier, and as Rousseau recounted, Voltaire had charged both writers with "insulting our evils by maintaining that all is well."[44] This, Voltaire had thought, indicated a distinct lack of compassion for the inhabitants of Lisbon blighted first by the earthquake and later by the tidal waves and fires it caused. However, Rousseau wrote to Voltaire that the effect of Pope and Leibniz's works was "the very opposite of what you intend."[45] He wrote that:

> This optimism which you find so cruel yet consoles me amid the very pains which you depict as unbearable.
>
> Pope's poem allays my evils and inclines me to patience, yours embitters my suffering, incites me to grumble, and, by depriving me of everything but a shaken hope, reduces me to despair.[46]

Indeed, for Rousseau, there could be no doctrine more consoling than that of optimism.

Natural and Moral Evils

As for so many thinkers who had gone before him, the central problem of evil was, for Rousseau, the problem of its origins. What made this problem a particularly tricky one, he recognized, was the fact that it could be more accurately described in terms of the two problems, the moral and cosmological problems introduced above. As Neiman writes however, although, like his predecessors, "Rousseau neither adequately distinguished nor made clear the connections between these kinds of problem of evil"; in addressing them in the way he did, he changed "the form of the problem itself."[47] Thus, Rousseau must be credited as the first to "treat the problem of evil as a *philosophical* problem."[48] Indeed, reflecting the central themes of the two problems of evil, Rousseau's two dominant lines of argument, particularly in his letter to Voltaire, concern the origin of evil and the nature of providence.

In Rousseau's view, the source of evil is not God but humankind. As the first line of *Émile* reads, "God makes all things good; man meddles with them and they become evil."[49] Thus, the source of moral evil cannot be found "anywhere but in man, free, perfected, hence corrupted."[50] By specifying that "moral evil" is the product of human actions, Rousseau here drew on an important distinction between moral and physical evils. Physical evils, otherwise known as natural disasters, were, in Rousseau's view, morally neutral on account of the fact that they are not the *direct* result of human actions. At the same time however, Rousseau also held human beings responsible for both natural and moral evils.[51] As he wrote in the "Letter to Voltaire" criticizing the population of Lisbon:

> I believe I have shown that except for death, which is an evil almost solely because of the preparations made in anticipation of it, most of our physical evils are also of our own making. To continue with your subject of Lisbon, you must admit, for example, that nature had not assembled two thousand six- or seven-story houses there, and that if the inhabitants of that great city had been more evenly dispersed and more simply lodged, the damage would have been far less, and perhaps nil. All would have fled at the first shock, and the following day they would have been seen twenty miles away, just as cheerful as if nothing had happened; but they were set on staying, on stubbornly standing by hovels, on risking further shocks, because what they would have left behind was worth more than what they could take with them. How many unfortunates perished in this disaster for wanting to take, one his clothes, another his papers, a third his money? Does not everyone know that a man's person has become his least part, and that it is almost not worth the trouble to save when he has lost everything else?[52]

Thus, for Rousseau, a natural connection between suffering and sin could be said to exist despite the distinction he made between physical and moral evils.

In order to explain this connection, it is necessary to consider Rousseau's understanding of Providence and the created order of things. What is particularly important to note is that Rousseau's understanding of the goodness of God was of a more absolute nature than that of either Leibniz or Pope before him. As Neiman explains, prior to Rousseau, thinkers concerned with the problem of evil "were forced into one of two positions."[53] On the one hand, optimists such as Leibniz and Bayle argued that evils are a necessary part of a greater, ultimately good plan, although they disagreed about whether or not human beings would ever be able to understand it. On the other hand, however, writers such as David Hume argued that evil defies understanding to the extent that it brings reasoning itself into question. Thus, to attempt to understand evil is to reject philosophy outright.[54] However, Rousseau presented two arguments that together provided an alternative to the dominant Enlightenment views, the first of which cemented the place of the problem of evil firmly within the bounds of philosophy.

Going beyond Leibniz's claim that this is "the best of all possible worlds" and Pope's argument that "what is, is right," Rousseau argued that "it might be preferable to say *The whole is good* or *All is good for the whole.*"[55] Thus, it is not the case that everything is good and hence God must be good, as Pope's reasoning seemed to imply, but rather that within the good whole "each material being" is "arranged in the best way possible in relation to the whole."[56] However, as Rousseau made clear in his "Letter to Philopolis," neither the goodness of God nor his providence need to be defended in the face of evil as Leibniz had done. Indeed, Rousseau went so far as to suggest that providence cannot possibly need the "help of the Leibnizian, or indeed, of any other Philosophy for its justification."[57] As Rousseau asked the recipient of his letter: "Do you yourself seriously think that any System of Philosophy whatsoever could be more blameless than the Universe, and that a Philosopher's arguments exonerate providence more convincingly than do God's works? Besides, to deny the existence of evil is a most convenient way of excusing the author of that evil; the stoics formerly made themselves a laughingstock for less."[58] What this seems to suggest then is that evil is a philosophical or moral problem and not, as it were, a cosmological problem. Interestingly however, in attempting to present a naturalistic account of the origins of evil, Rousseau takes Augustine's free will defense as his starting point.

To quickly recap, we recall that Augustine's solution to the problem of evil was presented in terms of his notions of free will and original sin. For Augustine, human beings suffer because they freely choose to sin. As such, sin is not the result of evil but evil, conceived in terms of suffering, is the result of sin. In Augustine's account, the Fall thus plays a central role as the action that, by first bringing evil into the world, became conceived as original sin. With Augustine, Rousseau also maintained that the free will defense provides the best means by which God can be absolved of all responsibility for evil. Despite sharing this starting point with Augustine however, here is where the similarities end. For Rousseau, the Fall, and the ensuing existence of evil that followed from it, could be explained in natural, meaning scientific, terms.

Rousseau's naturalistic account of evil argued, with Aquinas, that although "Evil is our own doing," human beings often commit evil actions unintentionally or by mistake.[59] That is, Rousseau conceived evil not as the result of specific individual intentions epitomized by the Fall, but as emerging out of a collective process. This process is, to a great extent, the central theme of his *Second Discourse*, otherwise known as the *Discourse on the Origin and Foundations of Inequality Among Men*. In this work, Rousseau introduced the "noble savage" who, from an original existence devoid of all evil, in becoming "civilized" produced evil. For Rousseau, "all the vices that currently plague us could be explained through a few developmental principles" and could be attributed to the emergence of factors such as vanity and self-alienation that came with civilized society.[60] Thus, evil was not a matter of intent for Rousseau and did not involve "sin," understood in an Augustinian sense. Rather, it was the result of collective processes of civilization borne of human weakness. As Rousseau demonstrated in the *Second Discourse*, at each stage in its development, human society could have made different choices that would have avoided the perpetuation of evil.[61]

Thus, Rousseau maintained that if all creation is good and if evil is the result of a particular process of civilization according to which the noble savage became corrupted, then the remedy to evil can also be found in the process of civilization. In this, *Émile*, the work in which Rousseau explains how a child ought to be raised and educated, may be conceived as the remedy to the ills diagnosed in the *Second Discourse*. What is more, it is in this work that Rousseau makes a firm natural connection between sin and the suffering that is evil. Suffering, in Rousseau's view is neither baseless nor is it the result of divine punishment. Rather, we suffer because attached to every sin is a natural consequence, a natural penalty for the sin committed. By thus arguing, Rousseau ultimately made it possible to answer the moral problem of evil without reference to the cosmological problem, a move finally achieved in Immanuel Kant's later works.

Evil in the Thought of Immanuel Kant

Kant's admiration for Rousseau is well-known, bestowing the title of "Newton of the mind" upon him:

> Newton was the first to see order and regularity combined with great simplicity, where disorder and ill-matched variety had reigned before. Since then comets have been moving in geometric orbits. Rousseau was the first to discover in the variety of shapes that men assume the deeply concealed nature of man and to observe the hidden law that justifies Providence. Before them, the objections of Alfonso and the Manichaeans were valid. After Newton and Rousseau, God is justified, and Pope's thesis is henceforth true.[62]

Despite this pronouncement however, in his earlier works Kant aligned himself more directly with Leibniz's understanding of theodicy. In particular, in the 1759 *Considerations on Optimism*, Kant perpetuated a "streamlined" version of the idea that "we live in the best of all possible worlds."[63] That is, he argued that "evil ultimately plays a role in the production of good."[64] However, Kant's early discussions of evil are not entirely consistent and in his lectures on the *Philosophy of Religion* delivered in the 1780s, but only published in 1817, he argued that "evil is a mere negation and an instrument in the progress of good."[65]

As Michael Despland notes, the "decisive turning point" in Kant's thought appeared in the 1791 essay *On the Failure of All Attempted Philosophical Theodicies* in which he not only rejected all forms of theodicy but finally divorced himself from the Leibnizian notion of evil.[66] In order to demonstrate the goodness of God in spite of the existence of suffering in the world, Kant argued that "the so-called advocate of God . . . must prove one of three things" in what he termed the "tribunal of reason": either that what one deems contrary to purposefulness in the world is not so; *or*, that while it is indeed contrary to purposefulness, it must be considered not as a positive fact but as an inevitable consequence of the nature of things; *or*, finally, that while a positive fact, it is not the work of the supreme Creator of things, but of some other reasonable being, such as man or superior spirits, good or evil."[67] Kant went on to demonstrate that no established theodicy had managed to achieve this. All theodicy, he argued, "must be an interpretation of nature and must show how God manifests the intentions of his will through it."[68] However, just what God's intentions are and how they are manifested in the world is something of a mystery; with regard to the intentions of God's will, the world is something of "a closed book."[69] Referring to the book of Job, the book he believed to be the "most philosophical book of the Bible," Kant argued, "God in His infinite wisdom has reasons which our weak and feeble minds cannot hope to comprehend."[70] From this he concluded, "Theodicy is not a task of science but is a matter of faith."[71] That is, individuals can *believe* that despite the abundance of suffering in the world, a benevolent deity exists, but they cannot *prove* the existence of this deity by observing an imperfect world.[72] This of course bears the hallmarks of David Hume's empiricism, which not only signaled the beginning of the end of theoretical theodicy but also exerted a demonstrable influence on Kant's thought.

David Hume's Problem of Evil

Focusing on the evidential "problem of evil," Hume (1711–1776) argued that since the existence of suffering, and hence evil, could not be reconciled with the Judeo-Christian characterization of God, the reality of innocent suffering could be said to disprove the existence of God. An empiricist who, on occasions, harbored a distinct "distaste for Christianity," Hume argued that the only knowledge we have is derived from empirical observation.[73] Thus miracles and apparently "rational" explanations for the goodness of God derived from evidence of human suffering were considered beyond the realm of empirical proof. As he wrote in *An Enquiry Concerning Human Understanding*, "Whoever is moved by *Faith* to assent to [a miracle], is conscious of a continual miracle in his own person, which subverts all the principles of his understanding, and gives him a determination to believe what is most contrary to custom and experience."[74]

However, it was in the context of his claim that "there is no view of human life or of the condition of mankind, from which, without the greatest violence, we can infer the moral attributes, or learn that infinite wisdom, which we must discover by the eyes of faith alone"[75] that Hume presented his version of the problem of evil. For Hume, the problem of evil was necessarily based on the assumption that if God does in fact exist then the suffering of humankind must necessarily be explained in terms of his character. As he famously wrote, inverting the classical presentation of the "problem of evil":

Epicurus's old questions are yet unanswered. Is he willing to prevent evil, but not able? then he is impotent. Is he able, but not willing? then he is malevolent. Is he both able and willing? whence then is evil?[76]

Although Hume entertained the possibility that the Judeo-Christian God may be a benevolent God, he concluded that all the available evidence of suffering suggested otherwise. Rather, imbuing God with benevolent characteristics amounted to nothing more than a baseless exercise in anthropomorphism. Thus, for Hume, the answer to the problem of evil was that empirical evidence of suffering indicated not the existence of an all-good, all-powerful, and all-knowing God but rather that the world we live in is an imperfect one.

By following Hume and breaking his bond with Leibniz, Kant began to pave the way for his more famous discussion of "radical evil" in the 1793 work *Religion Within the Boundaries of Mere Reason*. This work was written for the purpose of demonstrating that "the Christian religion, in its historic lineaments, is conformable with what he calls 'moral theology,' resting on a new metaphysics of the practical reason."[77] It was, in short, a "reinterpretation of Christianity solely in terms of moral values" that came face to face with the "struggle between good and evil in human nature."[78] As such, in this work Kant began to consider the moral question of why humans commit evil acts in isolation from the theological question of why God allows suffering in the world.

Kant on "Radical Evil"

For Kant, humans are not innately good or evil; that is, they are not born morally good or morally evil. Rather, as Kant explained:

> The human being must make or have made *himself* into whatever he is or should become in a moral sense, good or evil. These two [characters] must be an effect of his free power of choice. For otherwise they could not be imputed to him and, consequently, he could be neither *morally* good nor evil. If it is said, The human being is created good, this can only mean nothing more than: He has been created for the *good* and the original *predisposition* in him is good; the human being is not thereby good as such, but he brings it about that he becomes either good or evil.[79]

Good and evil therefore "lie only in a rule made by the will [*Willkür*] for the use of its freedom, that is, in a maxim."[80] The *Willkür*, as Bernstein writes, is "the name we give to the capacity to choose between alternatives" and is "neither *intrinsically* good nor *intrinsically* evil; rather, it is the capacity by which we freely choose good or evil maxims."[81] It is the "faculty of free spontaneous choice," an idea that, as we will see in Chapter 6, Hannah Arendt draws upon in her own determination of what constitutes "radical evil."[82]

According to Kant's reasoning therefore, "we call a human being evil . . . not because he performs actions that are evil (contrary to law), but because these are so constituted that they allow the inference of evil maxims in him."[83] As we will see in Chapters 5 and 6, in later scholarship, particularly in the post–World War II era, this notion that the individual could be directly deemed evil was replaced by the idea that it was in fact their actions, and not the individual, that were "evil." The ability of the human individual to make evil choices is explained by what Kant called the human "propensity for evil," a propensity that exists in constant tension with the "original predisposition to good in human nature."[84] This propensity to evil is, as Kant explained, "the possibility of an inclination" and is not, he argued, a natural "predisposition."[85] Evil is, rather, something that is "*acquired*," or more accurately, "*brought* by the human being *upon* himself."[86] This is a necessity if, according to Kant's wider project, human beings are to be held responsible for their actions. Thus, Kant argued that "the statement, 'The human being is *evil*,' cannot mean anything else than that he is conscious of the moral law and yet has incorporated into his maxim the (occasional) deviation from it."[87] Evil is thus not a complete abandonment of the law, but stems from the "all too human tendency to make exceptions for oneself . . . the propensity to subordinate moral considerations to those stemming from self-love."[88] It is, in short, to reverse moral priorities or, "in Kant's terms 'the order of incentives.'"[89] Evil is thus not, in any sense, a privation, as it was for Augustine, but "a positive reality" that becomes real "in the course of maxim-making."[90]

Rather than constituting an extreme form of evil, for Kant "radical evil" is nothing more than "a *radical* innate *evil* in human nature" that is "not any the less brought upon us by ourselves."[91] That is, even in a "radical" sense, human beings are wholly responsible for the evil they commit. However, Kant appears to be making a set of contradictory claims here, arguing on the one hand that human beings are innately evil and on the other, that they are wholly responsible for the evil acts they commit in the exercise of their free will. However, it is an innate *propensity* for evil that humans possess and, as such, it is not an unavoidable feature of human nature but a mere possibility. "Radical evil" is thus not a type of evil nor is it synonymous with natural inclinations.[92] It is similarly not "to be identified with any *intrinsic* defect or corruption of human reason" but is solely related "to the corruption of the will."[93] For writers such as Allen Wood and Stephen R. Grimm, Kant's explanation of the human propensity for radical evil can be conceived as an anthropological account of evil. However, where Wood argues that Kant's argument is "essentially a restatement" of Rousseau's claim that "human beings are by nature good and only come to be corrupted by their social interaction with others," Grimm interprets Kantian radical evil as predating the individual's interactions with others.[94]

Despite continuing debate over the interpretation of his writing, Kant's general understanding of evil and, in particular, the idea that evil deeds are presupposed by evil motives, came to dominate subsequent thinking about the problem of evil. In particular, it was to the Kantian notion of "radical evil" that Hannah Arendt turned in attempting to explain the suffering inflicted by the totalitarian death camps, although, as we will see in Chapter 6, she came to use the term in a distinctly different manner to Kant.

Conclusion

In the eighteenth century, accounts of the problem of evil, addressed under the banner of theodicy, were marked by two events. In the first instance, the Lisbon earthquake was not only the defining natural event of the century but one that brought with it a set of significant intellectual responses. In particular, the earthquake brought into question Leibniz's monist account of evil that maintained that despite the existence of evil, this was the best of all possible worlds. Evidence of the suffering inflicted by the earthquake seemed to suggest that this was not the case. In addition, it also inspired thinkers to challenge the firm connection between sin and suffering that had dominated accounts of evil since well before the works of Augustine. No longer did it seem reasonable to hold individuals personally responsible for the otherwise meaningless suffering inflicted upon them. The result of this, in the first instance, was that a distinction was drawn between natural evils, conceived in terms of natural disasters, and moral evils, caused directly by human actions. As we saw in this chapter however, it was some time before thinkers accepted that human sin in general could not be held responsible for natural evils.

The second event that had a lasting influence on discussions of the problem of evil during this period was an intellectual one, the Enlightenment. The dominant slogan of the Enlightenment, "have the courage to use your own understanding," expressed in Kant's famous 1784 essay "What Is Enlightenment?" was especially borne out in thought concerning evil.[95] In particular, by imploring individuals to replace superstition and so-called authoritative accounts of the world provided in most instances by the church, with reason, as evident in the work of David Hume, the Enlightenment made it possible to answer the question of why human beings knowingly commit evil without any reference to God. The result was the emergence of a fully independent moral problem of evil conceived exclusively in terms of human moral agency, the subject matter of Chapter 5.

5

Moral Monsters

I also do not understand the faith of the believer; nor do I comprehend the absence of faith in those who are not believers. I once asked the Lubavitcher Rebbe: How can you have faith after what happened? And he answered: how can you not have faith after what happened? Now, I accept his answer as a question, but not as an answer.[1]

They were made of our same cloth, they were average human beings, averagely intelligent, averagely wicked: save the exceptions, they were not monsters, they had our faces.[2]

Despite the undeniable horrors of recent years that have reawakened "evil" discourse and scholarship, understandings of the term, at least in contemporary Western thought, are still most commonly associated with the Holocaust. Not only do the atrocities of the Nazi concentration camps remain one of the most extreme examples of the human capacity for evil in history (if not *the* most extreme example) but, on an intellectual level, the meaningless suffering endured by millions of Jews, gypsies, and other minorities precipitated some of the most powerful and important reflections on evil in both theological and secular thought.[3] Although, in the first instance, the horrors of the Holocaust were met with a profound reluctance to confront its reality, born in part of the shock that something this grotesque could happen in the heart of civilized Europe and in part out of a misguided sense of Holocaust piety, with time intellectual responses began to emerge.

The ongoing significance of the Holocaust for the development of thought about evil has been two-fold. First, for many, with the Holocaust came an effective end of theodicy as a means of justifying the otherwise meaningless suffering of millions of individuals. Thus, while some theologians remained focused on the cosmological "problem of evil," general scholarship and discourse was marked by a widespread turn to the moral problem of evil. That is, the suffering of the Jews was to be explained in secular terms by answering the moral question of why human beings inflict such appalling suffering upon one another. Thus, for many prominent figures, including Hannah Arendt, Hans Jonas, and Emmanuel Levinas, Auschwitz, the representative embodiment of the Holocaust, "signifie[d] a rupture and break with tradition." "After Auschwitz," they argued, "both the meaning of evil and human responsibility" needed to be reconceived.[4] Thus, Levinas questioned the very notion of morality itself and asked whether we can even "speak of morality after the failure of morality" on the scale of the Holocaust.[5] Similarly, Arendt argued that a "rethinking" of evil and human responsibility was necessitated by the emergence of a new moral universe that had been brought about by the "total collapse of all established moral standards in public and private life during the 1930s and 40s."[6] As Berel Lang notes, "After Auschwitz" has thus come to signify for many "a metonymic line of (chronological) demarcation—a transformative moment in moral and social and religious history."[7] As we will see in this chapter however, such claims must be tempered by the realization that although a "turn" can be discerned in several aspects of moral and social thought about the Holocaust, in others, particularly those of religious derivation, the shift has not been quite as dramatic.

However, more than simply turning attention from the theological problem of evil to its moral counterpart, what also made the Holocaust particularly significant is that it brought into question the very relationship between evil and human moral agency itself. Before the Holocaust, the dominant secular mode of thinking about evil, derived from Kant's understanding of "radical evil," was based on the assumption that evil deeds presuppose evil motives.[8] Evil acts, in this mode of thinking, are committed by individuals who intentionally seek to bring about the harm they cause.[9] However, the range of individuals implicated in the extermination of the Jews, from Franz Stangl to Heinrich Himmler, and, of course, Adolph Eichmann, "confuted two centuries of modern assumptions about intention."[10] No longer was it possible to suggest that the absence of evil intentions absolved the participants of responsibility for their actions in an act as heinous as the Holocaust. Thus, what the Holocaust demonstrated with alarming clarity is that in some circumstances individuals contribute to the perpetration of evil without directly intending the evil they cause.

With this in mind, this chapter is concerned with the two major shifts that took place in discourse concerned with evil in the aftermath of the Holocaust. The first section of the chapter is concerned with the range of theological responses that emerged after the Holocaust, while the remainder of the chapter is concerned with the relationship between evil and human moral agency, particularly as it manifested itself in discourse that sought to make sense of the suffering of the Holocaust. The second section therefore addresses the relationship between agency and intention that stands at the center of one of the most profound shifts in thinking about evil to date. In doing so, it establishes a connection between agency, intention, and responsibility, and explains how moral evils can be distinguished from nonmoral evils.[11] However, as the third section turns to the range of evil agents that may be implicated in any one instance of evil, it becomes apparent that even in apparently clear-cut cases the relationship between agency and intention is often unclear. Thus, what emerges from the discussion is the realization that intention exists in varying forms and degrees and, accordingly, can be variously related to moral agency.

The End of Theodicy?

Despite the damage done to traditional notions of theodicy by Hume, Kant, and Nietzsche, it was the Holocaust that provided the most serious challenge to this mode of understanding the meaningless suffering that afflicts the human population. Although Richard Harries notes that in its immediate aftermath the Holocaust was met with "a stunned, appalled theological silence"[12] to match that which took place in discourse more generally, this does not seem to have been exclusively the case. While many theologians certainly did shy away from discussing the theological implications of the Holocaust, others, including the Christian theologian Karl Barth, did not. In his 1944 lecture "The Promise and Responsibility of the Christian Church," Barth spoke of the "innumerable Jews who were shot or buried alive, suffocated in overcrowded cattle wagons or murdered with poison gas."[13] Like many of his Orthodox Jewish counterparts, however, he did not "shrink from the affirmation that God [was] to be found even in the Holocaust." Indeed, for Barth the three greatest temptations that confronted the Christian world in 1944 (and presumably the post-Holocaust era as well) were "complacency, denial of God, and the worship of false gods."[14] However, at the same time, Barth sought to overcome one of the central problems afflicting traditional theoretical theodicies, the temptation to conceive God not simply as permitting evil, but as actually creating it.[15] The logical problem was, at its heart, this: traditional theodicies, including his own, tell us that "sin is the concrete form of nothingness." Sin is not created but emerges from turning away from God and "believing that we ourselves are gods." At the same time, however, evil cannot be simply equated with human sin because in equating it with nothingness, we fail to take it as seriously as we ought to.[16] Thus, acknowledging the limitations of this area of theological thought, Barth argued in his response to G. C. Berkouwer's critique of it: "It will always be obscure, unfathomable and baffling that something which is merely opposed to the will of God can have reality. We do not understand how this can be. But it is of a piece with the nature of evil that if we could explain how it may have reality it would not be evil."[17] With this, Barth attempted to uphold the character of God in the face of those challenges posed by the evil of the time by appealing to its mysterious nature.

However, with the immense suffering that came with the Holocaust, both materially and symbolically embodied in Auschwitz, it is not surprising that for others the goodness of God and the rationality of faith came to be seriously questioned. As Elie Wiesel famously wrote in *Night*, the flames of the mass graves at Auschwitz not only incinerated the bodies of its victims but also brought his faith into question. "If I told you I believed in God," he wrote, "I would be lying; if I told you I did not believe in God, I would be lying."[18] As Rubenstein and Roth note, Wiesel's pronouncement represents the tendency common in Holocaust survivors to question God's inherent goodness while retaining a belief not simply in his existence but in his acting in history.[19] However, it is important to note that no "one" response to the problem of evil posed in such stark terms by the events of the Holocaust can be identified. For some of its victims, the suffering of the Holocaust led to an intensified devotion, while for others it drew away the final vestiges of faith.[20] For others still, Auschwitz presented a range of serious theological problems that stood outside simple questions of faith. Among them was Emmanuel Levinas.

For Levinas, the uselessness of suffering, in particular that he witnessed in the twentieth century, necessarily signaled the end of theodicy—

understood in both theological and secular terms—as the attempt to justify human suffering. The "temptation" of theodicy, he argued, is that it seeks to render suffering meaningful by associating it with notions of faith and progress.[21] However, Levinas questioned its success in doing so: "Certainly one may ask if theodicy, in the broad and narrow senses of the term, effectively succeeds in making God innocent, or in saving morality in the name of faith, or in making suffering—and this is the true intention of the thought which has recourse to theodicy—bearable."[22] Of course, for him, it did not. And yet, in Levinas's view:

> Perhaps the most revolutionary fact of our twentieth-century consciousness—but it is also an event in Sacred History—is that of the destruction of all balance between the explicit and implicit theodicy of Western thought and the forms which suffering and its evil take in the very unfolding of this century. This is the century that in thirty years has known two world wars, the totalitarianism of right and left, Hitlerism and Stalinism, Hiroshima, the Gulag, and the genocides of Auschwitz and Cambodia. This is the century which is drawing to a close in the haunting memory of the return of everything signified by these barbaric names: suffering and evil are deliberately imposed, yet no reason sets limits to the exasperation of a reason become political and detached from all ethics.[23]

He continued to argue that "among these events the Holocaust of the Jewish people under the reign of Hitler seems to us the paradigm of gratuitous human suffering, where evil appears in its diabolical horror."[24] In particular, the "disproportion between suffering and every theodicy was shown at Auschwitz with a glaring, obvious clarity."[25] Auschwitz, and in particular, the extermination of millions of human beings "least corrupted by the ambiguities of the world" and, more than this, a million innocent infants, "renders impossible and odious every proposal and every thought which would explain it by the sins of those who have suffered or who are dead."[26] Theodicy is, in short, a vulgar impossibility in the era after Auschwitz.

Although it is often assumed outside the field of theology that after the Holocaust religious explanations no longer had a place in thought about evil, this is not strictly the case. Although some Holocaust survivors and commentators certainly did turn, as most scholarship in the social sciences did at that time, to wholly secular explanations for what had happened, theodicy remains alive and reasonably well. Indeed, despite suffering a period of relative downturn in the first half of the twentieth century, the 1960s saw a resurgence of interest in the fields of theodicy and its adversary aetheodicy. Thus, while some philosophers and theologians began, once again, to consider the traditional logical and evidential problems of evil, others began to alter and develop its central premises, assumptions, and ultimately, its form.[27]

For example, despite sharing Levinas's scepticism, Hans Jonas modified the traditional approach to theodicy to exclude the omnipotence of God from its calculations. God, he maintained, is "a personal, caring God who is beneficent," but to make the further claim that he is omnipotent is radically incoherent.[28] As Jonas wrote, "The disgrace of Auschwitz is not to be charged to some all-powerful providence or to some dialectically wise necessity, as if it were an antithesis demanding a synthesis or a step on the road to salvation."[29] On the contrary, according to Jonas, at the point of creation:

> [God] abandoned Himself and his destiny entirely to the outwardly exploding universe and thus to the pure chances of the possibilities contained in it under the conditions of space and time. Why he did this remains unknowable. We are allowed to speculate that it happened because only in the endless play of the finite, and in the inexhaustibility of chance, in the surprises of the unplanned, and in the distress caused by mortality, can mind experience itself in the variety of its possibilities. For this the deity had to renounce His own power.[30]

Thus, at Auschwitz, Dews writes, God, "handed over responsibility for history to human beings, and both the nameless evil of the Holocaust and the solitary acts of devotion and sacrifice which mitigated against it must be attributed to human beings alone."[31] Herein lies a direct transposition of the cosmological problem of evil to the moral problem, although, unlike its more common transformation, this one takes place *within* a theological account of suffering.

For Rubenstein and Roth however, the most important religious question posed by the concentration camps of the Holocaust is not whether or not "the existence of a just, omnipotent God can be reconciled with radical evil," for that is, they argue, "a philosophical question."[32] The religious question they contend was raised by the Holocaust is as follows: "*Did God use Adolph Hitler and the Nazis as his agents to inflict terrible sufferings and death upon six million Jews, including more than one million children?*"[33] Of course, this speaks directly to the question of God's moral agency and brings with it the assumption that God does not just act in history but is "the ultimate author of the drama of history."[34] In this vein, some Orthodox Jewish and Christian explanations situate the Holocaust in the wider sacred history of Jewish suffering. However, as Rubenstein writes in opposition to these arguments:

> I fail to see how this position can be maintained without regarding Hitler and the SS as the instruments of God's will. The agony of European Jewry cannot be likened to the testing of Job. To see any purpose in the death camps, the traditional believer is forced to regard the most demonic, anti-human explosion of all history as a meaningful expression of God's purposes. The idea is simply too obscene for me to accept.[35]

As Richard Harries writes, Rubenstein in particular became "loosely associated with the Christian so-called 'Death of God' movement." This movement attempted, at the same time to "assert the death of God" in contemporary secular society and encourage the "full assumption of human responsibility" as a Christian response to what had happened.[36] As Rubenstein wrote:

> No man can really say that God is dead. How can we know that? Nevertheless, I am compelled to say that we live in a time of the "death of God" . . . When I say we live in the time of the death of God, I mean that the thread uniting God and man, heaven and earth, has been broken. We stand in a cold, silent, unfeeling cosmos, unaided by any purposeful power beyond our own resources. After Auschwitz, what else can a Jew say about God?[37]

However, accounts of the "death of God" proved to be somewhat premature. On April 8, 1966, the cover of *Time* magazine asked "Is God Dead?" and the edition carried a highly controversial article on the subject titled "Toward a Hidden God." However, apparently reversing the claim that God no longer played a significant role in secular society, the cover of the December 26, 1969, issue asked "Is God Coming Back to Life?"[38] Indeed, in the second edition of *After Auschwitz*, Rubenstein confessed that he no longer thought that the cosmos was "cold, silent, unfeeling."[39]

Presenting an alternative view of God's role in the Holocaust, Paul van Buren writes that God was "trying to awaken His creatures to their irresponsibility . . . trying, by simply suffering with His people, to awaken His church to a new understanding of love and respect for them," although he concedes that the "cost" of this endeavor "seems out of proportion to the possible gain."[40] Alternatively, Ignaz Maybaum suggests that the Holocaust represents "*one of God's most important interventions*" in history, its victims not being punished for any particular transgression but acting as a "divinely chosen sacrificial offering."[41] In Maybaum's view: "It was the awesome fate of six million Jews, *precisely because they were God's chosen people* to become sacrificial victims in the death camps so that God's purposes for the modern world might be understood and fulfilled: 'The Golgotha of modern mankind is Auschwitz. The cross, the Roman gallows, was replaced by the gas chamber.'"[42] However, as Harries writes, this sort of view that conceived the "suffering of the Shoah as something done for the benefit of others and the redemption of the world was, understandably, not part of the main Jewish response."[43] Indeed, for many, he argues, attempts to impose meaning on the suffering endured by the Jews amounted to an "indignity . . . which would detract from the sheer evil of what happened."[44] However, as discussed briefly in Chapter 2, in the aftermath of the Holocaust many theologians did, in fact, attempt to locate a theological meaning in the events that had taken place. Although disagreement emerged as to the precise nature of the sin, for some, particularly ultra-Orthodox Jews, the Holocaust could be understood as punishment for the sins of the Jewish people.

Providing yet another response, Emil Fackenheim argued that the Holocaust was the most important "epoch making event" in Jewish history. The reason for this, he suggested, was that through the Holocaust, God issued a new commandment to the Jews, the 614th commandment to complement the 613 traditionally accepted. The 614th commandment specified that "the authentic Jew of Today is forbidden to hand Hitler yet another, posthumous victory." Thus:

> We are, first, commanded to survive as Jews, lest the Jewish people perish. We are commanded, second, to remember in our very guts and bones the martyrs of the Holocaust, lest their memory perish. We are forbidden, thirdly, to dent or despair of God, however much we may have to contend with him or with belief in him, lest Judaism perish. We are forbidden, finally, to despair of the world as the place which is to become the kingdom of God, lest we help make it a meaningless place in which God is dead or irrelevant and everything is permitted. To abandon any of these imperatives, in response to Hitler's victory at Auschwitz, would be to hand him yet another, posthumous victory.[45]

For Maybaum and possibly van Buren, the suffering of the Holocaust has a distinct meaning, a purpose, be it conceived in terms of punishment, redemption, sacrifice, or as an event of particular significance in the unfolding sacred history of the Jewish people. However, for Levinas, Jonas, and Rubenstein this is not the case. The suffering of the Holocaust lacks tangible meaning and, to repeat the sentiments of both Levinas and Rubenstein, to attempt to imbue it with meaning by reference to a benevolent deity seems a vulgar obscenity. Rather, for them, the imposition of meaning on acts of otherwise meaningless suffering, understood to constitute "evil," must be associated with human responsibility, intentions, and agency.

Evil and Agency

The second major shift in thinking about evil in the post-Holocaust era focused specifically on the relationship between evil and human moral agency. In the first instance, understandings of evil and agency drew upon the distinction between natural and moral evils that had been established in the eighteenth century by King, Leibniz, and, in particular, Rousseau. Indeed, what the early modern thinkers of the eighteenth century recognized was that not all suffering is the same. As discussed in Chapter 2, some forms of suffering are justly inflicted as punishment for an act that is in contravention with acceptable standards of behavior. Other forms of suffering are endured with the promise of redemption or with reward in mind. However, as was the central point of Chapter 2, in some instances, suffering appears meaningless, that is, it does not serve a readily understood purpose.

Let us consider two cases. Between 1975 and 1979 the Cambodian leader Pol Pot together with his supporters enacted a genocide that resulted in the deaths of more than 1.7 million people.[46] For the victims and survivors of the genocide, the suffering inflicted by Pol Pot's regime was simply meaningless. Death was simply the result of membership, in many cases unconscious membership, of the group marked for eradication. These individuals had not necessarily committed acts deserving of punishment, nor could their suffering be conceived as part and parcel of the meaning of their lives or as something endured in anticipation of future reward. Rather, they were made to suffer for no reason other than their group membership. Indeed, in an extreme example, it has been alleged that among those groups of people the Khmer Rouge singled out for extermination were those people who wore spectacles. The wearing of spectacles, as Berel Lang explains, was thought to signify membership of the dangerous, dissenting "intellectual" sector of society.[47] For the average spectacle-wearing member of the general population, to be summarily executed for nothing more than attempting to compensate for far- or near-sightedness is beyond comprehension. The death of the spectacle-wearer *qua* spectacle-wearer, like the death of the Jew *qua* Jew during the Holocaust, does not refer to acts that the individual may or may not have enacted; it is simply meaningless. Just as the vast majority of spectacle-wearing Cambodians were not disloyal intelligentsia, so too the vast majority of Jews murdered in Hitler's "Final Solution" had not committed acts deserving of death.

The second case to consider is that of the tsunami that devastated much of Southeast Asia on December 26, 2004. Killing upwards of 230,000 people and injuring many thousands more, the tsunami cannot, by itself, be said to serve a purpose or have meaning for its victims. We can offer a scientific *explanation* for what happened: in layman's terms, an earthquake off the coast of the Indonesian island of Sumatra caused a significant enough movement between two plates that make up the earth's crust to displace a large volume of water—the wave that struck the coasts of Thailand, Sri Lanka, India, Indonesia, Burma, and so on. What the scientific explanation cannot offer the victims of the tsunami is an answer to the question, why do I suffer? The vast majority of the people affected by the tsunami had not committed acts deserving of such severe suffering or even death; they were ordinary people living ordinary lives. Like the sufferings of the victims of the Cambodian genocide, the sufferings endured by the victims of the tsunami were meaningless.[48]

However, these two events, though both examples of the mass infliction of meaningless suffering, can be distinguished from one another in at least one important way: we do not attach the same moral significance to suffering inflicted by a natural disaster, such as an earthquake or tsunami, to that of suffering that is deliberately inflicted by other human beings, such as genocide. This is the case even despite the fact that each of these incidents may result in death or suffering of an equal magnitude. The distinction at play here is, of course, between natural and moral evils introduced in Chapter 4. As Bruce Reichenbach explains in what are fairly conventional terms, natural evils include "all instances of suffering—mental or physical—which are caused by the unintentional actions of human agents or by non-human agents" and include diseases, natural disasters, and the unintended effects of human activities.[49] Moral evil, on the other hand, may be said to include "all instances of suffering—mental or physical—which are caused by the intentional and willful actions of human agents." That is, they are actions "for which human agents can be held morally blameworthy."[50]

It is important to note here that the distinction between natural and moral evils does not rest exclusively on human agency; both natural and moral evils may involve human agents, although the former can also be caused by nonhuman agents. Nonhuman actions, however catastrophic their consequences, cannot be considered instances of moral evil. Indeed, it would seem rather pointless and more than a little silly to treat a wave with moral indignation or to say that it behaved unethically. Ethical judgement is something that is reserved for human beings; it is concerned, on a fundamental level, with human conduct. It thus makes no sense to talk about the morality of an inanimate object such as a chair, or the ethical conduct of a nonhuman entity such as a tree. The old adage, "guns don't kill people, people kill people" speaks to the same idea. As Nina Jørgensen writes, it would be "ridiculous to prosecute a tangible object such as a gun for manslaughter."[51] At the same time however, not all human conduct falls under the remit of ethical judgement. For example, there is a distinct difference between unknowingly passing on an influenza virus to a fellow passenger on the bus, and intentionally injecting an innocent commuter with a virus-filled syringe. Both may result in identical outcomes, the victim becoming infected with the virus, and both involve human agents, but critically, only the second action can be deemed an "immoral" act. That is, only the second activity falls within the remit of human moral agency.

Moral Agency and Moral Evil

The distinction between human agency and human moral agency stands at the center of moral judgements about human actions. As Toni Erskine explains, moral agency is constituted by two capacities: the capacity for "deliberating over possible courses of action and their consequences" and the capacity to act "on the basis of this deliberation."[52] The most important implication of this for our current discussion is that "not all agents are *moral* agents." For example, "adults who are severely mentally ill and young children . . . are agents, but they are not generally considered to be moral agents."[53] On a fundamental level, these two groups of people are not considered moral agents because they lack either the capacity for deliberation or the capacity for purposive action, or both. However, for some writers, moral agency requires more than the capacities for deliberation and purposive action. Conceptualizations of moral agency thus variously include "the possession of consciousness, an 'inner life,' rationality, sentience, intentionality, and self-awareness; the capacity to transcend mere feelings and passions and act in accordance with moral law; the ability to act on the basis of altruism; and the capacity for remorse and empathy."[54] However, for the purposes of this work, we will put these more complicated understandings of moral agency aside, as Erskine does herself, and focus on the more general definition discussed above.

Following on from the preceding discussion, we are now in a position to say that moral evil, apart from being simply distinguished from natural evil, may be defined in terms of those attributes considered essential to moral agency: deliberative and purposive action. Those actions that despite causing evil are not the result of deliberation or purposeful actions may thus be considered nonmoral evils. It may therefore be the case, as John Kekes argues, that the relationship between evil and agency is better explained by dividing evil into its "moral" and "nonmoral" forms than by its more traditional "natural" and "moral" forms. As he writes, explaining this distinction:

> Evil that is not caused by human agency is nonmoral, while evil caused by human agency may or may not be moral, depending on the answer to the difficult questions about the moral status of unchosen but evil-producing human actions. Thus, the distinction between moral and nonmoral evil can be said to rest on human agency being an indispensable condition of moral evil, while nonmoral evil involves human agency and may also involve some unchosen human acts.[55]

It is important to note at this juncture that while natural evils are nonmoral in form, they are not the only nonmoral evils. For example, as Kekes explains, "mass starvation caused by drought is an instance of contingency and nonmoral evil, provided the drought is due to adverse climactic conditions and not to human stupidity or viciousness."[56] Similarly, unintended "structural evils," for example, the extreme poverty that is in some senses a by-product of the functioning of the international political economy, are also forms of nonmoral evil on the strict assumption that they are unintended and in some senses unavoidable.

However, when we think of "evil" in international relations, we do not usually concern ourselves with nonmoral evils. Rather, the term "evil" often draws us to those individuals whose actions stand at the very extreme of the moral spectrum, perpetrators of genocides, the mass abuse of human rights, and terrorist attacks. These individuals are often referred to as "monsters" or described in demonic terms on account of the extreme heinousness of their deeds. Although, as we will see, some thinkers caution against the demonization of the evil agent, for others, Kekes among them, the label "moral monster" is an apt one. What sets the moral monster apart from other evil agents is, in Kekes's view, the extent to which they "systematically choose . . . to acquire a knowledge of evil . . . [and] to act on that knowledge."[57] Moral monsters act with express knowledge and intent of the acts they perpetrate, they exhibit clear capacities for deliberative and purposive action, and, in this sense, may be viewed as quintessential moral agents.

In a Kantian sense then, underlying understandings of the relationship between evil and moral agency is the explicit assumption that the "moral monster" must harbor intent to cause the harm they inflict. However, in the post-Holocaust era, this account of evil and moral agency has proven to be particularly problematic. In theoretical terms, the problem concerns the very concept of "intent" itself. "Intent," as it turns out, is not nearly as straightforward as our everyday understanding of it would seem to suggest. As Berel Lang explains, "intention may be conceived as a mental 'act'" (conceived as "deliberation") "chronologically prior to what is intended and thus also physically separated from it."[58] However, this definition of intent is not necessarily compatible with the understanding of human moral agency discussed above. In particular, although both deliberation and purposive action are essential components of moral agency, it does not necessarily follow from these definitions of intent that "deliberation is accompanied . . . by an intention to do evil."[59] Thus, "an act that turns out to be evil . . . may have been directed toward a specific end without having been intended *as* evil; and it seems clear, in fact, that many actions later judged to be evil initially have this character of innocence in the eyes of its agent."[60] That is, an action intended to be good or, at the very least not intended to be evil, may bring with it an unintended evil consequence. The problem with this is that it would seem to suggest that all such actions fall outside the remit of "moral evil" and as such, cannot bring with them a sense of responsibility for perpetrating the action. In contemporary international criminal law, this problem has been partially resolved by defining responsibility in terms of both "intent," described by the Latin expression *mens rea* ("guilty mind"), and knowledge.[61] As Article 30 of Rome Statute of the International Criminal Court, explains:

a person has intent where:

(a) In relation to conduct, that person means to engage in the conduct;
(b) In relation to a consequence, that person means to cause that consequence or is aware that it will occur in the ordinary course of events.[62]

Following from this, knowledge is defined in the Statute as "awareness that a circumstance exists or a consequence will occur in the ordinary course of events."[63] Thus, contemporary international criminal law establishes a connection between deliberation, intent, and the act by assuming that if individuals understand the likely outcome of their actions and choose to enact them, they can be said to have intended the outcome they brought about. However, as Michael Shapiro has argued, this, in effect, makes the concept of "intention" little more than a tool in both the interpretation and perpetration of acts:

> If we pursue the idea that what actors plan as their accomplishments does not wholly control what their actions become, we must reconstrue the concept of intention, for intentions are conceived by many as deliberate plans. Intention as it related to the concept of action becomes clarified if we realize that the interpretation of someone's conduct, such that it becomes one or another kind of action, does not involve treating intentions as mental causes of the resulting behaviour. Intention is ascribed as part of the interpretation that creates actions.[64]

Without delving any further into the philosophical complexities of the concept of intent, it suffices to say here that it is not at all surprising that the related "concepts of *motive* and *intention* . . . create headaches for lawyers" and philosophers alike, for intentions and actions do not always correspond.[65] As we will see in Chapter 6, this was particularly borne out in the fact that many of the most notorious perpetrators of the Holocaust did not exhibit explicitly evil intentions. Thus, for Hannah Arendt, what marked the notorious figure of Adolph Eichmann was not particularly heinous intent, but that he was driven by readily comprehensible, ordinary motivations that, in other circumstances, are generally commendable. Indeed, as will be the focus of the following section, what became particularly apparent in the aftermath of the Holocaust was just how few moral monsters—individuals who acted with evil intent—could actually be identified.

The Search for Evil

Even before the formal end of hostilities the international community began to search for the monsters who could be held responsible for the humanitarian atrocities that marked the particular barbarity of the World War II and, in particular, the genocide perpetrated against the Jews. The initial result of their endeavor was, of course, the Nuremberg Trial conducted from November 20, 1945, to October 16, 1946, when those sentenced to death were finally executed. Although many of the main players in the Nazi machine, including Adolph Hitler, Heinrich Himmler, Joseph Goebbels, Reinhard Heydrich, and Fritz Todt were already dead, and the involvement of others, most notably Adolph Eichmann, was only to be realized during the proceedings, twenty-four individuals were included on the original indictment list finalized in October 1945. Although several of the defendants did not agree with the characterization, the language of the Nuremberg prosecutors was smattered with references to the "evil" committed by those on trial and their associates. In particular, the American Chief Prosecutor, Justice Robert H. Jackson, emphasized on several occasions the particular evil committed by those who planned and led the Nazi project. In his opening address he stated:

> The common sense of mankind demands that law shall not stop with the punishment of petty crimes by little people. It must also reach men who possess themselves of great power and make deliberate and concerted use of it to set in motion evils which leave no home in the world untouched.[66]

Following in a similar vein, he continued:

> They were men who knew how to use lesser folk as tools. We want to reach the planners and designers, the inciters and leaders without whose evil

architecture the world would not have been for so long scourged with the violence and lawlessness, and wracked with the agonies and convulsions, of this terrible war.[67]

Similarly, the British Deputy Chief Prosecutor, David Maxwell Fyfe, argued after the proceedings that "the fanaticism of the Nazis . . . produced a singleness of mind directed to ruthlessness and evil."[68] Finally, in his argument to the trial chamber on February 1, 1946, the French Deputy Chief Prosecutor, Charles Dubost, argued that "Evil masters came who awakened [Germany's] primitive passions and made possible the atrocities" for which the defendants were being tried.[69] Thus, for the Nuremberg prosecutors, evil provided an apt description for both the defendants they saw before them in the dock and their actions.

Among the defendants it was Hans Frank, the Minister for Justice from 1933 and Governor-General of Poland from 1939 to 1944, who most readily described the Nazi activities and, in particular, Adolph Hitler, as evil. As G. M. Gilbert, the psychologist assigned to monitor the behavior of the prisoners in Nuremberg jail during the trial noted in his diary, Frank often referred to Hitler as "evil." "Hitler," Frank maintained, "did not just represent 'the spirit of evil on earth' but the embodiment of 'satanical evil.'"[70] However, what confirmed his particularly evil demeanor in Frank's view was less the heinous nature of the Final Solution or the terror meted out in the conduct of the war, but his own sense of being duped by Hitler. As he lamented to Gilbert in his cell one evening:

> I began to come to my senses in 1942, and realised what evil was embodied in him. When I protested against terror measures in public at that time, he deprived me of military rank and political power—but he let me sit as the figurehead Governor-General of Poland, to go down in history as the symbol of the crimes in that miserable country . . . And so here I sit—but it serves me right—I was in league with the devil in the beginning.[71]

Indeed, Frank did not confine his use of the term "evil" to Hitler, turning it on himself on several occasions. In particular, on one occasion Gilbert asked him how he could have made the speeches he had, and written about what he had done in his diary when he knew them to be wrong. He responded: "I don't know—I can hardly understand it myself—There must be some basic evil in me—in all men."[72] In this sense, evil became the means of explaining otherwise baffling actions. Several weeks later

Frank repeated this sentiment but with reference to Hitler once more when he conceded, "we do have evil in us—but do not forget that there is always a Mephistopheles who brings it out."[73] In a similar manner, Wilhelm Keitel, the chief of the Supreme Command of the Armed Forces from 1938 to 1945, did not hesitate when questioned, to describe Hitler as "a demonlike man."[74]

Although the evil committed by the Nazis was not in doubt, the nature of the so-called "evil agent" certainly was. In particular, what was most striking about the search for the masterminds behind the evil activities of the Nazi war machine was just how few of them conformed to existing notions of evil. Indeed, although some "monsters" were identified and found, in the end they were relatively few in number. Even many of those tried at Nuremberg and in the subsequent war crimes trials turned out not to be monstrous individuals at all.[75] That is, many (but of course not all) of the individuals held responsible for the Holocaust either did not intend to bring about the harm they caused at all or harbored other intentions, the by-products of which were the harm and suffering they caused. Indeed, although the American psychiatrist assigned to monitor the defendants and witnesses at the Nuremberg Trial, Leon Goldensohn, "arrived . . . convinced that some, perhaps many, Nazis were sadists, even those who did not engage directly in cruel actions," he was forced to concede that they were not sadistic but rather "all too 'normal.'"[76] As such, they could not be described in the sort of demonic terms according to which the evil agent is often referred.

Moral Monsters

Conceived in the terms described above, even among the perpetrators of the Holocaust, very few moral monsters actually exist. Indeed, when John Kekes, the foremost proponent of the label, discusses the "moral monster" in his work *The Roots of Evil*, it is not to an international figure he turns but the American psychopath, John Allen. Responsible for a range of crimes including "theft, rape, assault, armed robbery, and holdup" Allen exhibited the sort of explicit intent that marks the "moral monster."[77] As Allen explained in a tract of his autobiography, *Assault with a Deadly Weapon*, quoted by Kekes:

It really was something, but it was a lot of fun. I know one thing: out of all the cruel things I've done—and I done more bad than good—I done some cruel things, I done some unnecessary things, but I am not really sorry for maybe three things I done my whole life. 'Cause I like to have fun in my life.[78]

Allen certainly appears to have acted cruelly with explicit intent. Of course, the phenomenon that Allen describes here is a form of "sadism," "the derivation of pleasure from inflicting harm," although it is of a less extreme sort than the sadomasochism associated with individuals such as the Marquis de Sade after which it was named.[79]

However, individuals such as Allen, who systematically choose to commit evil acts, are actually quite rare. Even survivors of the Nazi concentration camps agree that "only a small minority of guards, of the order of five or ten percent, could legitimately be called sadists."[80] Somewhat surprisingly, some have even raised doubts about the characterization of Hitler as a "moral monster," despite the obvious intentions of the Final Solution. Indeed, although the name of Hitler is often conceived as being synonymous with "evil," a "pronounced reluctance" to label him as such remains.[81] For example, in Hugh Trevor-Roper's view, Hitler did not consciously commit evil but was "convinced of his own rectitude."[82] According to this reasoning, Hitler cannot be considered a moral monster acting with deliberate evil intent even though his actions were recognized by others at the time to be so. As we will see shortly however, there is a distinct difference between *doing* what is generally accepted as right and believing that you are *in* the right. The second of these positions is, as we will see, fraught with problems of delusion and self-deception and, in many cases, constitutes evidence of a profoundly warped moral compass. Thus, responding to claims that Hitler was compelled to act in the way he did by his sense of being morally right, Milton Himmelfarb, the author of the 1984 essay, "No Hitler, No Holocaust," argued that Hitler did not murder the Jews because "he *had* to" but "because he *wanted* to."[83] Significantly, however, regardless of whether or not he is viewed as a "moral monster," it remains the case that his actions, along with those of a great number of his subordinates, are readily described as evil, thereby bringing into further question the conventionally conceived relationship between evil and intention discussed above.

Despite on-going debates about Hitler's intentions, it remains the case that there are just "not that many people who habitually choose to cause undeserved harm."[84] The reason for this, Kekes suggests, is that "being a moral monster is very difficult." It requires not only avoiding legal sanctions but also ignoring what are, in most cases, the "extremely strong social pressures" that dissuade people from behaving in a monstrous manner.[85] Thus, rather than possessing direct, uncomplicated intent, those guilty of immoral actions commonly exhibit hypocrisy or self-deception in continuing to pursue what are commonly deemed to be morally unacceptable acts. The evil hypocrite knows "perfectly well what they are doing" but manages somehow to "hide from it."[86] As Philippa Foot writes, the successful hypocrite is "a very cunning liar and actor . . . he is prepared to treat others ruthlessly, but pretends that nothing is further from his mind."[87]

This type of behavior was most prominently displayed by Rudolph Hoess, the Commandant of the Auschwitz concentration camp from 1940 to 1943, where, by his own over-inflated estimation, some 2.5 million internees were exterminated.[88] For example, in an interview with Leon Goldensohn conducted while he was in Nuremberg to give evidence in the trial of Ernst Kaltenbrunner, Hoess was asked whether he was, in his "own opinion . . . a sadist?" He replied: "No, I never struck any internee in the entire time I was commandant. Whenever I found guards who were guilty of treating internees too harshly, I tried to exchange them for other guards."[89] Thus, the man responsible for designing and operating the gas chambers and crematoria of Auschwitz, noted for their efficiency in exterminating and disposing of up to 1800 people a day (in his own estimation), seemed somehow to dissociate himself from the grotesque nature of his actions by comforting himself with the knowledge that he had never personally hit anyone in the camp.[90] Taking this reasoning even further, when asked in a separate interview two days later whether "the fact that [he] put the phenomenal number of 2.5 million men, women and children to death . . . upset [him] a little at times" he responded, in part, as follows: "I don't know what you mean by being upset about these things because I didn't personally murder anybody. I was just the director of the extermination program in Auschwitz."[91] Thus, Hoess managed to console himself by engaging in the practice of self-deception so effectively that he convinced himself that what Foot terms his "habitual evildoing" was actually morally acceptable.[92] Indeed, Hoess maintained that in "obeying orders," however "unnecessary and wrong" they later seemed, he "thought he was doing the right thing." As such, in his view, it was Hitler, Himmler, and Eichmann who were to be held responsible for the exterminations.[93]

There is an interesting contradiction at play in Hoess's reasoning that serves to further highlight the extent of his self-deception. On one hand, he absolved himself of all responsibility for the brutality and mass murders that occurred under his authority at Auschwitz on the grounds that he never struck or murdered anyone himself. According to this reasoning, the direct perpetrators of these acts can be presumed responsible for them. On the other hand, Hoess also held his superiors responsible for planning and ordering the exterminations. However, what is interesting and indeed contradictory here is that he did not view his own orders and plans, orders and plans that resulted in the development of the most notorious and efficient killing apparatus of the Nazis' Final Solution, in the same light. Thus, through a quite remarkable act of self-deception, Hoess managed to blame all of those around him while affording himself only minimal responsibility for what he had done.

This sort of self-deception was also exhibited by Franz Stangl, the Commandant of Treblinka, a Nazi extermination camp in German-occupied Poland. After fleeing to Syria and then Brazil after the war, Stangl was extradited to West Germany in 1968, found to be complicit in the murder of nine hundred thousand people and sentenced to life imprisonment. Upon the sentencing of Stangl on December 22, 1970, the so-called "Nazi hunter" Simon Wiesenthal remarked, "If I had done nothing else in my life but get this evil man, I would not have lived in vain."[94] In her lengthy interviews with Stangl while he was in prison, published as *Into that Darkness: An Examination of Conscience*, Gitta Sereny pushed her interviewee to justify his actions. Pressing the issue, Sereny asked Stangl the following question: "You . . . months before, had acknowledged to yourselves what was being committed here was a crime. How could you, in all conscience, volunteer, as you were doing now, to take any part in this crime?"[95] Stangl replied as follows:

> It was a matter of survival—always of survival. What I had to do, while I continued my efforts to get out, was to limit my actions to what I—in my conscience—could answer for. At police training school they taught us . . . that the definition of a crime must meet four requirements: there has to be a subject, an object, an action and intent. If any of these four elements are missing, then we are not dealing with a punishable offence.[96]

At this point Sereny interjected and said "I can't see how you could possibly apply this concept to this situation?" to which Stangl replied:

> That's what I am trying to explain to you; the only way I could live was by compartmentalizing my thinking. By doing this I *could* apply it to my own situation; if the "subject" was the government, the "object" the Jews, and

the "action" the gassings then I could tell myself that for me the fourth element, "intent" [he called it "free will"] was missing.[97]

In such instances, by engaging in self-convincing intellectual deceit, some individuals may, in Kekes's view come to be the agents of habitual unchosen evil. As he explained earlier in the work, although "unchosen evil is clearly not nonmoral . . . it does not seem to be clearly moral either, because human beings do not choose to cause it."[98] However, if we return to Stangl's claim that "the absence of intent prevents his actions—which even he conceded were evil—from reflecting on him and making him an evil person," as Kekes does, then there may be a way through this confusion.[99] A person has intent, we recall, when they mean "to engage in [particular] conduct" and either "mean to cause [the] consequences" of that conduct or are "aware that it will occur in the ordinary course of events."[100] For Stangl, the question of intent is one of choice; did he mean to bring about the consequences of his actions or were his options so limited as to eliminate the possibility of choosing a course of action other than the one he followed? As Stangl argued, "My conscience is clear about what I did, myself . . . I have never intentionally hurt anyone," maintaining earlier on that he was effectively a "prisoner" of his superior Globocnik, the SS Polizeiführer or Chief of Police.[101] Sereny did not accept this justification of Stangl's behavior and argued that "we know now, don't we, that they did not automatically kill men who asked to be relieved from this type of job."[102] Indeed, it seems that Stangl did, in fact, choose to bring about the outcome of his actions, only he seemed to associate intent with a far greater project than the simple murder of those under his jurisdiction.

This type of evil that in some cases is the result of moral self-deception is quite closely related to evil that is conceived as a duty to be endured, perhaps for the realization of a greater good. This motivation is particularly evident in Heinrich Himmler's famous speech to an asscmbly of senior SS officers at Posen on October 4, 1943, in which he stated:

> Most of you know what it is like to see 100 corpses side by side, or 500 or 1,000. To have stood fast through this and—except for cases of human weakness—to have stayed decent that has made us hard . . . We had the moral right, we had the duty towards our people, to destroy this people that wanted to destroy us. But we do not have the right to enrich ourselves by so much as a fur, as a watch, by one Mark or a cigarette or anything else. We have exterminated a bacterium because we do not want in the end to

be infected by the bacterium and die of it. I will not see so much as a small area of sepsis appear here or gain a hold. Wherever it may form, we will cauterize it. All in all, however, we can say that we have carried out this most difficult of tasks in a spirit of love for our people. And we have suffered no harm in our inner being, our soul, our character.[103]

Himmler was, as Richard Breitman writes, "in his own eyes a moralist to the end."[104]

In a similar vein, Rudolph Hoess wrote, in a fit of self-pity:

I had to watch coldly, while mothers with laughing or crying children went into the gas chambers . . . I had to see everything. I had to watch hour after hour, by day and by night, the removal and extraction of bodies, the extraction of the teeth, the cutting of the hair, the whole interminable business. I had to stand for hours on end in the ghastly stench, while the mass graves were being opened and the bodies dragged out and burned . . . my pity was so great I longed to vanish from the scene.[105]

These types of evil, pursued "with grim determination" or out of deluded motivations have, at the heart of their driving force, a misguided sense of morality.[106] Indeed, the majority of people who commit evil do so believing that they are acting in the interests of the good, however perverted their understanding of it might be. Although these individuals "knowingly and intentionally perform evil actions . . . they do not realize that their actions are evil."[107] They may intend to cause suffering that will be retrospectively deemed "evil," but do not specifically intend to cause evil itself.[108] As such, the specific connection between evil intentions and evil actions cannot be maintained if we are to describe the perpetration of atrocities such as the Holocaust as evil.

Conclusion

As we have seen in this chapter, the experience of the Holocaust brought traditional Kantian understandings of the relationship between evil intentions and evil actions into question. No longer was it possible to argue at the same time that events such as the Holocaust were evil *and* that all of its perpetrators explicitly intended the evil they caused. Thus, thinkers were forced to adopt one of two positions: either the actions that contributed to the Holocaust were not all evil for they were not all driven by evil intent, or, nonevil intentions could result in evil outcomes. The general sentiment of the time was that the Holocaust was indelibly evil and as such, it was the relationship between evil intentions and actions, and not the description of the Holocaust as evil that required rethinking. In particular, recognition of the idea that evil acts are not always presupposed by specifically evil intentions brought into question how responsibility for evil acts was to be attributed. The question, posed starkly, is this: Can individuals be held responsible for the unintended but foreseeable consequences of deliberate actions?

Responsibility, as J. R. Lucas explains, has etymological roots in the Latin word *respondeo* meaning, "I answer." Thus, to be responsible for an action is to be "answerable . . . or accountable for it."[109] Taking the definition a little further, Michael S. Moore adds that *moral* responsibility may be conceived as responsibility "for those harms that we *cause*."[110] Resting his understanding on a distinction between causation and correlation, Moore thus conceives an agent who is morally responsible for an act to be answerable for their role in causing it.[111] As Lucas continues, to be answerable for an act is to be required to provide a response to the question "Why did you do it?"[112] Of course, not any old answer will do, as Martin Buber famously argued, "genuine responsibility exists only where there is real responding."[113] Rather, what is required of the agent is a justification for their action on which others will make a moral judgment, a judgment as to whether the action is deemed acceptable or unacceptable in accordance with generally accepted moral standards.[114]

In common legal parlance, notions of responsibility are generally expressed in terms of intentionality, although, as we have seen in this chapter, that is an extremely problematic concept. In order to navigate his way around the problem of intent, Manus Midlarsky argues that moral judgments must be based on actions and not intentions. He therefore writes: "Notwithstanding their intent, unless perpetrators are genuinely deranged, are psychologically disconnected from their surroundings, or are coerced with deadly force, judgements are based on actions, not motivations."[115] That is, individuals can be held morally responsible for the evil they cause regardless of whether they explicitly intended it or not. With this, thinkers have attempted to navigate their way around the problematic relationship between evil actions and intentions while retaining the ability to hold perpetrators of evils, such as the Holocaust, responsible for their actions.

6

Evil as Thoughtlessness

The greatest evil is not now done in those "sordid dens of crime" that Dickens loved to paint. It is not done even in concentration camps and labour camps. In those we see its final result. But it is conceived and ordered (moved, seconded, carried and minuted) in clean, carpeted, warmed and well-lighted offices, by quiet men with white collars and cut fingernails and smooth-shaven cheeks who do not need to raise their voice.[1]

Monsters exist, but they are too few in number to be truly dangerous. More dangerous are the common men, the functionaries ready to believe and not without asking questions.[2]

The problematic relationship identified between notions of intention, motivation, moral agency, and responsibility are perhaps most pronounced in the works of Hannah Arendt, the foremost philosopher of the Holocaust and the focus of this chapter. Arendt was born in Hanover, Germany, in 1906, studied at the Universities of Marburg, Freiburg, and Heidelberg where she received her doctorate in philosophy under the supervision of Karl Jaspers. Although not a victim of the Nazi concentration camps herself—Arendt escaped to France in 1933 and then to America in 1941—she devoted much of her intellectual energy to understanding the atrocities that took place during the Holocaust. In fact, it is probably fair to say that Arendt remains the most influential philosopher of the Holocaust to date. Of course, she is most famous, in scholarly and popular circles alike, for her 1963 work, *Eichmann in Jerusalem: A Report on the Banality of Evil*, an account of the 1961 trial of the Nazi bureaucrat Adolph Eichmann that was first published in serial form in *The New Yorker*. Although this work has exerted an immense influence on subsequent discourse about evil, it is important to note that Arendt's discussions of evil began much earlier in her 1951 work *The Origins of Totalitarianism* and her correspondence with Karl Jaspers in the 1940s.

In 1946, Arendt and Jaspers began to correspond about the question of whether or not the evil of the Holocaust could be considered a "crime" in the conventional sense of the word. Although, as discussed in Chapter 5, perpetrators of evil actions are commonly understood to have committed particular crimes forbidden in either domestic or international law, when we say that someone has committed an "evil" act, the implication is that they have done something far worse than commit a mere "crime." In this vein, in the aftermath of the Holocaust, many commentators, Arendt among them, questioned the extent to which the attempted annihilation of the Jewish people ought to be considered a "crime" and, following from this, whether its perpetrators could be described as mere "criminals." In her 1948 article "The Concentration Camps," Arendt asked: "What meaning has the concept of murder when we are confronted with the mass production of corpses?"[3] It was a subject she had broached in her exchange with Jaspers regarding his work on the subject of German guilt, *De Schuldfrage*. In a letter dated August 17, 1946, Arendt argued that the guilt associated with the Holocaust, "in contrast to all criminal guilt, oversteps and shatters any and all legal systems," and concluded that "we are simply not equipped to deal, on a human, political level, with a guilt that is beyond crime and an innocence that is beyond goodness or virtue."[4] In his reply Jaspers questioned the broader implications of what Arendt was arguing:

> You say that what the Nazis did cannot be comprehended as "crime"—I'm not altogether comfortable with your view, because a guilt that goes beyond all criminal guilt inevitably takes on a streak of "greatness"—of satanic greatness—which is, for me, as inappropriate for the Nazis as all the talk about the "demonic" element in Hitler and so forth. It seems to me that we have to see these things in their total banality, in their prosaic triviality, because that's what truly characterizes them. Bacteria can cause epidemics that wipe out nations, but they remain merely bacteria. I regard any hint of myth and legend with horror, and everything unspecific is just such a hint . . . The way you so express it, you've almost taken the path of poetry. And a Shakespeare would never be able to give adequate form to this material—his instinctive aesthetic sense would lead to falsification of it—and that's why he couldn't attempt it.[5]

Although Arendt did not concur with all of Jasper's points, she did concede that she had "come dangerously close to that 'satanic greatness'" in
describing the actions of the Nazis, adding that she "totally reject[ed]"
such a characterization.[6] However, she did not, at least at this stage,
wholly adhere to Jasper's view, writing:

> There is a difference between a man who sets out to murder his old aunt
> and people who without considering the economic usefulness of their
> actions at all (the deportations were very damaging to the war effort) built
> factories to produce corpses. One thing is certain: We have to combat all
> impulses to mythologize the horrible, and to the extent that I can't avoid
> such formulations, I haven't understood what actually went on. Perhaps
> what is behind it all is only that individual human beings did not kill indi-
> vidual other human beings for human reasons, but that an organized
> attempt was made to eradicate the concept of the human being.[7]

What is perhaps most significant about this exchange is that it signaled
the first moves in what became one of the most important shifts in thinking about the nature of evil in social and political thought, that from a
discourse dominated by notions of "radical evil" to one focused on the
now commonplace notion of the "banality of evil." With this came a shift
in ideas about the motivations driving evil actions and the intentions of
those who pursue evil ends. Thus, in her earlier work, *The Origins of
Totalitarianism*, Arendt explored the idea that the evil embodied by the
concentration camps was not the result of evil intentions as such, but
rather that comprehensible motives were absent from the evil acts that
took place. More famously, in *Eichmann in Jerusalem*, the figure of
Adolph Eichmann displayed not so much a lack of intent to contribute to
the atrocities in which he was involved, but rather explained his actions
in terms of readily understandable motivations not ordinarily associated
with evil behavior.

With this in mind, this chapter begins by discussing Arendt's conceptualization of evil in *The Origins of Totalitarianism*. The discussion
demonstrates the extent to which Arendt deviated from the dominant
mode of thinking about evil at the time, which drew a direct connection
between evil actions and evil motivations but argued that the evil of
totalitarianism could be conceived as "radical" because it was "irreducible to any set of recognizably human motivations."[8] In short, the
suffering of those interned in the concentration camps was rendered
meaningless and led, in turn, to a reconsideration of the relationship

between intention, motivation, and moral agency, epitomized in Arendt's discussion of the trial of Adolph Eichmann, the subject matter of the second part of the chapter. The final part of the chapter then considers Arendt's legacy in the latter part of the twentieth century.

The Radical Evil of Totalitarianism

In *The Origins of Totalitarianism* "radical evil" denotes an unprecedented type of evil, an evil associated with the "systematic dehumanization of human beings." This, as we saw in Chapter 4, was not what Kant meant by "radical evil." For Kant, "radical evil" was not "a particularly great or deeply rooted demonic evil," but the "universal propensity to evil, which serves as the precondition of the adoption of maxims contrary to the moral law and, therefore, of evil actions in the familiar sense."[9] However, for Arendt, the source of evil was not "self-love," as Kant had argued, but in making human beings superfluous, that is, removing the spontaneity that is central to both her and Kant's understandings of the human being as a free rational agent.[10] As Arendt wrote in a letter to Karl Jaspers on March 4, 1951:

> Evil has proved to be more radical than expected. In objective terms modern crimes are not provided for in the Ten Commandments. Or: the Western tradition is suffering from the preconception that the most evil things human beings can do arise from the vice of selfishness. Yet we know that the greatest evils or radical evil has nothing to do anymore with such humanly understandable, sinful motives. What radical evil really is I don't know, but it seems to me it somehow has to do with the following phenomenon: making human beings as human beings superfluous (not using them as a means to an end, which leaves their essence as human beings untouched and impinged only on their human dignity; rather, making them superfluous as human beings). This happens as soon as all unpredictability—which, in human beings, is the equivalent of spontaneity—is eliminated. And all this in turn arises from—or better, goes along with—the delusion of the omnipotence (not simply the lust for power) of an individual man. If an individual man qua man were omnipotent, then there is in fact no reason why men in the plural should exist at all—just as in monotheism it is only God's omnipotence that makes him ONE. So, in the same way, the omnipotence of an individual man would make him superfluous.[11]

This letter raised a number of points central to Arendt's understanding of radical evil. The first is the notion that radical evil seeks to render human beings superfluous.[12] For Arendt, the "insane manufacture of corpses" achieved in the concentration camps was "preceded by the historically and politically intelligible preparation of living corpses."[13] This process, she argued, had three main steps: the killing of the juridical person in man, the murder of the moral person in man, and the destruction of individuality, the last of which is most distinct. To destroy individuality, Arendt argued, "is to destroy spontaneity," and is intimately related to the manner in which victims of the Holocaust were often denied meaningful choice.[14] Thus, in *The Origins of Totalitarianism*, she wrote:

> When a man is faced with the alternative of betraying and thus murdering his friends or of sending his wife and children, for whom he is in every sense responsible, to their death; and when even suicide would mean the immediate murder of his own family, how is he to decide? The alternative is no longer between good and evil, but between murder and murder. Who could solve the moral dilemma of the Greek mother, who was allowed by the Nazis to choose which of her three children should be killed?[15]

The success of the totalitarian death camps in achieving both the destruction of spontaneity and the removal of meaningful choice from the lives of their victims helps to explain, in Arendt's view, why "those individually condemned to death very seldom attempt[ed] to take one of their executioners with them, that there were scarcely any revolts, and that even in the moment of liberation there were very few spontaneous massacres of the SS men."[16] As Maria Pia Lara writes, Arendt described this "initial understanding of evil as an effort to grasp why 'systematic torture and systematic starvation *create an atmosphere of permanent dying, in which death as well as life is effectively abstracted*' making the normative idea of human beings become superfluous."[17]

However, the second important element of Arendt's idea of radical evil was the notion that the death and suffering inflicted in the concentration camps was "irreducible to any set of recognizable human motivations."[18] It was, as Arendt wrote in the original "Concluding Remarks" of *The Origins of Totalitarianism*, omitted from subsequent editions, "absolute evil which could no longer be understood and explained by the evil motives of self-interest, greed, covetousness, resentment, lust for power and cowardice."[19] This, of course, directly contradicted Kant's claim that radical evil is the result of an easily understood human motivation: selfishness. As Richard Bernstein notes, in subsequent editions of *The Origins of Totalitarianism*, Arendt included parts of her original "Concluding Remarks" in the chapter titled "Total Domination." What is more, she also made, what Bernstein has described as, "a very significant *addition*":

> It is inherent in our entire philosophical tradition that we cannot conceive of a "radical evil," and this is true both for Christian theology, which conceded even to the Devil himself a celestial origin, as well as for Kant, the only philosopher who, in the word he coined for it, at least must have suspected the existence of this evil even though he immediately rationalized it in the concept of a "perverted ill will" that could be explained by comprehensible motives. Therefore, we actually have nothing to fall back on in order to understand a phenomenon that nevertheless confronts us with its overpowering reality and breaks down all standards we know. There is only one thing that seems to be discernible: we may say *that radical evil has emerged in connection with a system in which all men have become equally superfluous.*[20]

Evil then, in its absolute or radical form, is, in a sense, incomprehensible. Although philosophers as eminent as Kant have attempted to rationalize and explain it in terms of readily comprehensible motives, the reality of absolute evil is its very incomprehensibility. This, for Arendt is displayed most forcefully by the lack of utility of the concentration camps:

> The incredibility of the horrors is closely bound up with their economic uselessness. The Nazis carried this senselessness to the point of open antiutility when in the midst of the war, despite the shortage of rolling stock, they transported millions of Jews to the east and set up enormous, costly extermination factories. In the midst of a strictly utilitarian world the obvious contradiction between these acts and military expediency gave the whole enterprise an air of mad unreality.[21]

Thus, the extent to which the functioning of the concentration camps actually hampered the German war effort contributes to the idea that the suffering inflicted there was irreducible to recognizable human motivations. It was, in short, incomprehensible.

However, with the trial of Adolph Eichmann came yet another reason for Arendt to question the assumption that individuals responsible for evil acts are driven by evil intentions and motivations.

The Trial of Adolph Eichmann

The trial of Adolph Eichmann was, for Arendt, a matter of justice. "Justice," she wrote, "insists on the importance of Adolph Eichmann, son of Karl Adolph Eichmann, the man in the glass booth built for his protection: medium-sized, slender, middle-aged, with receding hair, ill-fitting teeth, and nearsighted eyes."[22] In this sense, the Eichmann trial was nothing more, and nothing less than "the last of the numerous Successor trials which followed the Nuremberg Trials" and, in this, sought to render nothing more than justice.[23]

On April 11, 1961, in the District Court of Jerusalem to which he had been brought after being kidnapped from his Argentinean hiding place, Eichmann "stood accused on fifteen counts: 'together with others' he had committed crimes against the Jewish people, crimes against humanity, and war crimes during the whole period of the Nazi regime and especially during the period of the Second World War."[24] Although not directly responsible for the death of a single person,[25] Eichmann was in charge of the Nazi transport system, thereby ensuring that the concentration camps received a steady flow of victims for extermination. He was, as Arendt described him, "the most important conveyer belt in the whole operation."[26] What the prosecution had hoped when the trial began was that Eichmann would come to represent the embodiment of the radical evil that had taken place during the Holocaust.[27] What he came to represent instead was the most significant shift in thinking about evil in the late-modern period.

For Arendt, what was curious about the figure of Eichmann was just how ordinary he was. He was, as were many others like him, "neither perverted, nor sadistic" but was, and remained, "terribly and terrifyingly normal."[28] The evil he committed was, as the catchphrase goes, simply "banal." Indeed, rather than being a monstrous individual, here was a fairly boring white-collar bureaucrat who, in his understandable desire to advance his career, helped to perpetrate one of the most atrocious evils of human history. Thus, although Arendt confessed that "it would have been very comforting indeed to believe that Eichmann was a monster,"[29] she was forced to confront a very different type of man:

> Eichmann was not Iago and not Macbeth, and nothing would have been farther from his mind than to determine, with Richard III "to prove a villain." Except for an extraordinary diligence in looking out for his personal

advancement, he had no motives at all. . . . He *merely*, to put the matter colloquially, *never realized what he was doing*.[30]

It was an assessment shared by many others, including Elie Wiesel who, some years later, admitted that he "wanted to picture Eichmann as a monster. I wanted him to be a man like the Minotaur by Picasso—with three ears, four noses. But he was human."[31] Indeed, the overwhelming impression of those at the trial was that Eichmann was all too human, an observation that, as we will see in the final section of this chapter, came to have a significant impact on later discussions of evil. Indeed, Arendt described the prosecution's portrayal of Eichmann as a "perverted sadist" as being "obviously mistaken."[32]

Not only did Eichmann fail to represent the sort of moral monster it had been assumed would make the sort of significant contribution to the Holocaust that he had, but he continually maintained his innocence. Indeed, in making his plea in response to each of the fifteen counts on which he was being tried, Eichmann stated: "Not guilty in the sense of the indictment."[33] As Arendt later explained, what he meant by this seemingly strange phrase was that "the indictment implied not only that he had acted on purpose, which he did not deny, but out of base motives and in full knowledge of the criminal nature of his deeds."[34] This he disputed.

The Eichmann trial thus forced Arendt to rethink her understanding of evil and with it, the related concepts of agency, intention, motivation, and responsibility. In short, the suffering Eichmann inflicted upon the victims of the Holocaust could not be explained by reference to the concept of radical evil presented in *The Origins of Totalitarianism*. The evil committed by Eichmann did not lack motivation but on the contrary, was driven by readily comprehensible motives not ordinarily associated with criminal behavior. More than that, it did not even seem reasonable to describe the man himself as "evil" for he was not, in any sense, a moral monster inflicting harm with explicit intent outside the bounds of normal human comprehension. Thus, as Arendt wrote in the Epilogue to *Eichmann in Jerusalem*, among the broader issues raised by the Eichmann trial was concerning the "assumption current in all modern legal systems that intent to do wrong is necessary for the commission of a crime."[35] Thus, as she continued, "where this intent is absent, where, for whatever reasons, even reasons of moral insanity, the ability to distinguish between right and wrong is impaired, we feel no crime has been committed."[36] The apparent crime with which Eichmann was charged was, it was argued, "a crime only in retrospect,"[37] and one for which he harbored no explicit intent.

On the contrary, Eichmann appeared not only to be driven by readily comprehensible motives, the desire to advance his career, but to act in accordance with moral principles. According to his own reasoning, Eichmann had "always been a law-abiding citizen" on the grounds that he obeyed Hitler's orders, orders that "possessed 'the force of law.'"[38] As it is famously told, Eichmann went so far as to argue that "he had lived his whole life according to Kant's moral precepts, and especially according to a Kantian definition of duty."[39] Upon hearing this statement, Arendt wrote, one of the judges began to question Eichmann's use of Kant in defense of his actions: "To the surprise of everybody, Eichmann came up with an approximately correct definition of the categorical imperative: 'I meant by my remark about Kant that the principle of my will must always be such that it can become the principle of general laws.'"[40] Of course, what Eichmann promulgated here was a "perverted understanding of duty" that rested on a notion of morality devoid of all judgment and hence some way from Kant's understanding of the term.[41] Indeed, as Arendt noted, what Eichmann had done was reformulate the categorical imperative to read: "Act as if the principle of your actions were the same as that of the legislator of the law of the land" or, as Hans Frank put it: "Act in such a way that the Führer, if he knew your action, would approve it."[42] What is more, Eichmann failed to acknowledge that although he may not have intended to cause suffering or evil, those who gave the orders he chose to follow certainly did.

Evil and Thinking

In Arendt's assessment therefore, Eichmann displayed not evil intent as such, but a lack of judgment coupled with utter thoughtlessness. This lack of judgment was borne out in explicit terms in Eichmann's own account of his response to the proceedings of the Wansee Conference at which the execution of the "Final Solution" was deemed the best course of action for the Nazis to take. Prior to the Wansee Conference, Eichmann had displayed some attributes of moral deliberation and decision making. On occasions he had deliberately diverted particular groups of people away from the extermination camps.[43] After the Wansee Conference had declared the merits of the Final Solution, however,

Eichmann put aside all moral judgment, arguing at his trial: "*Who was he to judge?* Who was he 'to have [his] own thoughts in this matter?'"[44] "At that moment," Eichmann explained, he experienced what he described as a "Pontius Pilate feeling," a feeling that he was now "free of all guilt."[45] Eichmann's guilt, Arendt argued, actually "came from his obedience," a characteristic most often "praised as a virtue."[46] In Eichmann's view, his obedience to the "ruling clique" who masterminded the murder of the Jews, made him a victim, "abused by the Nazi leaders" and therefore not deserving of punishment.[47] As he argued in his final statement to the Court, "I am not the monster I am made out to be . . . I am the victim of a fallacy."[48] What is more, Eichmann also seemed to comfort himself with the knowledge that no one around him seemed to be against the Final Solution; "no one protested, no one refused to cooperate. "*Immerzu fahren hier die Leute zu uhrem eigenen Begräbnis*" (Day in day out the people here leave for their own funeral).[49] The moral universe in which Eichmann found himself seemed to be suggesting that obeying orders and contributing to the Final Solution was the right thing to do.

Eichmann's ability to make moral judgments, it seems, had contracted to the point where the only decisions he was able to make concerned whether or not to follow the orders he was given (which, of course, he chose to do). It was, as Arendt explained some years after the publication of *Eichmann in Jerusalem*, brought about by "a curious, quite authentic inability to think."[50] "Thinking" occupies a place of relative prominence in several of Arendt's other works. It is, in a Socratic sense, what makes us moral. As Bernard Bergen explains, for Arendt, "the principles by which we act and the criteria by which we conduct ourselves depend ultimately on the life of the mind."[51] Thus, in *The Life of the Mind*, she distinguished between two different types of thought: intellectual, which is "oriented to obtaining knowledge about the world" and has as its ultimate end the pursuit of truth, and thinking that is concerned with meaning.[52] In Arendt's view, it is the "process of thinking" and its associated attempt to establish meaning that "generates the individual *conscience*."[53] Explaining the connection, she wrote that the thinking ego's "criterion for action will not be the moral rules, recognised by multitudes and agreed upon by society, but whether I shall be able to live with myself in peace when the time has come to think about my deeds and words. Conscience is the anticipation of the fellow who awaits you if and when you come home."[54] What Socrates had done, in Arendt's view, was "make public, in discourse, the thinking process—the dialogue that soundlessly goes on within me, between me and myself."[55] As we will see shortly, it was against Socrates that Arendt contrasted Eichmann in his unthinking character. However, before addressing Arendt's discussion of Eichmann's thoughtlessness, it is worth briefly exploring her other famous and controversial discussion of the subject, which came in the form of an essay written for the occasion of Martin Heidegger's eightieth birthday. In this essay, Arendt defended Heidegger's involvement with National Socialism in the 1930s as an "error in judgment," thereby seemingly letting him "off the hook" for his association with those responsible for the Holocaust. As Arendt wrote in her controversial piece:

> We who wish to honor the thinkers, although our abode may lie in the midst of the world, can hardly help thinking it striking and perhaps infuriating that Plato and Heidegger, when they got mixed up in human affairs, turned to tyrants and Führers. This should be imputed not only to the circumstances of the time and still less to a preformed character, but rather to what the French call a *déformation professionelle*.[56]

Arendt's apparent defense of Heidegger has generated a great deal of debate since its publication. As we will see shortly, whereas the Jewish community condemned Arendt for her action, cast her out, and made of her a pariah, others took a more sympathetic view and interpreted the statement as an attempt "to preserve Heidegger's 'rightful place in the history of thought.'"[57] Indeed, as Dana Villa writes, it is certainly the case that Heidegger "present[ed] Arendt with a problem." The problem with Heidegger was that he forced Arendt to choose between two unsatisfactory alternatives: "Either she must give up her tradition-inspired association of philosophy with virtue, thinking with judgement, or she must make an exception in the case of Heidegger."[58] However, disagreeing with Bernasconi's assessment, Villa argues instead that "Arendt's 'defense' of Heidegger is, in fact, an attack on philosophy and the activity of thinking in its pure unadulterated form."[59] As she had previously argued in *The Life of the Mind*, Heidegger represented the sort of "pure thinking" that "is the enemy of 'ordinary' (Socratic) thinking and oddly harmonious with everyday thoughtlessness."[60]

At the opposite end of the spectrum to "pure thinking" is the sort of thoughtlessness epitomized by Adolph Eichmann. However, the problem of thoughtlessness was not simply one that occurred to Arendt at the trial but had appeared in her earlier work, *The Human Condition*, in which she wrote that "thoughtlessness—the heedless recklessness or hopeless confusion or complacent repetition of 'truths' which have become trivial and empty—seems to me among the most outstanding characteristics of our time."[61] What makes thinking crucial for moral judgment, in Arendt's view, was the fact that it "inevitably has a destructive, under-mining effect on all established criteria, values, measurements for good and evil, in short on those customs and rules of conduct we treat of in morals and ethics."[62] The "saving power" of thinking is thus found in the challenge it poses to established ideas of right and wrong. Transposed to Eichmann's context, the ability to think would have allowed Eichmann to make moral judgments about the situation in which he found himself: rather than accept that he was not in a position to judge, it would have allowed him to question the morality of what he was being asked to do.

However, it was precisely the "total absence of thinking" in Eichmann that attracted Arendt's interest. As she wrote in the 1971 lecture, "Thinking and Moral Considerations":

> Is our ability to judge, to tell right from wrong, beautiful from ugly, dependent upon our faculty of thought? Do the inability to think and a disastrous failure of what we commonly call conscience coincide? The question that imposed itself was: Could the activity of thinking as such, the habit of examining and reflecting upon whatever comes to pass . . . could this activity be of such a nature that it "conditions" men against evil-doing?[63]

What the Eichmann trial had revealed to Arendt was that there is "an inner connection between the ability or inability to think and the prob-lem of evil."[64]

Eichmann's thoughtlessness was, in Arendt's view, most prominently displayed in his entrapment in standard preprepared answers and clichés:

> The longer one listened to him, the more obvious it became that his inabil-ity to speak was closely connected with his inability to think, namely to think from the standpoint of someone else. No communication was possi-ble with him, not because he lied but because he was surrounded by the most reliable of all safeguards against the words and presence of others, and hence against reality as such.[65]

For this Eichmann was unapologetic, claiming that his "only language" was now "Officialese [*Amtssprache*]."[66] However, as Arendt explains, what is important to note about this claim is that "officialese became his language because he was genuinely incapable of uttering a single sentence that was not a cliché."[67] As she later noted, even Eichmann's final statement upon the parapet before his execution was "a cliché used in funeral oratory." "After a short while, gentlemen," he said, *we shall meet again. Such is the fate of all men. Long live Germany, long live Argentina, long live Austria. I shall not forget them.*"[68] This unthinking, unjudging individual gave rise to Arendt's now commonplace phrase, the "banality of evil." That the evil he committed was "banal" did not indicate that it was not severe, horrific, or even interesting, but simply sought to describe the individual that Arendt saw before her at the trial. Arendt explained this some years later in "Thinking and Moral Considerations":

> Some years ago, reporting the trial of Eichmann in Jerusalem, I spoke of "the banality of evil" and meant with this no theory or doctrine but something quite factual, the phenomenon of evil deeds, committed on a gigantic scale, which could not be traced to any particularity of wickedness, pathology, or ideological conviction in the doer, whose only personal distinction was a perhaps extraordinary shallowness. However monstrous the deeds were, the doer was neither monstrous nor demonic.[69]

A very similar tract is found in *The Life of the Mind*, the last section of which reads:

> The deeds were monstrous, but the doer—at least the very effective one now on trial—was quite ordinary, commonplace, and neither demonic nor monstrous. There was no sign in him of firm ideological convictions or of specific motives, and the only notable characteristic one could detect in his past behaviour as well as in his behaviour during the trial and throughout the pre-trial police examination was something entirely negative: it was not stupidity but *thoughtlessness*.[70]

In describing Eichmann in these terms, Arendt's work reflected two of the most significant shifts in thinking about evil in the modern period: first, the move from the notion that individual perpetrators of evil could themselves be evil, to the idea that it is the action and *not* the individual that is described as evil, and second, recognition that perpetrators can be held responsible for their evil actions even in those instances, such as the case of Eichmann, where they harbor no specifically evil intent. That this is the case is made clear in Arendt's 1964 article in *The Listener*, "Personal

Responsibility Under Dictatorship" in which she refutes the claim that Eichmann was simply a cog in the Nazi machine and thus could not possibly know or feel that what he was doing was wrong:

> When I went to Jerusalem to attend the Eichmann trial, I felt it was the great advantage of the court-room procedure that this whole cog business makes no sense in its setting, and therefore forces us to look at all these questions from a different point of view. To be sure, that the defense would try to plead in this sense was predictable—Eichmann was but a small cog—that the defendant himself would think in these terms was probable—he did up to a point—whereas the attempt of the prosecution to make out of him the biggest cog ever—worse and more important than Hitler—was an unexpected curiosity. The judges did what was right and proper: they discarded the whole notion, and so incidentally, did I—all blame and praise to the contrary notwithstanding. For, as the judges took pains to point out, in a court-room there is no system on trial, no history or historical trend, no "ism," anti-Semitism for instance, but a person: and if the defendant happens to be a functionary, he stands accused precisely because even a functionary is still a human being, and it is in this capacity that he stands trial.[71]

Both the preceding discussion and her exchange with Jaspers, discussed earlier, raises the hotly debated question of whether or not Arendt actually changed her mind about the nature of evil. At the center of claims that she did indeed do so, discarding her early conceptualization of evil as "radical" in favor of the new concept of the "banality of evil," is her response to Gershom Scholem's criticisms of *Eichmann in Jerusalem*. As Scholem wrote:

> I remain unconvinced by your thesis concerning the "banality of evil"—a thesis which, if your sub-title is to be believed, underlies your entire argument. This new thesis strikes me as a catchword: it does not impress me, certainly, as the product of profound analysis—and analysis such as you gave us so convincingly, in the service of a quite different, indeed contradictory thesis, in your book on totalitarianism. . . . Of that "radical evil," to which your then analysis bore such eloquent and erudite witness, nothing remains but this slogan.[72]

It was in her reply that Arendt seemed to indicate that she had, in fact, changed her mind about radical evil, writing, "You are quite right:

I changed my mind and do no longer speak of 'radical evil.'"[73] As she continued:

> It is indeed my opinion now that evil is never "radical," that it is only extreme, and that it possesses neither depth nor any demonic dimension. It can overgrow and lay waste the whole world because it spreads like a fungus on the surface. It is "thought-defying," as I said, because thought tries to reach some depth, to go to the roots, and the moment it concerns itself with evil, it is frustrated because there is nothing. That is its "banality."[74]

Although, in light of this statement, the question of whether or not Arendt changed her mind seems easily resolved, Bernstein argues that her reply to Scholem is "extremely misleading." "Arendt," he writes, "*never* repudiated the thought-trains that went into her original discussion of radical evil, especially her claim that radical evil involves making human beings as human beings superfluous, as well as a systematic attempt to eliminate human spontaneity, individuality, and plurality. On the contrary, the phenomenon that she identified as the banality of evil *presupposes* this understanding of radical evil."[75] In a similar vein, Robert Pippen also argues that Arendt's "notorious claim about the 'banality' of evil in *Eichmann in Jerusalem* (and the all-too-human origins of such evil in 'thoughtlessness') must be read together with a much fuller, more historically detailed attempt to make sense of such total or totalitarian evil in her earlier book, *The Origins of Totalitarianism*."[76] However, Bernstein does concede that Arendt "did change her mind about one crucial aspect of evil—the *motivation* for committing these crimes."[77] This, as I have argued previously, constitutes the most important change in Arendt's thinking, both for her own work and for the general idea of evil in twentieth-century social and political thought.[78]

Beyond Banality?

With the publication of *Eichmann in Jerusalem*, Arendt "unwittingly unleashed a firestorm" that cast a dark shadow over the remainder of her life.[79] Indeed, as Bernard Bergen writes, in the period after its publication, "an unforgiving war" broke out over "the right to define what Arendt meant by associating the words *banal* and *evil* in the context of the most massive moral failure of the century."[80] In particular, interpreters of *Eichmann in Jerusalem* were divided into two contending camps, each of which attracted Jews and non-Jews alike. The first group interpreted the work and, in particular, the phrase "*the banality of evil*" that stood at its core, as an "egregious insult to the Jewish victims of the Nazi genocide."[81] Proponents of this view generally presented three main criticisms of Arendt's work. First, they challenged Arendt's claim that the Eichmann case was a show trial.[82] Indeed, Arendt had written early on that the courtroom in which the trial was to take place was "not a bad place for the show trial David Ben-Gurion, Prime Minister of Israel, had in mind when he decided to have Eichmann kidnapped in Argentina and brought to the District Court of Jerusalem to stand trial for his role in the 'final solution of the Jewish question.'"[83] In the eyes of many however, by describing it as a "show trial" Arendt diminished the place of justice in the proceedings.

Second, many survivors of the Holocaust felt extremely aggrieved by a suggestion made by Arendt that the Jewish Councils had played a critical role in facilitating the deportation of the Jews to the camps and participating in their extermination.[84] Indeed, Arendt argued explicitly that the "role of the Jewish leaders in the destruction of their own people" must undoubtedly be, for a Jew, "the darkest chapter of the whole dark story."[85] In particular, she told of the Jewish *Sondercommandos* (special units) who "had everywhere been employed in the actual killing process." These Jews, she wrote, "had committed criminal acts 'in order to save themselves from the danger of death.'"[86] However, Arendt was less sympathetic to the plight of the Jewish Councils of Elders who, she counted, "were informed by Eichmann or his men of how many Jews were needed to fill each train, and they made out the list of deportees."[87] "The Jewish Councils and Elders," she wrote, "had cooperated because they thought they could 'avert consequences more serious than those which resulted.'"[88] The general response to this assertion in the Jewish community was extremely critical. For example, in a letter to Arendt, Gershom Scholem wrote on the matter: "What perversity! We are asked, it appears, to confess that the Jews too had their 'share' in these acts of genocide."[89] In her response, Arendt emphasized her feeling that "wrong done by my own people naturally grieves me more than wrong done by other people."[90]

As Seyla Benhabib notes, in an interview with Samuel Grafton dated September 19, 1963, for *Look* magazine, Arendt sought to defend her position on the Jewish Councils. Thus, to a question "about when the community leaders should have urged: "Cooperate no longer, but fight!" Arendt responded:

> There never was a moment when "the community leaders [could] have said: 'Cooperate no longer, but fight!'" as you phrase it. Resistance, which existed but played a very small role, meant only: we don't want that kind of death, we want to die with honor. But the question of cooperation is indeed bothersome. There certainly was a moment when the Jewish leaders could have said: We shall no longer cooperate, we shall try to disappear. This moment might have come when they, already fully informed of what deportation meant, were asked to prepare the lists for the Nazis for deportation . . . I answered your question with respect to this point, but I should like to point out that it was never my intention to bring this part of our "unmastered past" to the attention of the public. It so happened that the *Judenräte* came up at the trial and I had to report on that as I had to report on everything else. Within the context of my Report, this plays no prominent role . . . It has been blown up out of all reasonable proportions.[91]

As Julia Kristeva notes, many tracts of Arendt's work appeared twisted and misconstrued in the critical literature that followed the publication of *Eichmann in Jerusalem* and were ultimately used to argue that Arendt was anti-Semitic. For example, Elisabeth Young-Bruehl recounts a speech given by Nathan Goldmann, the then President of the World Zionist Organization, the evening before the work was published, that argued that "Hannah Arendt had accused European Jews of letting themselves be slaughtered by the Nazis and of displaying 'cowardice and lack of will to resist.'"[92] Such was the vitriol to which Arendt was subjected that on October 26, 1966, the French newspaper, *Le Nouvel Observateur*, published "a letter signed by prominent Jewish intellectuals entitled 'Is Hannah Arendt a Nazi?'"[93] When Arendt died in 1975, she had almost completely "fallen out of favor with the Jewish community" and very few eulogies appeared in the Jewish press. As Ron Feldman argues, she was, in a sense, "subjected to a modern form of excommunication" from which she never recovered.[94]

Finally, many critics fundamentally disagreed with the description of the Holocaust as banal. As Bergen writes, "to associate the word *banal* with the Nazi genocide against the Jews" was seen to dissipate "its singular horrors by merging them into the stream of commonplace horrors that marks the movement of human history."[95] Of course, as she explained at length after the publication of the work, Arendt did not describe the Holocaust as "banal" but used the word to characterize the individual she found before her at the trial. However, in doing so, she attempted to use Eichmann as the exemplar of the new form of evil she had identified. Defending Arendt against her critics, Tzvetan Todorov argued, "To call this evil banal is not to trivialize it: precisely what made this evil so dangerous was that it was so easy, that no exceptional human qualities were required for it to come into being. The wind had only to blow in the right direction, and the evil spread like wildfire."[96] Thus, following from this, the opposing camp interpreted *Eichmann in Jerusalem* as presenting a warning "that we are all Eichmanns—that is, that there is an Eichmann in each of us waiting only for the correct sociohistorical conditions to be released."[97] Although Arendt explicitly denied that this was the case,[98] the claim gave rise to a new set of psychologically and sociologically driven debates about the nature of evil.

The Extraordinary Evil of Ordinary People

Explicitly deriving the starting point of his work *Ordinary People and Extraordinary Evil* from Arendt, Fred Katz argues that "even evil on an horrendous scale can be," and most often is, "practiced by very ordinary sorts of persons."[99] Indeed, the finding that evil intent is not necessary for participation in evil acts opened up the possibility, not simply that many evil-doers are "ordinary people" with ordinary, comprehensible motives, but that we are all capable of committing evil acts. Although he confesses that Arendt's work is a precursor to his own, Katz criticizes Arendt for not "spell[ing] out for us how human ordinariness can be so readily harnessed for evil," the task he sets himself.[100] For Katz, the reason that ordinary people commit extraordinary evils is that they become "mentally locked into a particular context where 'outside' values are excluded and locally generated values dominate," what he terms a "local moral universe."[101] Alongside the Holocaust, of which he was a survivor, Katz cites the Vietnam War and, in particular, the My Lai massacre, as a pertinent example of this. He writes that the "young American who was drafted into the army in the Vietnam era did not start out thinking that he might indiscriminately kill innocent men, women, and children."[102] Rather, through processes of "localized incremental decision making" insulated from dissenting opinions, the ordinary soldier became involved in "profound evil":

Following the death of a close buddy or after seeing a horribly mutilated body of an American soldier who had been ambushed, our youthful, idealistic American soldier became less innocent. He might then, with a clear conscience set fire to a Viet Cong village, even when no enemy soldiers but only unarmed women and children were found. It might all happen within a day's incremental exchange of atrocities.[103]

The incremental establishment of a moral vacuum facilitated, in Katz's view, the My Lai massacre:

> Evil became morally invisible because, for some hours, an abbreviated culture of cruelty reigned. Here cruelty was enjoyed precisely because it was cruel. Yet it was an "abbreviated" culture of cruelty because there was no time for specialized roles in cruelty to emerge and become stabilized, as happened at Auschwitz. There was no time for individuals to gain a reputation for repeatedly enacting a particular form of cruelty. But there was joy in acting cruelly and, for a flickering moment providing a rewarding forum for cruelty, there flourished an exuberant culture of cruelty.[104]

Despite standing accused of murdering more than a hundred civilians however, the military commander in charge of the My Lai massacre, Lt. William Calley maintained that he was just an ordinary person: "I was a run-of-the-mill average guy: I still am, I always said, *The people in Washington are smarter than me.*"[105] Thus, central to his defense was the claim that he was not in a position to question the superior wisdom of those in higher positions: "If intelligent people told me, 'Communism's bad. It's going to engulf us. To take us in,' I believed them. I had to. I was sure it could happen: the Russians could come in a parachute drop. Or a HALO drop or some submarines or space capsules even."[106] Calley thus committed what Kelman and Hamilton have called a "crime of obedience." Crimes of obedience, they argue, are those in which "the actor knows that the order is illegal, or . . . any reasonable person—particularly someone in the actor's position—'should know' . . . is illegal."[107] For Kelman and Hamilton, along with the routinization of killing and the dehumanization of its victims, sanctioned massacres, such as the one that took place at My Lai, require "a different kind of morality, linked to duty to obey orders . . . to take over."[108]

In a similar vein, Christopher Browning's *Ordinary Men: Reserve Police Battalion 101 and the Final Solution in Poland* details the process of "habituation" undergone by members of the police battalion in question, from their initial physical revulsion at the tasks they were set, to not only proficiency in executing civilians including women and children but a sense of enjoyment in doing so.[109] In a tract quoted in the works of both Clendinnen and Browning, Ervin Staub discusses this phenomenon with regard to an incident that occurred during the Vietnam War and, in doing so, highlights the role of authority in the process of habituation:

> The pressure of authority can result in a relatively sudden shift of attitude, as exemplified in the story of a Vietnam veteran (personal communication from Seymour Epstein, who interviewed this veteran). Flying over a group of civilians in a helicopter, he was ordered to fire at them, an order he did not obey. The helicopter circled over the area and again he was ordered to fire, which again he did not do. The officer in charge then threatened him with court-martial, which led him to fire the next time around. He vomited, felt profoundly distressed. The veteran reported that in a fairly short time firing at civilians became like an experience at a target-shooting gallery, and he began to enjoy it. This story also demonstrates what may be a frequent phenomenon: a conversion-type experience in which a final inhibition against killing, in this case of a certain type of victim, is overcome.[110]

As Clendinnen notes, works such as those of Browning and Staub rely to a great extent on the highly influential psychological experiments of Stanley Milgram and Philip Zimbardo that demonstrated not only the extent to which human beings are "blindly obedient to authority" but their propensity for inflicting suffering upon one another.[111] Similarly, Fred Katz also relies heavily on Milgram's findings in his theory of the "local moral universe," except he interprets their significance differently. As Katz explains, in the aftermath of the Holocaust, one of a number of explanations for its horrors suggested that the German people displayed a particular "proclivity to obeying authority, even when that authority has a horrifying message."[112] In order to test whether Americans were similarly obedient to authority, Milgram set up an experiment in which participants were ordered to inflict painful electric shocks "on entirely innocent individuals who" they had been told, were "taking part in a learning experiment."[113] While Milgram explained the fact that the participants in the study overwhelmingly inflicted pain on their subjects in terms of obedience to authority, Katz maintains that this finding was too limited. Rather, he writes:

I believe that Milgram created the circumstances—through his ingenious research strategy—where the participants in the experiment were made to believe that the moral standards of their personal lives were entirely irrelevant and inappropriate to their behaviour in the experiment. They were made to believe that the moral standards presented to them by the experimenter should fully govern their behavior in the experiment. These standards were presented as an entirely complete and self-contained system; they comprised a moral universe of their own.[114]

That is, what was created was "*a local, and self-contained moral universe that precluded the morality of the participant's personal private world*" that resembled, in Katz's view, the local moral universes that were at play in the My Lai and other massacres.[115]

Contrary to the claims of Browning and Katz however, is Daniel Goldhagen's famous, and controversial, work that also focuses on the activities of the Police Battalions during the Holocaust, *Hitler's Willing Executioners*. In it, Goldhagen argues: "The notions that the perpetrators contributed to genocide because they were coerced, because they were unthinking, obedient executioners of state orders, because of psychological pressure, because of prospects of personal advancement, or because they did not comprehend or feel what they are doing [are] . . . untenable."[116] Rather, as the title of the work suggests, ordinary Germans, driven by wild anti-Semitism willingly took part in the Nazis' genocidal plan. Attacking Arendt directly, Goldhagen goes on to argue that responsibility for the incorrect image of the reluctant, unthinking perpetrator fell wholly at her feet.[117] However, Goldhagen's work has been severely criticized from a number of different perspectives. In particular, historians have criticized Goldhagen's methodology, in particular, his "reconstruction of the actions and attitudes of the Hamburg Reserve Police Battalion 101 in Poland and Russia in the first years of the war."[118] Similarly, Gordon Craig argues that "the specificity and variety of history finds no place in Goldhagen's book . . . Goldhagen's relentless argument by implication that the population of Germany consisted exclusively of two groups, the Jews and the Germans who hated them, bears little resemblance to the facts of life."[119]

However, with the works of Goldhagen and Browning what has become known as the functionalist/intentionalist debate emerged. On one side, functionalists, such as Browning, Katz, and Staub, argued that the "ordinary" perpetrators of the Holocaust committed atrocities as a function of their position in the military, police force, or other organization.

The intentionalists, on the other hand, responded with the counter-claim that these same individuals specifically intended to carry out the acts of which they were guilty. In part, this debate is centered on two differing interpretations of how the "ordinary" perpetrators of the Holocaust viewed themselves but it is also derived from the immense confusion, discussed in Chapter 5, about the very concept of intention itself.[120] Thus, while intentionalists interpret deliberate behavior directed toward a specific end as intended, regardless of whether the perpetrators of the act agreed with it or not, functionalists do not consider coerced or habituated behavior as intended. Rather, for them, there is a sense that to be truly intended the perpetrator of an action must be at one with what they do. However, if intent is conceived as knowing and deliberate behavior, as it commonly is, then there is no reason why individuals cannot intend to commit acts they do not necessarily agree with. With this it appears that the functionalist/intentionalist debate leads us directly back into the quagmire that surrounds the very notion of intent discussed in Chapter 5.

Adam Morton's recent work, *On Evil*, manages to sidestep this problem while taking Arendt's notion of the banality of evil as the starting point of its psychosocial discussion of evil. From the outset, Morton's central argument maintains that although "we need to distinguish a special class of horrible actions whose causes are different in important ways from those of other wrong-doings," by viewing evil purely in terms of demonic or beyond-the-pale acts we run the risk of neglecting the fact that evil is most often committed by ordinary people.[121] What is particularly interesting about Morton's argument is that for him the banality of evil is not just empirically verifiable (although he does devote a significant amount of attention to demonstrating this) but it is a *necessary* characterization of evil if we are to be able to respond to it ethically. As will be seen as this discussion continues, this endpoint is visible throughout his work.

For Morton, a comprehensive and workable theory of evil must adhere to three conditions: comprehension, banality and reflexiveness. Contrary to the claim, discussed in Chapter 2, that the Holocaust "defies human capacities for understanding,"[122] Morton argues that "instead of depicting the motives of evil-doers as unintelligible, an enlightening theory of evil should help us to understand the variety of motives for performing evil actions, and the varied resemblances these motives have to those that operate in human life."[123] As will be seen shortly, Morton extends this notion in order to view the motivations behind evil actions as not simply intelligible in an abstract sense, but in terms of what we would ordinarily conceive as normal behavior.

The second condition of Morton's theory of evil is banality as described above, the claim that foremost among those who perpetrate evil are ordinary individuals who "are marked not by viciousness but by traits that would in other circumstances lead them to be useful members of society."[124] Herein lies the fundamental crux of Morton's argument and, as I will argue shortly, its most significant problem. However, before we get there, derived from the previous two conditions is the third, reflexiveness. Thus, Morton maintains that "a theory of evil should help us to understand how *we* can be seen as evil."[125]

Combining these three elements, Morton's "barrier theory of evil" maintains that evil motivation is derived from the malfunctioning of our "inbuilt barriers against harm" and is thus defined in psychological terms as the "failure to block actions that ought not even to have been considered."[126] An act is therefore evil "*when it results from a strategy or learned procedure which allows that person's deliberations over the choice of actions not to be inhibited by barriers against considering harming or humiliating others that ought to have been in place.*"[127] But what about "nightmare people," as Morton terms them, perpetrators of mass violence such as Pol Pot, Adolph Hitler, and Osama bin Laden, serial killers and terrorists? Surely they cannot be viewed as ordinary people whose "harm barrier" has failed? Resorting to psychology once more, Morton argues that, when deconstructed, the motivations of these "nightmare people" are the motivations of you and me. Their actions may be extreme but they are driven by things that we can readily understand, even if we have no experience of them ourselves, for example, social isolation.[128] Evil, in this sense, can only be used to describe the *actions* and not the perpetrators of those actions themselves.

However, a number of writers have responded to this type of extended "banality of evil" thesis by arguing that although some atrocities can be described as "banal," it does not seem realistic to view *all* evil this way. Thus, although it is eminently sensible to incorporate "the extraordinary evil of ordinary people," into a broad understanding of the term, surely this cannot describe *all* evil acts. While it is certainly possible to see a figure such as Eichmann, as the embodiment of banality, it would seem bizarre to describe the acts of those who masterminded in Rwandan genocide or, indeed, the Holocaust as banal. Richard Bernstein agrees, arguing that "the banality of evil is a phenomenon exemplified by only *some* of the perpetrators of radical evil—desk murderers like Eichmann."[129] This was a point that Karl Jaspers had made in a letter to Arendt dated December 13, 1963, in which he wrote that "the point is that *this* evil," meaning the evil of Eichmann, "not evil per se, is banal."[130] As such, it seems clear that "evil" must be a term that refers to *both* "nightmare people" and "desk murderers," a suggestion that Morton does not disagree with in principle.

Conclusion

At the beginning of the twenty-first century, the works of Hannah Arendt remain massively popular and influential. International conferences are filled with countless panels discussing, critiquing, and developing her work, her appeal extending from graduate students to established academics. For our purposes however, the significance of Arendt's work is found in the way in which she illustrated, whether consciously or otherwise, the failings of the agent-centered approach to evil. Thus, in her early work, *The Origins of Totalitarianism*, Arendt demonstrated not that the horrors of totalitarianism were driven by specifically evil intentions, but that they were devoid of all rational motives. However, it was with her "banality of evil" thesis, devised as a specific description of Adolph Eichmann, that Arendt made her most significant impact on thought about evil. Here she demonstrated, with alarming clarity, that the perpetrator of one of the most extreme evils of human history did not harbor evil intent. Rather, his intentions were readily comprehensible: the desire to succeed in his job.

What makes Arendt's finding particularly significant is that it reveals the extent to which the self-conscious intentions of the perpetrators of evil acts can become detached from the outcomes they intend. Thus, while Eichmann knowingly and deliberately sent millions of Jews to their deaths in the extermination camps, he only conceived intent on the level of doing his job properly. The fact that he intended to kill millions of Jews, in the sense that he knowingly and deliberately sent them to that fate, did not resonate as "intent" in his mind. In a similar manner, Joseph Stangl, discussed in Chapter 5, also managed to detach the actions he willingly undertook from the concept of intent. Thus, both he and Eichmann reveal that a point of disjuncture exists between what is conceived as "personal intention" (for example, doing one's job properly, or getting a promotion) and "intended action" (sending millions to die), which allows individuals to disassociate themselves from their actions. By reasoning that they would not have personally devised a plan like the Final Solution themselves, figures such as Eichmann and Stangl seem to absolve themselves of any guilt for their part in enacting that plan. As we saw in this chapter, a similar phenomenon was addressed, in part, by the functionalist/intentionalist debate. Thus, although many soldiers did not personally want to kill those they were ordered to shoot, they nonetheless did so deliberately.

As with the discussion in Chapter 5, the findings of this chapter bring the modern notion of evil, conceived in terms of moral agency, into serious question. Evil, we recall, is commonly conceived in terms of moral agency in most modern thought. Moral agency, in turn, is understood to entail deliberate and purposive action, and is usually equated with intent. However, as we have seen in Chapters 5 and 6: (i) evil actions are not always the result of evil intentions and, (ii) individuals are routinely held responsible, in moral terms, for evil actions that reside outside the bounds of explicit intent. As such, the much theorized association between evil and moral agency is, in fact, a false one.

This leaves us with the question of what a satisfactory alternative to the modern, agent-centered, conception of evil is. Could it be that what is actually needed is a return to the theologically-derived understandings of the term that became marginalized in the nineteenth and twentieth centuries? This is a question that Arendt seemed to be concerned with when she wrote in a letter to Kenneth Thompson in 1969, "How can we approach the problem of evil in an entirely secular setting?"[131] Thus Dana Villa posits that:

> Arendt's change of mind on the nature of evil reflected her own awareness that the concept of "radical evil" (at least as she had deployed it in *The Origins of Totalitarianism*) was irreducibly theological. Evil can be radical, can have metaphysical depth and reality, only within a theological framework that posits transhuman forces working for good or evil.[132]

Indeed, it would seem, in light of the preceding discussion, that the concept of evil must have a metaphysical aspect to have any real meaning.

However, when it comes to questions of religion, Arendt seems particularly agnostic. On one hand, her works are littered with religious references, some of which are derived from her doctoral thesis on Augustine's understanding of love. Famously, she also identified "the loss of religious

reference points and the secularization of European society" as important factors, alongside the rise of technology, in the "crystallization of
totalitarianism."[133] On the other hand, however, Arendt also dismissed
religion as a quick fix for the ills of society. This is particularly revealed in
her response to Eric Voegelin's interpretation of her work. Voegelin had
argued that "fascism and Communism stemmed from a 'spiritual disease
of agnosticism' and from an 'immanentist sectarianism' [that developed]
since the high Middle Ages and reached its peak in the eighteenth century."[134] However, when he attempted to associate Arendt with his view,
she responded by arguing: "Those who conclude from the frightening
events of our times that we have got to go back to religion and faith for
political reasons seem to me to show just as much lack of faith in God as
their opponents."[135] As we will see in the following chapter however, the
return to faith, whether for political or spiritual reasons, has certainly
marked ideas about evil at the beginning of the twenty-first century.

7

The War on Evil

This will be a momentous struggle of good versus evil, but good will prevail.[1]

This is a new kind of—a new kind of evil. And the American people are beginning to understand. This crusade, this war on terrorism is going to take a while.[2]

On September 11, 2001, nineteen terrorists commandeered four commercial airliners and, in a coordinated attack, crashed them into the Twin Towers of the World Trade Center in New York, the Pentagon in Washington, D.C., and, following the courageous intervention of the passengers on board American Airlines Flight 93, a field in Pennsylvania. Killing more than 2600 people, the September 11 attacks remain the most shocking event of the, as yet, short twenty-first century. In the five and a half years that have followed, terrorists have struck a range of targets around the world. Most notably, on October 12, 2002, a series of bombs in the Indonesian beach resort of Bali killed 202 people; in March 2004, ten train bombs in the Spanish capital of Madrid, left 191 people dead; and in London, on July 7, 2005, three bombs detonated on the Underground and one on a bus at Tavistock Square killed fifty-six people. As we saw in Chapter 1, in the aftermath of each of these incidents, both the attacks and their perpetrators were roundly condemned as "evil." Indeed, at the beginning of the twenty-first century, evil has been indelibly, though not exclusively, associated with what has become known as "mass casualty terrorism."[3]

Terrorism, variously defined as "political violence that intentionally targets civilians (noncombatants) in a ruthlessly destructive, often predictable manner,"[4] or as "the unlawful use of—or threatened use of—force or violence against individuals or property to coerce or intimidate governments or societies, often to achieve political, religious, or ideological objectives,"[5] is nothing new. With (notably positive) origins in the French Revolution—the phrase *régime de la terreur* (1793–1794) described the attempt to establish order after the 1789 uprisings—and in particular, the activities of the revolutionary leader Maximilien Robespierre, the term "terrorism" was popularized by the British writer Edmund Burke in his polemic against the French Revolution, *Reflections on the Revolution in France*.[6] For much of its history, terrorism has retained its revolutionary association; for example, in the 1960s, '70s, and beyond, "disenfranchised or exiled nationalist minorities—such as the PLO, the Québecois separatist group FLQ (Front de Libération du Québec), [and] the Basque ETA (Euskadi ta Askatasune, or Freedom for the Basque Homeland) . . . adopted terrorism as a means to draw attention to themselves and their respective causes."[7] In the 1980s, 5431 international terrorist attacks, conceived in both revolutionary terms and as "a calculated means to destabilize the West"[8] killed 4684 people.[9] By the 1990s, the concept of terrorism had expanded even further to include criminal organizations that were employing strategic "violence for specifically political ends" and to refer to "wider pattern[s] of non-state conflict."[10] In that decade, 3824 terrorist attacks brought about the deaths of some 2468 people.[11]

However, what makes September 11 stand out in this long history of terrorist atrocities is that it changed the course of world politics in a way that the regular Palestinian suicide bombs on Israeli buses, or the bombing of Pan Am Flight 103 over Lockerbie, Scotland in December 1988 that killed 270 people, could not. In particular, unlike any other terrorist attack, September 11 has precipitated a so-called "war on terror," also known as a "war on evil," fought across many different theaters from Iraq to Afghanistan, and even within the United States and its ally Britain, against an enemy that remains as elusive as it was the day it first struck.[12] Although it is perhaps going too far to suggest, as Louis Pojman does, that the "history of the United States and the entire world will henceforth be divided into Before 9/11 and After 9/11"[13]—as we saw in Chapters 5 and 6, "ruptures and breaks" even of the magnitude of the Holocaust, are never as complete as they first appear—September 11 has had a significant impact on the way in which "evil" is used and conceived in contemporary discourse.

Although of a completely different material nature and, indeed, magnitude, the intellectual impact of the September 11 terrorist attacks on the concept of evil has been comparable to that which followed the Lisbon earthquake in the eighteenth century and the Holocaust in the twentieth. For one, recent scholarship has witnessed a proliferation of works on the subject of evil, some revisiting the question of its origins,[14] others engaging with its use in contemporary political rhetoric,[15] and still others providing historical and philosophical accounts of the concept.[16] However, more significant is the fact that the events of September 11 have brought with them yet another turn in how evil is understood in social and political discourse. In particular, the terrorist attacks of September 11 have brought Arendt's "banality of evil" thesis and its progeny, discussed in Chapter 6, into serious question. Indeed, it does not seem realistic to describe the terrorists, who, after years of training and planning, hijacked aircraft and directed them into their targets in full knowledge of the death and destruction they would personally inflict, as banal. These were, after all, individuals who acted with explicit intent to bring about the harm they caused. Although some, such as Adam Morton, have maintained that the suicide bombers' actions could be deconstructed to reveal a range of motivations compatible with everyday behavior, for others, it is simply inconceivable that such terrorists escape being described as evil.[17] Alongside their actions, therefore, the perpetrators of the September 11 attacks have been roundly condemned as "evil" themselves, thus returning to a much older, pre–twentieth century understanding of the term that equates most closely to Kant's notion of "radical evil."

At the same time, older religious notions of evil that were largely subsumed by secular, agent-oriented understandings of the concept in the twentieth century, have also risen to the fore once more. Although originally conceived in response to otherwise meaningless suffering however, this association has been largely overlooked in contemporary discourse and rhetoric. Rather, religious notions of evil now appear as instruments in the search for moral absolutes and, posed in opposition to "good," are used to justify all manner of actions in the international sphere. Thus, what has regained a particular level of prominence in recent years is the idea that evil is a dark and malevolent force to be reckoned with and, following from this, that a good/evil dualism is at play in the world. However, unlike the early apocalyptic writers and, indeed, the Manichaeans who conceived the cosmic war between good and evil in response, at least in part, to the problem of meaningless suffering, this battle is now being presented in predominantly moral terms. This, in large part, can be attributed to the personal beliefs and public rhetoric of George W. Bush, the central focus of this chapter.[18] However, as we will see in this chapter, although Bush can be attributed with the greatest responsibility for bringing the term "evil" to the forefront of contemporary political discourse, he is not the first American president to favor the term nor is his use of it out of step with broader socio-religious movements within the United States.

A Christian President

George W. Bush's Christian credentials are well known. Although he was born into a regular church-going Presbyterian family, religion did not begin to play a significant role until much later in his life. After marrying Laura in 1977 he joined the Methodist church she attended; however, for the next eight years or so found himself in the grip of alcohol, although he has never considered himself an alcoholic as such. The story of his final conversion, or his being "born again," is a famous one highlighted in most biographies of his life and indeed, in his autobiography. As Bush tells in *A Charge to Keep*, the turning point came for him on a summer weekend at the family's holiday house in Kennebunkport, Maine. The renowned Evangelist Billy Graham had been invited to stay with the family and during his time there took a walk on the beach with the junior George Bush. As the story goes, Graham asked Bush if he was "right with God," to which Bush replied that he was not sure, but he would like to be. As Bush writes, at that moment Graham "planted a mustard seed in my soul" that ultimately led him to "recommit [his] heart to Jesus Christ."[19] Interestingly, in his 2003 *Newsweek* article, "Bush and God," Howard Fineman plays down the role that Billy Graham played in Bush's recommitment to Christianity, focusing instead on the Community Bible Study group he attended with his friend, and later Commerce Secretary, Don Evans. Either way, Bush "quit drinking in the summer of 1986, after his and Evans's 40th birthday. 'It was "goodbye Jack Daniels, hello Jesus,"' said one friend from those days."[20]

It is well-known that, as the President of the United States, Bush rises early each morning to devote himself to reading from a set of mini-sermons, *My Utmost for His Highest*, by the early twentieth-century Scottish Baptist preacher, Oswald Chambers, before the business of the day commences. As his former speechwriter David Frum also makes clear in his insider's account, Bush's White House is one "where attendance at Bible study [is] if not compulsory, not quite *uncompulsory*, either."[21] What is less clear is the extent to which faith dictates the policymaking decisions of the man named "Methodist Layman of the Year" in 2001.[22] Some Presidential aides argue that the President's "faith gives him strength but does not dictate policy."[23] Others, including his closest friend and Commerce Secretary, Don Evans, suggest that "It gives him a desire to serve others and a very clear sense of what is good and what is evil."[24] Further along the spectrum however, Greg Thielman, who worked for the State Department's Bureau of Intelligence and Research, famously argued, with specific regard to the question of whether or not Iraq possessed weapons of mass destruction, that the Bush administration "has had a faith-based intelligence attitude: 'We know the answers, give us the intelligence to support those answers.'"[25]

However, most significant of all is Bush's sense, magnified in the aftermath of September 11, that he is on a mission from God. As Kevin Phillips argues in *American Theocracy*, "in some ways George W. Bush . . . approached the 2000 election as a cross between political project and biblical mission."[26] Indeed, although he does not admit it openly to the electorate at large, Bush "regularly conveys" the claim that God called him to be president to his "core constituency—the religious right"[27] in 1999, telling "an assemblage of Texas pastors that he believed God had called him to run."[28] Recounting a meeting with Bush and his political strategist Karl Rove shortly after this event, the televangelist James Robison recalls that Bush had said: "I feel like God wants me to run for President . . . I can't explain it, but I sense that my country is going to need me."[29] More than this, on occasions Bush has also referred to himself as a sort of prophet who speaks on behalf of God; for example, in 2004 he told a group of Old Order Amish in Pennsylvania, "I trust God speaks through me. Without that, I couldn't do my job."[30]

Shortly after the September 11 attacks, Bush gathered together a group of "twenty-seven religious leaders, including Evangelical Christians, Catholics, Mormons, Muslims, Buddhists, Sikhs, and Hindus. The President of the Missouri Synod of the Lutheran Church said to Bush":

> "Mr President, I have just come from the World Trade Center site in lower Manhattan. I stood where you stood. I saw what you saw. I smelled what you smelled," [Gerald] Kieschnik said. "You not only have a civil calling, but a divine calling. . . . You are not just a civil servant; you are a servant of

God called for such a time as this." "I accept the responsibility," Bush said, nodding.[31]

However, as Ivo Daalder and James Lindsay write, Bush has also denied on occasion that "he ever told anyone that he believed God had chosen him to wage the war on terrorism."[32] Bush is thus reputed to have said: "It's not true. I think God sustains us, but I don't think I was *chosen*. I was chosen by the American people."[33] Whether or not Bush believes he was "chosen" by God or is on a "mission" from God, his speeches are laden with Biblical invocations that seek to explain and justify his actions to the American people. In particular, his understanding of evil is profoundly religious if, at times, theologically confused.

Evil in the Political Rhetoric of George W. Bush

There is little doubt that "evil" is among President George W. Bush's favorite watchwords. As Peter Singer notes, between taking up office on January 20, 2001, and June 16, 2003, he spoke about evil in some 319 speeches—current estimates suggest that by March 2007 he had used the term in more than 800 speeches. Using the term "as a noun far more than . . . as an adjective," Singer argues that Bush does not generally conceive evil as a type of act, or even a type of person, but as a "*thing*, or a force, something that has a real existence apart from the callous, brutal, and selfish acts of which human beings are capable."[34] However, what is interesting, although not surprising, is that despite making this claim, Singer does not devote a great deal of attention to unraveling Bush's varied understanding of the term "evil." Rather, what Singer focuses on is an extremely black-and-white view of evil in Bush's rhetoric that, although sometimes well-founded, at other times appears almost caricature-like. That is, by failing to consider the range of different ways in which Bush uses the term and choosing to focus on a set of extreme examples, Singer blinds himself (and his readers) to the nuances of the president's rhetoric and thought. In large part, this can be attributed to Singer's reluctance to take religion seriously. Thus, the weakest chapter of his work is the one that addresses Bush's faith. And yet, as we will see shortly, it is here that the crux of the President's understanding of evil lies.

The word "evil" did not suddenly appear from nowhere in the public rhetoric of George W. Bush on that fateful day in September 2001. Rather, it was a term to which he had referred on many occasions during his years as the Governor of Texas and the early months of his presidency. Referring to Ronald Reagan's famous "evil empire" speech in an address titled "A Distinctly American Internationalism" given in 1999, Bush argued that "America has determined enemies, who hate our values and resent our success. The Empire has passed, but evil remains."[35] Similarly, at a memorial for the victims of the Oklahoma bombing on February 19, 2001, he cited St. Paul's admonition to the Romans to "Be not overcome of evil, but overcome evil with good," before telling the congregation that "the presence of evil always reminds us of the need for vigilance. All of us have an obligation to confront evil, wherever and whenever it manifests itself."[36] What is particularly interesting about these speeches is that they present themes that, as we will see shortly, have been echoed strongly in Bush's post–September 11 "evil" rhetoric: the idea that America's evil enemies hate its values, the Biblical instruction to "overcome evil with good," and the "obligation to confront evil" in all of is forms. As Daalder and Lindsay note however, it is important to mention that despite his long-term partiality for the term, "Bush invoked the word *evil* sparingly in his public comments before the attacks in New York and Washington."[37] After September 11 this has clearly no longer been the case.

In contemporary discourse, George Bush is most famous for his association of evil with the September 11 terrorist attacks, and his discussion of the "Axis of Evil" in his 2002 State of the Union Address. In particular, on the evening of September 11, the President addressed the nation with the following remarks:

> Today, our fellow citizens, our way of life, our very freedom came under attack in a series of deliberate and deadly terrorist attacks. The victims were in airplanes, or in their offices; secretaries, businessmen and women, military and federal workers; moms and dads, friends and neighbors. Thousands of lives were suddenly ended by evil, despicable acts of terror.
>
> . . . Today, our nation saw evil, the very worst of human nature. And we responded with the best of America—with the daring of our rescue workers, with the caring for strangers and neighbors who came to give blood and help in any way they could.
>
> . . . The search is underway for those who are behind these evil acts. I've directed the full resources of our intelligence and law enforcement communities to find those responsible and to bring them to justice. We will make no distinction between the terrorists who committed these acts and those who harbor them.

. . . America and our friends and allies join with all those who want peace and security in the world, and we stand together to win the war against terrorism. Tonight, I ask for your prayers for all those who grieve, for the children whose worlds have been shattered, for all whose sense of safety and security has been threatened. And I pray they will be comforted by a power greater than any of us, spoken through the ages in Psalm 23: "Even though I walk through the valley of the shadow of death, I fear no evil, for You are with me"[38]

Thus, in a single speech, Bush not only referred to evil four times, but used it in three different ways; twice to describe the acts that had taken place, once as a noun, and once in the context of a Biblical quote. However, in many ways it is an unremarkable speech. In the immediate aftermath of what was a truly shocking act, references to evil invoked the sense of bafflement and mystery that often surrounds such events. It also provided an immediate answer to the otherwise incomprehensible question of why so many innocent victims were made to suffer; the victims of September 11 suffered and died because there is evil in the world. In this, Bush's initial speech can be seen as a fairly typical reaction to a large-scale humanitarian atrocity. Although the speech, composed by Bush's long-time speech-writer Karen Hughes, was widely regarded as a rhetorical disaster by members of the White House staff for failing to be war-like enough and capture the senses of fear, fury, and revenge that many victims and observers in America and around the world felt,[39] with this Bush opened the floodgates of evil discourse once more. As we will see however, from his initial claim that "the search is underway for those who are behind these evil acts," to his declaration that the United States would "make no distinction between the terrorists who committed these acts and those who harbor them," the term *evil* soon took on a distinctly different purpose in Bush's rhetoric that has taken it quite some way from its traditional association with suffering.

Of course, Bush's use of the term "evil" came under sustained criticism in the months and years since his use of it began to increase. As discussed in Chapter 1, many commentators argued that the term *evil* was vague, obfuscating and even dangerous when used in the context of foreign policy decision making. Responding to his critics however, Bush maintained his position: "When we see evil," he said, "I know it may hurt some people's feelings, it may not be what they call, diplomatically correct, but I'm calling evil for what it is, evil is evil, and we will fight it with all our might."[40] This steadfast position has been reiterated on numerous occasions, Bush refusing to back away from describing what he sees as evil, as "evil." Indeed, as David Frum notes, the use of "evil" in his political rhetoric came naturally to the President. This was particularly the case, Frum writes, with regard to Bush's famous "Axis of Evil" speech.[41]

In his State of the Union Address to Congress in January 2002, Bush began to reveal the extent of his plans for the so-called "war on terror" for the first time. In it he described "a terrorist underworld—including groups like Hamas, Hezbollah, Islamic Jihad, Jaish-i-Mohammed—[that] operates in remote jungles and deserts, and hides in the centers of large cities."[42] However, Bush also argued that the terrorist threat to America included a set of rogue states, including Iran, Iraq, and North Korea, he called the "Axis of Evil." "States like these," Bush argued, "and their terrorist allies, constitute an axis of evil." He continued:

> By seeking weapons of mass destruction, these regimes pose a grave and growing danger. They could provide these arms to terrorists, giving them the means to match their hatred. They could attack our allies or attempt to blackmail the United States. In any of these cases, the price of indifference would be catastrophic.
>
> . . . Time is no longer on our side. I will not wait on events, while dangers gather. I will not stand by, as peril draws closer and closer. The United States of America will not permit the world's most dangerous regimes to threaten us with the world's most destructive weapons.[43]

As Frum, one of the speechwriters who worked on this State of the Union address explains: charged with devising a justification for a war he had suggested, early on in the drafting process, comparing Iraq to the Axis powers of the World War II. "No country on earth," he argued, "more closely resembled one of the old Axis powers than present-day Iraq."[44] Attempting to link Iraq to terrorism, if tenuously, this comparison was soon transformed to express the view that "the terror states and the terror organizations formed an axis of hatred against the United States."[45] In the days and weeks that followed leading up to the State of the Union, Condoleezza Rice and Steve Hadley from the National Security Council decided they wanted the speech to take on Iran as well.[46] North Korea, as Frum recounts, "was added to the axis last."[47] With this, the "axis of hatred" was formed. However, another of Bush's speechwriters, an Evangelical Christian by the name of Michael Gerson, replaced "hatred" with "evil" because he "wanted to use the theological language that Bush had made his own since September 11."[48] As Frum notes, although the phrase originated with Gerson, Bush used it so regularly that it "became his own."[49] For example, in a speech to the First-Responders in Greenville, at the end of March 2002, Bush took the opportunity to explain to the assembled group precisely what he had meant by the phrase "the axis of evil." He said, "Let me put it to you this way: We cannot allow nations that have got a history of totalitarianism and dictatorship—a nation, for example, like Iraq, that poisoned her own people—to develop a weapon of mass destruction and mate it up with terrorist organizations who hate freedom-loving countries."[50] Similarly, in discussing the nation's critical infrastructure later in the year, Bush explained that what the United States was fighting was "a new kind of war, because we're going to be confronted with the notion that the shadowy terrorist could hook up with a nation that has got weapons of mass destruction, the nations that I labeled the axis of evil, people who in one case have gassed their own people with a [sic] weapons of mass destruction."[51] From these beginnings in the immediate aftermath of September 11 and the "Axis of Evil" speech, Bush has come to use the term "evil" on a regular basis. However, contrary to the way in which he has been characterized in much contemporary thought, Bush does not always use the word in black-and-white terms, in a paired dualism with good. Rather, the President uses the term in a range of different, sometimes incommensurable, ways.

The Nature of Evil

In the speeches of George W. Bush the nature of evil is variously conceived. In a manner typical of its modern conception, "evil" is sometimes used as an adjective to describe a particular type of act. Thus, in his Address to the Nation on September 11, Bush spoke of the "evil acts" that had, that day, shattered America's sense of security.[52] Similarly, he has, on several other occasions, referred to the "evil deeds" and "evil acts" he believes his nation must confront. "We have a chance to turn this evil," he has argued, "to turn the evil deeds and the evil acts into incredible, long-term good for our nation."[53] Again, in launching his "Back to Work Plan" for the people of New York and Washington, D.C., on October 4, 2001, Bush spoke of the "evil deeds" and "evil actions" that had "changed a lot of lives" in the three weeks that had passed since the attacks.[54]

More commonly however, Bush uses the term to refer to "evil people" or, as we will see shortly, "evildoers." On September 16, 2001, he reassured the American people with the following statement: "We've been warned there are evil people in this world. We've been warned so vividly—and we'll be alert. Your government is alert. The governors and mayors are alert that evil folks still lurk out there."[55] By claiming that individuals do not just commit evil acts but are themselves evil, Bush made use of a much older understanding of evil that was subsumed, for much of the twentieth century, by the notion that only deeds and not individuals can be rightly considered evil. There is certainly a sense here that the thoroughly evil individual, incapable of rehabilitation, is literally beyond-the-pale, to be cast out of civilized society for good if caught.

Although he often refers to "evil people" or "evil folks" in general, Bush particularly characterizes Osama bin Laden as the embodiment of evil:

> I consider bin Laden an evil man. And I don't think there's any religious justification for what he has in mind. Islam is a religion of love, not hate. This is a man who hates. This is a man who's declared war on innocent people. This is a man who doesn't mind destroying women and children. This is a man who hates freedom. This is an evil man.[56]

What is particularly interesting about Bush's characterization of bin Laden here and on other occasions is that it combines the idea that bin Laden is himself inherently evil, with the claim that what makes him evil are the specific acts he has undertaken and plans to undertake. Thus, on one hand, Bush drawing, at least implicitly, on a version of Augustine's privation/corruption thesis, argues that "Osama bin Laden is an evil man. His heart has been so corrupted that he's willing to take innocent life."[57] That is, by turning away from the good and allowing himself to become corrupted, bin Laden has become "evil" itself. At the same time however, Bush also seems to derive his understanding of bin Laden's evil character from his specific actions:

> The dictator who is assembling the world's most dangerous weapons has already used them on whole villages—leaving thousands of his own citizens dead, blind, or disfigured. Iraqi refugees tell us how forced confessions are obtained—by torturing children while their parents are made to watch. International human rights groups have catalogued other methods used in the torture chambers of Iraq: electric shock, burning with hot irons, dripping acid on the skin, mutilation with electric drills, cutting out tongues, and rape. If this is not evil, then evil has no meaning.[58]

Considered together, already we have what is a rather confused understanding of evil. Evil is, for Bush, a type of action that, in some circumstances, is extreme enough to render the perpetrator of the action evil themselves. However, in what appears to be a somewhat circular argument, he also understands evil as the turning away from or corruption of good, which renders the individual evil and allows them, in turn, to perpetrate evil actions.

To further complicate matters, on other occasions Bush has spoken of the "instruments" or "servants" of evil, "criminals and terrorists who live by violence and make victims of the innocent."[59] In particular, he describes the September 11 hijackers as "instruments of evil who died in vain."[60] However, it is in describing the "evil" of which the hijackers were instruments that Bush reveals yet another understanding of the term. He has argued that behind the hijackers: "is a cult of evil which seeks to harm the innocent and thrives on human suffering . . . Theirs is the worst kind of violence, pure malice, while daring to claim the authority of God. We cannot fully understand the designs and power of evil. It is enough to know that evil, like goodness, exists. And in the terrorists, evil has found a willing servant."[61] Here we get a glimpse of the notion that evil is a type of malevolent force to be reckoned with in the world. Significantly however, it is only a glimpse, for Bush never explicitly articulates such a view but rather implies it. Indeed, Bush never makes it clear whether the hijackers were willing servants of an evil force, or an evil individual, namely bin Laden, or perhaps even both. Although he undoubtedly views bin Laden in this light, in the imagery Bush uses in other speeches, imagery that speaks of the darkness of evil, and the "dark threat" that hangs over "our age," it is fair to conclude that he does include an understanding of evil as an independent force in his thought.[62]

It thus seems clear that the nature of evil is, in Bush's mind, manifold. Evil at once describes the acts that individuals perpetrate, those individuals themselves, and a type of independent force that exists in the world. As such, in utilizing the term, Bush, whether consciously or otherwise, draws on the history of the term in the twentieth century agent-centered discourse discussed in Chapters 5 and 6, medieval and modern conceptions of the evil agent discussed in Chapter 4, and Judeo-Christian apocalyptic notions of a cosmic battle between good and evil outlined in Chapter 3. This last point of reference is particularly evident in Bush's demonization of the enemy as "evildoers" or "evil ones."

Demonizing the Enemy

The practice of demonizing one's adversaries has a long and esteemed history. As we saw in Chapter 3, not only did many Jewish sects of the first century CE demonize their Roman tormentors but, in the early Christian period, members of Jesus's movement characterized opposing Jewish sects in demonic terms. In the fifth century, the Romans demonized the Vandals and the Huns, while the Spanish kings and the Pope came to be viewed as the Antichrist by Protestants in the aftermath of the Reformation. Similarly, when the French "emerged as the major threat to Dutch power in 1672," Louis XIV came to be known to the Dutch as the Antichrist. In response, the Pope granted "crusadelike status to the Hapsburg Spanish battle against" what was seen as Protestant heresy.[63] Indeed, the tendency to demonize one's enemies appears to be a relatively common response to perceived threats in world history.

It is therefore not surprising that at the outset, Bush sought to distinguish between "us," the "civilized people" of the world, and "them" the "evildoers" responsible for the September 11 attacks. "Civilized people around the world," he stated, "denounce the evildoers who devised and executed these terrible attacks."[64] Indeed, in subsequent speeches, the term "evildoers" has been a relatively common one.[65] The casting of the "evildoer" in opposition to civilized people of the world echoed the President's September 11 statement that warned that "we will make no distinction between the terrorists who committed these acts and those who harbor them," and his later warning to the international community, "either you're with us or you're against us."[66] Again, by posing the evildoer in this sense, Bush provides himself with a justification for its "casting out" from civilized society; the logical corollary of this is, of course, the idea that those civilized societies that do not cast out the evil ones, but rather harbor and support them, are tainted by association.

In a manner typical of early and Medieval Christian thought then, Bush announced that he would undertake a "crusade" against the evil terrorists who had harmed his nation.[67] That he used the term "crusade" is, of course, significant. As Graham Maddox explains, "the word, of course, comes from the Latin for the cross, *crux*, and implies the warlike march of Christianity against the infidel."[68] As it turned out, it was, however, "an especially unfortunate use of the term given that the prime suspects in the terrorist attack were militant Muslims. . . . an off-the-cuff and politically inept remark from which Bush quickly withdrew."[69] Indeed, in subsequent speeches Bush went to great lengths to reassure the Muslim world that his complaint was not with the Islamic faith and that he was not intending to launch a twenty-first century crusade against Islam.[70] On the contrary, Bush has made it clear on several occasions that he believes that the terrorists have hijacked a great religion.[71] Despite these remonstrations however, an adversarial tone had been set, one that continues to mark Bush's discussions of the "enemy."[72]

Good Versus Evil

That President Bush conceives evil in absolute opposition to good has been made explicit on several occasions. Most notably, in an address to the United States Military Academy at West Point in June 2002, Bush argued, "We are in a conflict between good and evil, and America will call evil by its name."[73] Earlier that same year, in a speech to promote the merits of "Compassionate Conservatism," Bush stated that "Our war is a war against evil. This is clearly a case of good versus evil, and make no mistake about it—good will prevail."[74] For many, the characterization of the perpetrators of September 11 as evil is relatively unproblematic; the most extreme form of moral condemnation seems particularly suited to crimes as heinous as those that took place on that day. What is more so, however, is the concomitant claim, made explicit in Bush's dualist presentation of evil, is that the United States is, in its fight against evil, inherently good. As the President claimed, in announcing the establishment of a humanitarian aid package for Afghanistan less than a month after the September 11 attacks:

> We are engaged in a noble cause. And that is to say loud and clear to the evildoers that we reject you, that we will stand firm against terror, and that this great nation, along with many other nations, will defend freedom.
> . . . . There's no question that we're an angry people about what happened to our country. But in our anger, we must never forget we're a compassionate people as well. We will fight evil. But in order to overcome evil, the great goodness of America must come forth and shine forth.[75]

By presenting the fight against evil in this way, as Samantha Power argues, Bush "mutes criticisms" of the United States' response to the events of September 11. "Who, after all," she writes, "can be against combating evil?"[76] Similarly, Stephen Chan has noted, what follows from this dualist presentation is the claim that "those who fight evil are *ipso facto* good."[77] Indeed, Bush has gone to some lengths to affirm America's good character: "In the wake of great evil . . . Americans responded with strength, compassion, and generosity."[78] "Time and time again, our country has shown the strength of its character by responding to acts of evil with acts of good."[79] Bush's use of the term "evil" in post–September 11 rhetoric is marked by several often-repeated, sermon-like refrains. "Good," the President has argued on numerous occasions, "triumphs over evil."[80] Thus, the President has charged his citizens with responding to evil by doing good, referring, on numerous occasions to Paul's admonition to the Romans to "Be not overcome of evil, but overcome evil with good."[81] Indeed, as Bush has regularly commanded his listeners:

> . . . the truth of the matter is, if you want to fight evil—and make no mistake about it, this is good versus evil—if you want to fight evil, do some good.
>
> . . . If you're interested in fighting evil, tell your children you love them every day this year. If you want to fight off evil, get involved in the school system and make it as good as it can be. Teach a child to read. If you want to fight evil, go to your church or synagogue or mosque and start a program that will love a neighbor. If you want to fight evil, go see a shut-in and say, what can I do to help.
>
> . . . The evil ones struck, but out of this will come incredible good. The world will be more peaceful when we accomplish our mission. And this country will be more compassionate and more decent and more loving.[82]

These phrases are repeated, almost verbatim, in a large number of Bush's subsequent speeches, from that congratulating the Los Angeles Lakers for winning the 2001–2002 National Basketball League series, to that asking senior citizens to get involved in the USA Freedom Corps.[83]

As early as March 2002, Bush had begun to reach a verdict on the triumph of good over evil, arguing that "out of that evil has come some good."[84] That good, he argued, could be seen in "sincere appreciation and respect for the men and women who wear the uniform [of] the police and the fire and the emergency medical units all across the country" that had emerged after September 11.[85] It could be seen in Americans "taking a good hard look at what's important. Moms and dads taking an assessment of their—of what's important in their life, and that is to love your children with all your heart and all your soul."[86] It could also be seen in what he viewed as the increased compassion of the American people and their renewed commitment to "love their neighbor as themselves," another of Bush's favorite refrains.

For many contemporary writers, including Peter Singer, Bush's dualist understanding of evil is fundamentally Manichaean and, as such, heretical.[87] Indeed, Singer argues not only that "seeing the world as a conflict between the forces of good and forces of evil is not . . . the orthodox Christian view, but one associated with the heresy of Manichaeaism," but that this understanding of evil is part of what Walter Lippmann called "one of the great American traditions."[88] As Richard Hofstadter has argued, the division of social and political relations, both international and domestic, into the diametrically opposed positions of "good" and "evil" is a recurrent feature of what he has termed the "paranoid style in American politics." The "paranoid leader," Hofstadter writes, believes not simply that "history *is* a conspiracy" but that it is "set in motion by demonic forces of almost transcendent power." What follows from this is the belief that "the usual methods of political give-and-take" will be insufficient in attempting to defeat this malevolent force. Rather, what is required is "an all-out crusade."[89] The "enemy," as Hofstadter wrote, "is thought of as being totally evil and totally unappeasable" and must, as a result, "be totally eliminated—if not from the world, at least from the theatre of operations to which the paranoid directs his attention."[90] The similarities between Hofstadter's "paranoid leader," identified in the 1960s, and President Bush are, indeed, striking.

Although Singer is correct to identify a tradition of dividing the world into good and evil in American politics, his characterization of Bush's understanding of evil as Manichaean is not exactly accurate. As discussed in Chapter 3, central to the Manichaean faith was the claim that the independent forces of good and evil existed in perpetual conflict with one another. As Richard Bernstein writes, Bush's view can be more accurately described as "*quasi*-Manichaean, because the original Manichaeans believed that God is *coeternal* with Satan."[91] By maintaining, as he frequently does, that good triumphs over evil, Bush actually stops just short of out-and-out Manichaeanism.[92] Rather, Bush's understanding of evil actually corresponds more accurately to notions of evil that appeared in Jewish and early-Christian apocalyptic literature. With these groups Bush believes that the cosmic battle between good and evil will ultimately be won by something approximating the "Teacher of Righteousness" referred to by the early apocalyptic writers. As we will see shortly, this turn to apocalyptic imagery may possibly be linked to the general rise in apocalyptic theology that has been under way since the late twentieth century in American religion.

However, there is another more important reason why Bush's understanding of evil can be conceived as *quasi*-Manichaean at best. Although it is certainly the case that Bush uses the terms good and evil as nouns, as we saw earlier, he also implores his citizens to *do* good to combat evil; by doing good, he suggests, the American people will overcome evil. What this would seem to suggest is that in these instances at least, good is not a force actively combating evil in the world, as the Manichaeans would have it, but something that ordinary human beings enact in response to the evil committed by other human beings.

This is not to say, however, that there are not serious problems associated with Bush's characterization of America's war on terror. As Graham Maddox writes, "Bush's stark contrast between the claimed righteousness of his own cause and the alleged evil of his chosen enemies presents a narrow and judgmental version of Christianity, pronounced with dogmatism not far removed from the rhetoric of the terrorists themselves."[93] Indeed, by posing his struggle in terms of good versus evil, Bush is unable to conceive any of his own responses to evil as forms of evil themselves. For many contemporary thinkers, Richard Bernstein amongst them, this demonization of the enemy is among the most problematic aspects of Bush's use of the term evil. In Bernstein's view, "demonizing one's enemies as absolutely evil" leads to the distortion and corruption of politics. Explaining what he means by this he continues: "To speak in this way, to speak about the 'evil ones,' the 'servants of evil,' 'the axis of evil'—as Bush frequently does—may be highly successful in playing on people's fears and anxieties, but it blocks serious deliberation and diplomacy." In this context, the term "evil" is used to "*trump* serious consideration of alternatives in responding to real dangers."[94] Alternatively, both Stephen Chan and Farid Abdel-Nour associate Bush's demonization of the enemy in terms of "otherness"; that is, the attempt to cast the opposition as "other" or, as Abdel-Nour puts it, "absolutely-not-self."[95] Contrary to aspects of discourse about evil in the 1980s and 1990s that, drawing on the notion that ordinary people commit extraordinary evil, suggested that we are all capable of evil, "in this conception, evil is not only not-self, but the nature of its separation from self is absolute."[96] With this, an absolute duality between the good self, immune to criticism, and the evil other is established.

In an attempt to counter the claim that the fight against evil is inherently good, Michael Ignatieff's 2003 Gifford Lectures in Edinburgh, later published as *The Lesser Evil: Political Ethics in an Age of Terror*, sought to illustrate the extent to which responses to evil might constitute evils, albeit lesser ones, themselves. In particular, he recognizes that while protecting citizens from evil acts such as terrorist attacks is a fundamentally good thing to do, it remains the case that many of the activities this necessarily entails, such as the suspension of individual rights, preemptive strikes, interrogation, and detention, remain fundamentally wrong.[97] They are, in his view, "lesser evils," evils that, although of less extreme magnitude, nonetheless remain characterized as evil.

Religion and Politics in American Society

Although President George W. Bush remains the foremost proponent of evil discourse in American presidential history, when considered in that context, he is not as unusual as he first appears. Indeed, as the following table reveals, he is followed behind in these stakes by a number of other interesting contenders, some predictable, others less so.

There are a number of interesting observations to be made here about the use of the word evil by American presidents. The first is that although George W. Bush leads the way, he is followed by Ronald Reagan (351) and, perhaps surprisingly, Bill Clinton (309). Indeed, although Bush's use of the term is often compared to Reagan's, it is seldom compared to Clinton's. As we will see shortly, this is somewhat surprising for in many ways Bush's understanding of evil more closely approximates that of his immediate predecessor than the president he is more commonly thought to have followed. Second, this brief survey indicates that although American presidents have long relied on the term, its use increased sharply in the middle of the twentieth century. Thus, Roosevelt and Truman remain the fourth and fifth most prolific proponents of the term with 141 and 111 uses, respectively. Interestingly, during the same period, intellectuals and scholars shied away from discussions of evil, only returning to it briefly in the 1960s.

In his radio address to the American people following Japan's surrender from the war, President Harry S. Truman declared that "the evil done by the Japanese warlords can never be repaired or forgotten."[98] This followed his earlier call, after the surrender of Germany, that the "whole world must be cleansed of the evil from which half the world" had by then been freed.[99] Of course, as Scott Kline has recently pointed out, the

Table 7.1. References to "evil" in the speeches of American presidents

President	Term	References to evil
George Washington	1789–1797	8
John Adams	1979–1801	4
Thomas Jefferson	1801–1809	3
James Madison	1809–1817	7
James Monroe	1817–1825	6
John Quincy Adams	1825–1829	3
Andrew Jackson	1829–1837	22
Martin van Buren	1837–1841	8
William Henry Harrison	1841–1841	1
John Tyler	1841–1845	13
James K. Polk	1845–1849	8
Zachary Taylor	1849–1850	1
Millard Fillmore	1850–1853	5
Franklin Pierce	1853–1857	8
James Buchanan	1857–1861	13
Abraham Lincoln	1861–1865	8
Andrew Johnson	1865–1869	11
Ulysses S. Grant	1869–1877	15
Rutherford B. Hayes	1877–1881	10
James A. Garfield	1881–1881	1
Chester A. Arthur	1881–1885	9
Grover Cleveland	1885–1889	13
Benjamin Harrison	1889–1893	6
Grover Cleveland	1893–1897	9
William McKinley	1897–1901	6
Theodore Roosevelt	1901–1909	26
William Howard Taft	1909–1913	8
Woodrow Wilson	1913–1921	9
Warren G. Harding	1921–1923	2
Calvin Coolidge	1923–1929	24
Herbert Hoover	1929–1933	36
Franklin D. Roosevelt	1933–1945	141
Harry S. Truman	1945–1953	111
Dwight D. Eisenhower	1953–1961	78
John F. Kennedy	1961–1963	27
Lyndon B. Johnson	1963–1969	97
Richard Nixon	1969–1974	39
Gerald R. Ford	1974–1977	47
Jimmy Carter	1977–1981	87
Ronald Reagan	1981–1989	351
George H.W. Bush	1989–1993	63
William J. Clinton	1993–2001	309
George W. Bush	2001–	>800

"evil" of which Truman spoke was "cleansed" at a great cost, the bombing of Hiroshima and Nagasaki, arguably "evil" acts in and of themselves.[100] In the years that followed, Truman continued to refer to America's opponents as evil, announcing upon receiving the Franklin Roosevelt Award in 1948, "we will face the evil forces that are abroad in the world," and referring in his 1951 State of the Union Address to the Korean war as "an evil war by proxy."[101]

On November 27, 1963, Lyndon B. Johnson described the assassination of John F. Kennedy as an "evil moment . . . the foulest deed of our time,"[102] before going on to use the term almost one hundred times during his presidency, usually to refer to racism or the threat of the Cold War. Following in this vein, in 1983 Ronald Reagan famously denounced the Soviet Union as the "evil empire" in a speech to the Annual Convention of the National Association of Evangelicals in Orlando, Florida.[103] Less than a year earlier he had sought to assure the Western world that "the forces of good ultimately rally and triumph over evil" in a speech to Members of the British Parliament.[104]

Although not as prominent as Reagan's "evil empire" speech, the starkest presentation of a good/evil duality was presented by the current president's father during the first Gulf War. George H. W. Bush thus wrote in an open letter to college students on the Persian Gulf Crisis, dated January 9, 1991:

> There is much in the modern world that is subject to doubts or questions—washed in shades of gray. But not so the brutal aggression of Saddam Hussein against a peaceful, sovereign nation and its people. It's black and white. The facts are clear. The choice unambiguous—right vs. wrong.
>   . . . . there's no horror that could make this a more obvious conflict of good vs. evil. The man who used chemical warfare on his own people—once again including children—now oversees public hangings of dissenters.
>   . . . . A year after the joyous dawn of freedom's light in eastern Europe, a dark evil has descended in another part of the world. But we have the chance—and we have the obligation—to stop ruthless aggression.[105]

Less than a month later he reiterated the sentiment when he told the American people "At this moment, America, the finest, most loving nation on earth, is at war, at war against the oldest enemy of the human spirit: evil that threatens world peace,"[106] thereby reiterating the "good

America," "evil enemy" theme.

Most surprising of all however, is the frequency with which Bill Clinton referred to evil during his presidency. In particular, it was during the Clinton presidency that evil became especially associated with acts of terrorism, both at home and abroad. On numerous occasions Clinton referred to terrorist bombings in Israel as "evil." For example, set in the context of his efforts to achieve peace in the Middle East, in January 1995 he stated: "Once again, the enemies of peace have struck down innocent people in an evil effort to destroy the hopes of peaceful coexistence between Israelis and Arabs."[107] Similarly, he described the kidnapping of Corporal Nahshon Waxman by Hamas in October 1994 as a "cowardly and evil" action.[108] Although he often used the term in this context however, most of Clinton's references to evil appeared in the aftermath of attacks in America or on Americans. Thus, in 1995 and again in a radio address one year later, Clinton called the Oklahoma City bombing, which cost the lives of 168 people, evil.[109] Similarly, the Atlanta Olympics bombing on July 27, 1996, was condemned as an "evil act of terror."[110] Finally, on the eighth anniversary of the bombing of Pam Am Flight 103 over Lockerbie, Scotland, Clinton told the families of those killed, "You are not alone in your determination to see that the perpetrators of this evil deed are brought to justice."[111]

Even more surprising than the frequency with which Clinton used the word during his presidency, is the proximity of his understanding of evil to that of George W. Bush. In particular, Clinton seems to have favored Paul's instruction to the Romans, "Do not be overcome by evil, but overcome evil with good," as much as Bush.[112] The only real difference is that Clinton confined his reference to this Bible passage to National Prayer Breakfast meetings while Bush addressed it to a broader audience. More significant however, are the references to dark and evil forces in Clinton's speeches, in particular those in the aftermath of the Oklahoma City bombing. At a memorial service for the victims he said: "To all my fellow Americans beyond this hall, I say, one thing we owe those who have sacrificed is the duty to purge ourselves of the dark forces which gave rise to this evil. They are forces that threaten our common peace, our way of life."[113] Indeed, although Bush is often attributed with bringing the idea that evil forces exist in the world back into contemporary American politics, it was actually Clinton who did so in explicit terms. What Bush did, in the media spotlight of September 11 and its aftermath, was to raise its public profile. That Clinton's use of evil most closely approximates Bush's is particularly significant and, as we will see in the following section, is possibly symptomatic of wider trends taking hold in America in the late twentieth and early twenty-first centuries.

The Rise of Radical Religion

There are a number of factors particular to the United States that may account for not only the enthusiasm with which some sectors of the electorate have embraced George W. Bush's rhetoric of good and evil, but also for the use of evil in the political discourse of those presidents that immediately preceded him, in particular Clinton, Bush Senior, and Reagan. The first finds its roots in the very nature of religious adherence in the United States. America is, and has long been, the "world's leading Bible-reading crusader state."[114] From its beginnings as a religious safe haven for persecuted Protestant European sects, the United States has always been a particularly religious society. Americans, in their own view, "are God's chosen people . . . a people and nation chosen by God to play a unique and even redemptive role in the world."[115] With this, American Christianity has often taken on an evangelical and combative form,[116] pitting itself against those who challenge or ignore the central message of the Gospel. In recent years, this radical, combative version of Christianity has enjoyed a marked increase in popularity in the United States, with increasing numbers of people proclaiming to be "born again." Gallup Polls conducted in the mid-1980s and again in the early 2000s revealed that identification with being "born again" had increased from 33 percent to 44–46 percent during that period. As Kevin Phillips notes, polls conducted in the first five years of the new millennium indicate that the highest percentage of people identified themselves as "born again" in the two years following the September 11 attacks; that figure dropping slightly to 42 percent in 2005.[117]

What has accompanied this rise in religious identification in recent American history is the rise of conservative Protestant sects and associated decline of the older, more traditional denominations. Thus, while membership of Presbyterian, Episcopal, United Church of Christ, and Methodist congregations has suffered a marked decline, Southern Baptist, Mormon, Pentecostal Assemblies of God, and Church of God congregations have enjoyed a period of significant expansion over the past forty years or so. For example, while the Methodists lost around two million members in the period between 1960 and 1997, "the Southern Baptist Convention added 6 million members, the Mormons 3.3 million [and] the Assemblies of God, 2 million."[118] As Mark Noll writes, these increasingly popular Protestant sects are "nearly all characterized by such labels as Bible-believing, born again, conservative, evangelical, fundamentalist, holiness, Pentecostal, or restorationist."[119] Two aspects of this characterization are particularly important. First is that this type of fundamentalism has been transformed in contemporary thought to reflect the slogan often utilized by President Bush, "either you are with us or you are against us." Indeed, in its original form, fundamentalism was a form of "reactionary Evangelicalism," the "prime purpose" of which was "the defense and exaltation of traditional views of the Bible."[120] Largely defined in terms of *The Fundamentals*, a set of twelve paperback pamphlets published between 1910 and 1915,[121] its central claims could be summed up in the five "fundamentals":

1. The inspiration and infallibility of scripture.
2. The deity of Christ (including His virgin birth).
3. The substitutionary atonement of Christ's death.
4. The literal resurrection of Christ from the dead.
5. The literal return of Christ in the Second Advent.[122]

Drawing on its militant, reactionary roots, contemporary fundamentalism has taken on a particularly combative nature that is reflected in what might be termed Bush's "political fundamentalism," the combination of "a religious fundamentalist worldview with political language."[123] Second, associated with this radical form of fundamentalism and coupled with the evangelical zeal and belief in the literal truth of the Bible that marks this form of conservative Christianity, is a widespread belief in the idea that the world will end in an Armageddon battle between Jesus Christ and the Antichrist.[124] As we will see shortly, identification with this sort of belief has made a large sector of the American community particularly responsive not only to Bush's discussions of an ongoing battle between good and evil, but his demonization of the United States' adversaries.

As we have already seen, the demonization of perceived enemies has been a common feature of world history. Aside from the particular expression this type of discourse as found in the so-called "paranoid style" of American leadership, there is another aspect of it that is particular to the

American case. In the 1970s and early 1980s, the United States witnessed the convergence of the counter-reformation that, marked by the rise of the conservative Protestant sects, was taking place in the religious realm, and the politics, particularly those associated with the Cold War, of the time. Thus, in the late 1970s and early 1980s, America saw the emergence of a number of conservative religious organizations that sought to influence the policymaking process, including the "National Federation for Decency (1977), the evangelist Jerry Falwell's Moral Majority (1979), the Religious Roundtable (1979), the Christian Voice (1979), the National Affairs Briefing (1980), the Council on Revival (1980), and the Council for National Policy (1981)."[125] Known collectively as the New Christian Right, these organizations were "headed by fundamentalist ministers" who were vehemently anticommunist.[126] For many conservative evangelicals, the atheism of the Soviet Union stood in the way of their ultimate goal, the conversion of the entire world to Christianity. With this, the Soviet Union began to take on the role of the apocalyptic adversary in much politicoreligious discourse of the time. Indeed, it is no accident that President Ronald Reagan made his famous "evil empire" speech to the Annual Convention of the National Association of Evangelicals in Orlando, Florida.[127] Thus, the Soviet Union became characterized as "a biblical as well as ideological foe . . . end-times preachers nam[ing] the U.S.S.R. as the evil confederation supposedly referred to in the Bible" to be defeated at Armageddon.[128]

With the end of the Cold War however, the characterization of the Soviet Union as the evil adversary subsided in both political and religious terms. In response to this, searching for a new foe, some evangelical Christians "substituted Islam for the Soviet Union" and, as such, in some quarters, "Muslims have become the modern-day equivalent of the Evil Empire."[129] In particular, many religious conservatives have come to view "Islam as the primary evil force, and Iraq and Saddam Hussein, respectively, as (1) the re-embodiment of the evil Babylon; and (2) the leading new contender for the role of the Antichrist,"[130] although considering the former dictator's death in 2007, this last claim probably warrants reconsideration. Although manifested in the 2000s, however, as Paul Boyer suggests, the seeds of this transformation were planted as far back as the 1970s:

> Anticipating George W. Bush, prophecy writers in the late 20th century also quickly zeroed in on Saddam Hussein. If not the Anti-Christ himself, they suggested, Saddam could well be a fore-runner of the Evil One . . .

Prophecy believers found particular significance in Saddam's plan, launched in the 1970s, to rebuild Babylon on its ancient ruins. The fabled city on the Euphrates, south of Baghdad . . . owed its splendor to King Nebuchadnezzar, the same wicked king who warred against Israel and destroyed Jerusalem in 586 B.C.[131]

As a poll conducted by the *Washington Post* in September 2003 revealed, seventy percent of respondents believed that Saddam Hussein, described as "the evil one," was involved in the September 11 attacks.[132] Although it is possible that many respondents to this poll thought that they were answering a question about whether he was responsible for September 11, this would nevertheless seem to indicate that the association of Saddam Hussein with the Antichrist remained solid in the minds of many Americans at the time.

What has also accompanied the designation of Saddam Hussein as the "evil one" in both political and religious thought, is the continuation and expansion of the rhetoric of Armageddon that marked Reagan's Cold War presidency. Indeed, Paul Boyer suggests that more than forty percent of the American population "believe[s] that Bible prophecies detail a specific sequence of end-times events."[133] For many, this comes in the form of so-called "rapture" or "dispensationalist" theologies. As Barbara Rossing explains, dispensationalists commonly "identify the Bible's cosmic plan coming to life" in "world wars, bloody crashes, earthquakes, diseases and other violent cataclysms."[134] For example, the raptureready.com Web site devotes itself to calculating how close the world is to Armageddon by interpreting recent disasters in terms of end-times prophecies.

On a fundamental level, the rise of radical, conservative Christianity in the United States has made a large sector of the electorate fertile ground for promulgating views of evil such as those of President Bush. It is no surprise that conservative Christians are Bush's most fervent supporters; 87 percent of frequent-attending white voters who identify themselves as being on the religious right voted for Bush in 2000.[135] What is more, although his supporter base was not predominantly conservative white Christians, President Clinton's use of "evil" may possibly be attributed to his Southern Baptist roots. Thus, although it is certainly the case that the rise of what might be termed "fundamentalist evil rhetoric" can be attributed to George W. Bush, it remains the case that the general rise of radical religion has made a large sector of the American electorate open to such discourse.

Conclusion

In the immediate aftermath of the September 11 terrorist attacks, the turn to the concept of evil made by both President Bush and a large number of other world leaders and dignitaries helped to express the sense of bafflement that accompanied the meaningless suffering inflicted on that day. In this, and in the sense of mystery the concept embodied, the use of the term "evil" was, at this time, both unremarkable and relatively uncontentious. At the same time, the sheer wickedness of the attack and demonstrable intent of its perpetrators led some to return to a pre–twentieth century understanding of the evil agent, the moral monster who willingly and knowingly inflicts undeserved suffering on innocent victims. However, as we have seen in this chapter, before long, evil took on a range of other meanings and has become ultimately associated with the search for moral absolutes used to justify foreign policy decisions. In particular, although he uses the term in a manifold number of ways, it is President Bush's understanding of evil in paired duality with good that has exerted the greatest influence over thought about evil in the early twenty-first century. By conceiving evil in this manner, Bush not only appeals to an early apocalyptic understanding of the term but, in many ways, continues a long tradition of thought among American presidents. In addition, as we saw in the last part of this chapter, this understanding of evil concords well with more general trends present in contemporary American religious thought. Thus, although it undoubtedly remains the case that Bush is himself responsible for what Richard Bernstein calls the "abuse of evil" in contemporary politics, it remains the case that his use of the term must be considered in the broader context of the American presidency and the rise of radical religion in the United States.

Although predominantly an American response, the use of "evil" in political rhetoric is not, however, exclusively American. In the post–September 11 era the other world leader known for his prominent use of "evil" in political rhetoric is the British Prime Minister Tony Blair. In the immediate aftermath of September 11, Blair described the attacks on the United States as "hideous and foul events . . . an act of wickedness for which there can be no justification."[136] Within days however, Blair began to describe not only the attacks but also the "mass international terrorism" that confronted the world on that day as "evil."[137] Like President Bush, Prime Minister Blair has used the term "evil" in a range of different ways. Most commonly, evil is simply equated with terrorism in his rhetoric, and thus often appears as an adjective used to describe especially heinous acts.[138] However, Blair has also spoken of "evil people," with reference to the suicide bombers who continue to wreak havoc in Iraq and referred to the "sheer evil of bin Laden and his followers."[139]

More famously however, Blair has spoken of an "evil ideology" that is the driving force behind the terrorist attacks that have afflicted the world in recent years. In a speech to the House of Commons on July 13, 2005, some six days after the London bombings, Blair argued that "international cooperation would be needed to 'pull up this evil ideology by its roots.'"[140] Several days later, he explained that this "evil ideology" was "based on a perversion of Islam" that could only be defeated "by the force of reason."[141] However, Blair has never properly expanded upon this explanation and, to date, it remains very unclear precisely what this "evil ideology" entails.

Indeed, where President Bush has not flinched when questioned over his use of "evil," Blair has floundered, appearing to be increasingly uncomfortable with the term. In a BBC Radio 4 interview early in 2007, Blair's apparently Manichaean view of good and evil was challenged repeatedly. The extent to which he skirted around the question, ultimately failing to reveal whether or not he does, indeed, view the world in black and white, good and evil terms, betrayed either his discomfort with the term or, more plausibly, his sense that concern over the misuse of the term has made it politically inexpedient. At the same time, Blair's reluctance to discuss his understanding of evil is possibly also due to the fact that although he is also a committed Christian, his faith is of a far less radical variety than that of his American counterpart and in that, reflects wider British sentiments. Nonetheless, that he has turned to the concept of evil in times of crisis, to describe the very worst of human behavior, again reveals the very potency of the term in the aftermath of horrific events.

Conclusion

In the aftermath of World War II, Hannah Arendt predicted that "the problem of evil [would] be the fundamental question of postwar intellectual life in Europe."[1] However, as evidence would seem to suggest and, as Richard Bernstein has pointed out on several occasions, "she was wrong. Most post-war intellectuals avoided any direct confrontation with the problem of evil."[2] While the horrors of the Holocaust remained a permanent scar on the European psyche, concern with evil and the overt discussion of the range of problems associated with it largely disappeared in general Western political thought. Indeed, with a few rare exceptions—notably Arendt's own *Eichmann in Jerusalem* and Paul Ricoeur's *The Symbolism of Evil*[3]—the fifty years following the end of World War II was marked by deafening silence on the subject.

At the beginning of the twenty-first century however, "evil" is enjoying something of a renaissance—not, of course, in the material world (it hardly needed a renaissance there)—but among writers, intellectuals, scholars, and most notably, politicians. Beginning in the middle of the 1990s with the Rwandan genocide, followed just a year later by the massacre of some eight thousand Bosnian Muslim men at Srebrenica, the concept of evil began to make its return to popular rhetoric and discourse as the means to describe the very worst humanitarian atrocities. At the same time, revisionist accounts of the Holocaust and investigations of the historiographical assumptions that have underpinned many of the most common historical treatments of that, the most significant evil of the modern period, if not all human history, also began to revisit notions of "evil" that have often been used to describe that event. In particular, a massive upsurge in the popularity of Hannah Arendt's works in the late 1990s and early 2000s has also contributed to the sense that the problem of evil, if not *the* fundamental problem of contemporary social and political thought, has certainly emerged as *a* significant problem.

Most notably, of course, interest in the concept of evil and its associated "problems" has intensified since the events of September 11, 2001. As the events of that day demonstrated with alarming clarity, even the citizens of the world's only superpower are susceptible to the meaningless suffering that so often afflicts other sectors of the human population. Indeed, precisely what made the World Trade Center attacks especially shocking is that they shattered the sense of security that many in the West had, perhaps naïvely, assumed was sacrosanct. Prior to September 11, most of us had not considered that downtown New York could be the site of massacre on this scale; Tel Aviv, perhaps, Kigali certainly, but not New York. As Susan Sontag explained in *On Photography*, the ability of events, or more accurately, images of events, to shock is based on two factors that were certainly at play in most Western responses to September 11. The first is that photographs, or other images, "shock in so far as they show something novel." That is, she wrote, the "quality of feeling, including moral outrage, that people can muster in response to photographs of the oppressed, the exploited, the starving, and the massacred also depends on the degree of their familiarity with these images."[4] Indeed, I would hazard a guess that very few people (at least in those parts of the world where such destruction is not commonplace) who watched the footage of the airplanes slamming into the twin towers of the World Trade Center, the frantic office workers trapped in the burning buildings, waving from the windows in the vain hope of being rescued before leaping to their deaths, and the final dramatic collapse of the entire structure, did so with complete emotional detachment. The image of "The Falling Man" in particular seemed to inspire extreme emotional responses from horror, disbelief, and sadness to moral outrage in a large percentage of the population.[5]

Secondly, Sontag also argues that the very "possibility of being affected morally by photographs" is itself determined by "the existence of a relevant political consciousness."[6] Thus, the response of many in the West to the images of September 11 was determined by both the shock associated with the fact that footage such as this had not been seen before and by an understanding of its wider political significance. Sympathetic responses to September 11 within the United States were often derived from a sense of national solidarity, that is, from an understanding that as an act perpetrated against fellow nationals it was an act perpetrated against Americans more generally. For non-Americans, similar emotional responses could possibly be understood as being born out of a sense of political and cultural proximity. Sontag's discussion of responses to photographs and other images also helps to explain why many in war-torn regions of the world failed to understand the outpouring of grief that followed the September 11 attacks; pictures of destruction such as this are no longer shocking in those parts of the world where war is a continuing part of daily life. What is more, without a personal understanding of the "relevant political consciousness," it is difficult for outsiders to fully appreciate the shocking nature of this act. In the same way, reports of yet another suicide bomb on an Israeli bus, neither shocks many of us in the West nor does it enter the realm of our political consciousness.

With the sense of shock that accompanied the events of September 11 came the inevitable search for an answer to the question of why this happened. Why was such tragedy visited upon the people of New York, Washington, D.C., the passengers on the hijacked flights, their families, friends, and fellow nationals? Why did they suffer? Of course, the first to grapple for an answer to these questions was President George W. Bush who, in his Address to the Nation on the evening of September 11 turned to an age-old answer: America suffered because there is evil in the world. In the immediate aftermath, the designation of the September 11 attacks as "evil" seemed apt; the most extreme form of moral condemnation appeared to be the most appropriate way of describing what had happened. As both a shocked response and as a means of associating the attacks with other serious atrocities that had garnered the title in recent years, the claim made by President Bush that "today, our nation saw evil, the very worst of human nature," seemed entirely reasonable.[7]

As we have seen in subsequent years however, Bush's reference to evil was not simply an initial response to an extremely shocking event. Rather, it has come to signal the beginning of an ever-intensifying devotion to the term by the President and others in the international community. "Evil," particularly when used in conjunction with "good," has come to represent one extreme of the moral spectrum, the designation of one's adversaries in these terms thereby seeming to provide moral and religious impetus for particular foreign policy objectives.

However, the recent surge in popularity that "evil" has enjoyed at the hand of the American president, has been accompanied by an increasing sense of discomfort surrounding the term. As we saw in Chapter 1, critics of "evil" raise several sometimes well-founded objections to its use in contemporary political rhetoric and scholarly thought. First, on a practical and moral level, the designation of one's adversaries as evil and the associated assumption that all actions taken in response to it are inherently good is not only practically dangerous but morally hazardous. By posing their actions in terms of a fight against the forces of evil, states not only attempt to provide their actions with greater cosmic legitimacy but often fail to give due moral consideration to the means according to which they conduct that battle. As such, they are blinded to the fact that they too, despite their best intentions, may become the purveyors of evil themselves.

Second, in much contemporary discourse, evil has been criticized as a vague, confusing and ultimately obfuscating concept. Little consensus exists as to what it means, the form that it takes, or, indeed, whether it has real existence in the world. However, rather than attempt to clarify these issues as far as possible, many contemporary thinkers have made the frankly impractical claim that it ought to be abandoned. As we have seen in this work, throughout the past three thousand years or so human populations have regularly turned to the concept of evil in times of crisis. Attempting to abandon it would appear to be an ultimately futile exercise; the problem of its indeterminacy would perhaps be better served by efforts to elucidate precisely what the term means, the principal aim of this work.

Finally, and most significantly, many contemporary scholars have objected to the religious connotations associated with the term evil, even as it is used in much secular thought. Indeed, in the secular world of twentieth- and twenty-first–century scholarship, references to theological constructs, particularly of the Judeo-Christian variety, are commonly deemed unacceptable. This, as we have seen, poses a particularly thorny problem for the concept of evil, a concept that, despite appearing in secular forms in Western thought in the late modern period, remains grounded in Judeo-Christian ideas.

Despite these objections, the concept of evil remains alive and well in contemporary discourse of both the public and scholarly varieties. As such, the central aim of this work has been precisely to address those problems that surround the meaning of evil and its religious foundations.

The Meaning of Evil

Traditionally, the concept of "evil," as we have seen in its variety of forms, has at its heart the attempt the make otherwise meaningless suffering meaningful. It is the concept we turn to when we cannot find an answer to the question, why do I suffer? In its earliest forms, the answer to this question was often sought in reference to a deity or deities and thereby gave rise to the so-called problem of evil, the problem of how to reconcile the existence of an all-good God with the existence of suffering in the world, that area of scholarship known as theodicy. As we saw in Chapters 3 and 4 however, the practice of theodicy has been variously conceived over the millennia and as such, thinkers of differing faiths in different eras have constructed very different answers to the question "why do I suffer?" Thus, in many early accounts, evil is posed as the ultimate penalty for sin, the suffering human beings must endure as punishment for their sins. In this sense, the ancient Hebrews conceived evil as a term of moral condemnation, equated with the spoiled, worthless, or useless, and used to denote sinful actions, as opposed to particular entities. However, for others, most notably Job and the author of the *Babylonian Theodicy*, a connection, whether natural or metaphysical, between sin and suffering could not be identified as the authors did not conceive themselves as sinners worthy of the suffering to which they were subjected. Thus, both writers sought to explain their suffering by reference to the mysterious and ultimately unknowable wisdom of God, or in the case of the *Babylonian Theodicy*, the gods.

However, with the rise of Jewish apocalyptic literature in the second century BCE, the concept of evil began to take on a new type of meaning. Although still used to explain the meaning of otherwise meaningless suffering, and posed in terms of the "problem of evil," evil began to be understood as a sort of entity as opposed to a mere action. Thus, many Jewish apocalyptic sects conceived of a spiritual battle, fought on both earthly and cosmic levels, between the spiritual forces of good and evil, and posited that undeserved suffering was inflicted, not by a benevolent deity, but by the evil force itself. In early Christian thought, this notion of evil became personified in the figure of Satan, an adversary and servant over whom God retains ultimate power to defeat. However, the idea that evil is an independent entity wreaking havoc on Earth and in the cosmos was most forcefully and explicitly articulated by the Zoroastrians and, in particular, the Manichaeans of the third century CE. Here evil was conceived as an independent force, something that actually exists and is locked in a perpetual battle with good. Thus, by conceiving good and evil as independent, rival forces, the Manichaeans avoided having to answer the problem of suffering by reference to a good God.

Suffering, particularly of the meaningless variety, could be attributed to the force of evil in the world quite independently of God.

As we saw in Chapter 3 however, Augustine of Hippo roundly refuted the claim that an independent force of evil to rival God could be said to exist as blatant heresy. Evil, in Augustine's view, did not have a real, material existence, but was better conceived as the privation of good. What is more, Augustine turned on its head the view that evil was the cause of sin, by arguing that evil was in fact caused by sin. In doing so, Augustine placed on a more solid foundation the much earlier claim that suffering, conceived in terms of evil, was the result of sin and thereby placed responsibility for evil squarely with human agents. Thus, in the works of Augustine we find the beginnings what later became the more clearly defined distinction between the moral and cosmological problems of evil. Of course, for Augustine, the moral problem of why humans knowingly commit evil acts was answered by reference to the cosmological problem of why a good God allows evil and suffering in the world. By the middle of the eighteenth century however, many writers began to rethink this association.

As we saw in Chapter 4, eighteenth-century Europe was marked by two significant events: the Lisbon earthquake and, in intellectual terms, the Enlightenment. In particular, the 1755 earthquake inspired many thinkers to reconsider the firm connection between sin and suffering that had long dominated thinking about evil. Indeed, prior to the earthquake, thinkers answered the question "why do I suffer?" by arguing that individuals suffer because they sin. However, in the aftermath of the Lisbon earthquake, it did not seem reasonable to hold pious individuals personally responsible for the meaningless suffering inflicted upon them. Thus, thinkers were forced to concede that while some suffering is caused by human sinfulness, some is the result of the natural finitude of the created world. With this the now commonplace distinction between natural and moral evils was established.

Although he managed to retain a partially-Augustinian connection between suffering and sin, with the works of Rousseau came a firmer distinction between the moral and cosmological problems of evil. Indeed, what the earlier division of evils into its natural and moral forms allowed was for those evils caused directly by human actions to be considered in isolation from other forms of meaningless suffering in the world. With Kant, and the reason-driven approach of the Enlightenment, the final firm distinction between the moral and cosmological problems of evil was achieved. No longer was it necessary to answer the question of why human beings commit evil by reference to God. Rather, the answer to that question and the question, "Why do I suffer?" was to be found by exclusive reference to the human agent, more than that, the evil human agent. Evil was thus conceived as "radical" in Kant's view, not because it is extreme, but because it reveals an innate propensity within human nature. With this, the cosmological problem of evil became largely rejected from general thought, finding a place only within the more narrow confines of theological inquiry.

This trend continued well into the twentieth century and, in the aftermath of the Holocaust, accounts of evil generally focused on the moral, as opposed to theological or cosmological, problems raised by what had taken place. Again, the question, "why do I suffer?" was to be answered by reference to human agents alone, in this case the human agents who perpetrated the particular evils of the Holocaust. However, what the experience of the Holocaust and the subsequent investigation of those held responsible for its most horrific atrocities revealed was that it was not accurate to describe the perpetrators of evil as "evil" themselves. Rather, as the trial of Adolph Eichmann demonstrated, the perpetrators of evil, despite their actions, were not necessarily monstrous, demonic individuals but, as in the case of Eichmann, could be better described as banal. Thus came the recognition that in some instances it is more accurate to describe particular actions, and not the individual perpetrators of those actions, as evil. With the range of agent-centered, psychological, and psychosocial accounts of evil that followed in the late twentieth century it appeared that despite the manifold problems inherent in the modern concept of evil, that the ongoing tension between the moral and cosmological approaches to evil had been finally resolved.

However, at the beginning of the twenty-first century, parts of the Western world, particularly the United States, have witnessed the reemergence of theologically driven explanations for evil and answers to the question "why do I suffer?" Indeed, particularly in the political rhetoric of President George W. Bush, evil is most commonly used in religious or *quasi*-religious terms. Evil has thus come to refer, once again, to an independent force at play in the world and the privation of good in an Augustinian sense, and to describe the adversaries of the United States. At the same time, those agent-centered understandings of evil that dominated twentieth century thought have suffered a significant decline. In part, this can be attributed to the fact that, in the aftermath of September

11, it does not seem reasonable to absolve the perpetrators of evil acts of being characterized as evil themselves. However, it can also be attributed, in part, to the inability of the modern concept to account for metaphysical aspects of evil.

Evil, Religion, and Modernity

What the return to premodern notions of evil at the beginning of the twenty-first century would seem to reveal are some of the failings inherent in modern understandings of the term and, indeed, modernity itself. As Scott Thomas explains, the concept of "modernity" and the social theories of modernization that came with it commonly have three aspects. The first is the claim that a distinction can be made between "traditional" and "modern" societies, modernization thereby signifying the transition from traditional to modern. The modern state is, as we will see shortly, the secular state and, after the Peace of Westphalia, was granted ultimate control over its religious adherence. The second main aspect of modernization theory views modernization as "a linear, progressive conception of social change, a universal theory, applicable" not only to Western societies that had already modernized but "to all non-Western societies that were in the process of becoming 'modern.'"[8] That is, it conceives modernization as the universal process by which different societies make "an inevitable transition toward a common end."[9] There is thus no room in modernization theory for societies to revert back to more traditional forms or to take a path of development other than that which the theory specifies itself. Finally, and most importantly for our discussion, the third main aspect of modernization is secularization. Since the eighteenth century it has generally been assumed that modernization fundamentally entails secularization; modern society, as mentioned above, is fundamentally secular society, the modern state, a secular state.[10] Although there is growing recognition within some areas of social and political thought that the separation between Church and state "does not necessarily lead to the full-scale secularization of society"—the United States is the most obvious example of a secular state that represents an extremely religious society—secularization theory holds that formal separation to be essential.[11] Thus, in the modern, secular state, religion is effectively privatized or relegated to the private sphere. At the very least it is to have no overt bearing on the official capacities and activities of the state.

As Thomas explains, secularization theory has remained surprisingly persistent in recent thought despite what he views as "the global resurgence of culture and religion" in the contemporary world. The reason for this, he suggests, is that in attaching itself to elements of modernism, secularization theory has managed to replace certain religious ideas with its own set of beliefs. Thus, secularization theory explains the decline in religious belief in terms of another set of beliefs "about the nature of rationality, modernization, and progress . . . powerful images and assumptions of what many people in the West want to believe modernity is."[12] In intellectual terms this has amounted to a turn away from religious, faith-based explanations for phenomena, to what are presented as "rational" forms of reasoning. The ultimate result of this, along with a number of other factors associated with the secularization of scholarship in the social and political sciences, has been the marginalization of religion from serious consideration.

In terms of the development of thinking about evil, these phenomena began to become apparent from the works of Descartes, Hume, and Kant onward. In Kant's later works, following his outward rejection of theodicy, the search for an explanation for evil, and in particular the question of why human beings knowingly commit evil, could only be found by considering the human agent itself. Thus, although Kant conceded that one could *believe* in a theological explanation for evil, one could not *prove* it in what he conceived as "scientific" terms (of course, this distinction is based on a faulty understanding of what constitutes scientific enquiry, for Kant does not actually prove anything in scientific terms either). Through what Kant conceived as rational enquiry, he thus arrived at the answer to his question: human beings commit evil because they are predisposed to will it. Evil motivations, driven by the negative human characteristic of self-love, lead individuals to choose incorrect maxims to guide their behavior and thereby commit evil. Evil actions, in Kant's view, are therefore presupposed by the evil intentions to which human beings are presupposed.

There are, of course, a number of serious problems associated with Kant's understanding of radical evil. In the first instance, it is based on a *belief* in a particular form of rationality. Rationality, as Kant understands it, is the means to scientific proof. However, all Kant is able to achieve in reality is to demonstrate that his explanation for evil is rational, that is, that it is based on accepted principles of rationality. The claim that his explanation is therefore true, is no less an act of faith (in this case in rationality) than belief in a theistic explanation for evil.

More seriously however, as we saw in Chapters 5 and 6, this modern, secular notion of evil proved extremely problematic in the twentieth-century thought that tried to make sense of the Holocaust. In particular, the claim that a connection could be identified between evil actions and evil intentions that was central to the Kantian notion of radical evil proved, in some cases, to be fatally flawed. This was the case made particularly apparent in the works of Hannah Arendt. In her early work on the *Origins of Totalitarianism*, Arendt found that those responsible for establishing and administering the concentration camps were not driven by evil motivations, but that they had no motivations at all. This, the sheer useless of it, in Arendt's view, is what made their evil "radical." Of course in her later work on the trial of Adolph Eichmann she found that evil is not always devoid of all motivations, but can be driven by readily comprehensible motives that, in other circumstances, may even be considered laudable. Thus, Arendt made two separate but connected attempts to reconceive evil while retaining the sense of moral agency that marks the modern concept.

By the end of the twentieth century, these types of explanations for evil, and in particular, the "banality of evil" thesis, began to look extremely flawed. Although the "banality of evil" thesis was seen favorably because it allowed individuals like Eichmann, who were involved in the Holocaust through a lack of imaginative capacity—that is, the capacity to imagine how their actions might impact others beyond what they have directly observable evidence for—to be viewed as perpetrating evil, it soon became apparent that this description did not fit all, or even most, of the perpetrators of those incidents described as evil in the late twentieth and early twenty-first centuries. Just as the masterminds of the Final Solution could not be described as banal, so too dictators such as Idi Amin, Bokassa Pol Pot, and Saddam Hussein did not fit the description. Similarly, the description of the Rwandan genocide as evil brought with it the sense that those wielding machetes, knives, and guns, who see the consequences of their actions before their very eyes and, quite literally, have the blood of their victims on their hands, cannot be described as "banal" in any sense of the word. Finally, of course, the September 11 attacks also defy the label of banal; these attacks were conscious choices of those who committed them, part of a careful and well worked out plan, made in full awareness and indeed, the confident expectation of the suffering they would inflict.

Thus, despite significant problems associated with its conceptualization, at the beginning of the twenty-first century we have witnessed a partial return to the concept of radical evil. This, in itself, is relatively unproblematic. If we are to use the term evil to signify the extreme of moral condemnation, then it follows that evil, in this sense, ought to be conceived in terms of human moral agency. It would make little sense for it to be otherwise. However, at the same time we must recognize not simply that our understanding of human moral agency is flawed and incomplete, but that by extension, agent-centered accounts of evil cannot tell the whole story. The modern concept of evil, in both its radical and banal forms, can take us some way to answering the question, why do I suffer? We suffer because human agents, either through direct and explicit, or indirect intent, knowingly inflict harm upon us. This may be the result of their natural predisposition or, in some instances, the result of the psychosocial context in which they find themselves.

What the modern concept of moral evil cannot do is answer the bigger, metaphysical questions: Why do I suffer? Why is there suffering in the world? Why do horrible things happen to good people? and so on. As we have seen in this work, throughout history, humans have sought answers to these and other "big questions" by reference to religion, in its various varieties. In large sections of contemporary Western society it is no different; as responses to the events of September 11 demonstrate, in attempting to understand extreme meaningless human suffering, we often turn to both secular "moral" and sacred religious explanations. What this reveals is that despite the efforts of much eighteenth-century philosophy, a fundamental tension remains between cosmological or theological, and philosophical explanations for evil. Indeed, in light of the lengthy history of this tension in Western thought about evil, we might want to go so far as to say that the period from the late eighteenth to the late twentieth centuries represents something of an anomaly.

In its contemporary form, evil is both a secular and sacred concept. In order to fully understand the extremes of human suffering, the most heinous humanitarian atrocities, and the infliction of wanton, undeserved suffering, we need both sacred and secular understandings of the term. To return, in the final analysis to Augustine, we recall that this great thinker understood that two fundamental problems of evil could be said to exist: the problem of why human beings knowingly do what is wrong, and the problem of why a good God would allow evil to exist in the world. In contemporary thought, we readily identify the first of these problems as a moral problem, a problem of human behavior to be explained in secular, human terms. However, the second problem speaks not only to our understanding of evil in the wider cosmic order, but also to the mysterious and metaphysical aspects of its occurrence. If we want to provide answers to this broader set of questions (and, of course, some us may not) then we must look beyond the mere observation of human behavior. By doing so, we may develop a greater sense of evil in its entirety, as fundamentally human and yet ultimately mysterious, the means according to which, in both sacred and secular thought, we seek to make otherwise meaningless suffering meaningful.

Notes

Chapter 1

1. Joel Feinburg, *Problems at the Roots of Law* (Oxford: Oxford University Press, 2003), 144.
2. Prime Minister Tony Blair, Statement from Gleneagles, July 7, 2005, available at https://news.bbc.co.uk/1/hi/uk/4659953.stm (accessed March 22, 2007); "Blair speech on terror" at the Labor Party National Conference, July 16, 2005, available at http://news.bbc.co.uk/2/hi/uk_news/4689363.stm (accessed March 22, 2007).
3. George W. Bush, Speech from Gleneagles, July 7, 2005, available at https://www.cba.ca/news/background/london_bombing/bush_speech.html (accessed July 15, 2005); Michael Howard, July 11, 2005, available at http://uk.news.yahoo.com/050711/143/fn3yb.html (accessed July 15, 2005).
4. John Howard, condolence book message for the victims of the July 7 attacks on London, British High Commission, Canberra, July 8, 2005.
5. See Philip Gourevitch, *We Wish to Inform You That Tomorrow We Will be Killed With Our Families* (London: Picador, 2000); Bill Berkeley, *The Graves Are Not Yet Full: Tribe and Power in the Heart of Africa* (New York: Basic Books, 2001); Carlos Santiago Nino, *Radical Evil on Trial: Reflecting on the Rwandan Genocide* (New Haven: Yale University Press, 1996).
6. Graham Jones, "Srebrenica: 'A triumph of evil,'" CNN, May 3, 2006, available at http://www.cnn.com/2006/WORLD/europe/02/22/warcrimes.srebrenica (accessed March 23, 2007); Remarks by Ambassador Pierre Richard Prosper at the Tenth Anniversary Commemoration, Srebrenica, Bosnia and Herzegovina, July 11, 2005, Embassy of the United States of America, Belgrade, available at http://belgrade.usembassy.gov/archives/press/2005/b050712.html (accessed March 26, 2007).

7. Albert Likhanov, "Against Evil—In the Name of Good," 57th Conference of UN Associated NGOs. Available at https://www.un.org/dpi/ngosection/annualconfs/57/likhanov.pdf (accessed March 26, 2007)

8. George W. Bush, "Statement by the President in Address to the Nation," September 11, 2001, available at http://www.whitehouse.gov/news/releases/2001/09/20010911-16.html (accessed March 22, 2007).

9. George W. Bush, "President's Remarks at National Day of Prayer and Remembrance," National Cathedral, Washington, D.C., September 14, 2001, available at http://www.whitehouse.gov/news/releases/2001/09/20010913-2.html (accessed March 22, 2007).

10. George W. Bush, "State of the Union Address," United States Capitol, Washington D.C., January 29, 2002, available at http://www.whitehouse.gov/news/releases/2002/01/20020129-11.html (accessed March 26, 2007); see also Peter Singer, *The President of Good and Evil: The Ethics of George W. Bush* (New York: Dutton, 2004), 2.

11. George W. Bush, "State of the Union Address," United States Capitol, Washington D.C., January 23, 2007, available at http://www.whitehouse.gov/news/releases/2007/01/20070123-2.html (accessed March 27, 2007).

12. United Nations, Report of the Panel on United Nations Peacekeeping Operations, A.55.305, S/2000/809, August 21, 2000, par. 50, available at http://www.un.org/peace/reports/peace_operations (accessed March 22, 2007)

13. United Nations Secretary General Kofi Annan, "Address to the United Nations General Assembly," SG/SM7977, GA/9920, 1/10/2001, September 24, 2001, available at http://www.un.org/News/ossg/sg/stories/statements_search_full.asp?statID=34, (accessed March 22, 2007).

14. General Assembly President, "Terrorism Is Our Irreconcilable Enemy," 9/11/2002, GA/SM/289, September 12, 2002, available at http://www.un.org/News/Press/docs/2002/GASM289.doc.htm (accessed March 22, 2007).

15. Ri Yong Ho, Counselor, Minister of Foreign Affairs, Democratic Peoples Republic of Korea, World Conference Against Racism, Racial Discrimination, Xenophobia and Related Intolerance, South Africa, August 31–September 7, RD/D/34, available at http://www.un.org/WCAR.aconf189_12.pdf (accessed March 22, 2007).

16. President Bedjaoui argued at the International Court of Justice that nuclear weapons were the "ultimate evil," 103. "The Legality of the Threat or Use of Nuclear Weapons, International Court of Justice Advisory Opinion," July 8, 1996, http://www.un.org/law/icjsum/9623.htm (accessed March 22, 2007).

17. Newspaper headlines documenting the use of rape by Serbian forces read, "Serbian 'Rape Camps': Evil upon Evil"; "Sexual Violence and Armed Conflict: United Nations Response Division for the Advancement of

Women, Department of Economic and Social Affairs," http://www
.un.org/womenwatch.daw/public/cover.pdf (accessed March 22, 2007).

18. "International Security Includes 'Peaceful War' Against Aids, Economic and
Social Council Told," ECOSOC.5884, February 28, 2000, available at
http://www.un.org/News/Press/docs/2000/20000228.ecosoc.5884.doc.html
(accessed March 22, 2007).

19. Crime Congress High Level Segment, Bangkok, April 23, 2005, SOC/
CP/333, available at http://www.un.org/News/Press/docs/2005/soccp333
.doc.htm (accessed March 22, 2007).

20. Ibid.

21. *Prosecutor v. Radislav Krstic* (IT-98-33), Judgement of the Trial Chamber,
International Criminal Tribunal for the Former Yugoslavia, August 2, 2001,
par. 70.

22. Richard J. Bernstein, *Radical Evil: A Philosophical Interrogation*, (Cambridge:
Polity Press, 2002), x.

23. Singer, *The President of Good and Evil*, 2.

24. As Douglas Klusmeyer and Astri Suhrke point out, this phenomenon is not
simply confined to public discourse as increasing numbers of scholars are
being drawn to the term but find little cause to consider the concept itself.
Douglas Klusmeyer and Astri Suhrke, "Comprehending 'Evil': Challenges
for law and policy," *Ethics and International Affairs* 16, no. 1 (2002): 28. For
example, they highlight the fact that Carlos Santiago Nino "put 'evil' on the
title page of his book and uses the word prominently in the introduction,
where he acknowledges his debt to Hannah Arendt. Yet he makes no use of
it in his analysis of events or conclusions for dealing with the perpetrators."
Similarly, "Martha Minnow cites several other scholars who invoke the
term, although she herself does not us it either descriptively or as a tool in
her analysis of overcoming the legacy of massive violence." Finally, "after
declaring his book 'is about evil,' Bill Berkeley offers a definition that is so
broad as to be virtually useless," Berkeley, *The Graves Are Not Yet Full*, 5; see
Nino, *Radical Evil on Trial*; Martha Minnow, *Between Vengeance and
Forgiveness: Facing History After Genocide and Mass Violence* (Boston:
Beacon Press, 1998).

25. Catherine Lu, "Editor's Introduction," *International Relations* 18, no. 4,
(2004): 403.

26. Richard J. Bernstein, *The Abuse of Evil: The Corruption of Politics and
Religion Since 9/11* (Cambridge: Polity, 2005), 10–11.

27. Lu, "Editor's Introduction," 403.

28. Stephen Toope and Jutta Brunnée, "Slouching Towards New 'Just' Wars: The
Hegemon after September 11th," *International Relations* 18, no. 4, (2004):
405–23.

29. Inga Clendinnen, *Reading the Holocaust* (Melbourne: Text, 1998), 104.

30. Ibid., 101.
31. Thomas W. Simon, "Genocide, Evil, and Injustice: Competing Hells," in *Genocide and Human Rights: A Philosophical Guide*, ed. John K. Roth (Basingstoke: Palgrave Macmillan, 2005), 69.
32. Ibid.
33. Peter Dews, "Disenchantment and the Persistence of Evil: Habermas, Jonas, Badiou," in *Modernity and the Problem of Evil*, ed. Alan D. Schrift (Bloomington: Indiana University Press, 2005), 51.
34. Gil Bailie, "Two Thousand Years and No New God," in *Destined for Evil? The Twentieth-Century Responses*, ed. Predrag Cicovacki (Rochester: University of Rochester Press, 2005), 20. However, Thomas Simon concedes that the frequency with which thinkers have turned to the idea of evil can, at least in part, be attributed to the fact that there is no comparable word in the secular vocabulary. In the aftermath of the Holocaust, for example, "the concept of evil," whether conceived in a traditional religious sense or in wholly secular terms, "gave philosophers a way to deal with Auschwitz, for the term *evil* seemed to capture the extreme moral outrage needed to describe" its horrors. Simon, "Genocide, Evil, and Injustice," 71.
35. Scott M. Thomas, "Faith, History and Martin Wight: The Role of Religion in the Historical Sociology of the English School of International Relations," *International Affairs* 77, no. 4 (October 2001): 907.
36. See Vendulka Kabalkova, "Towards an International Political Theology," *Millennium: Journal of International Studies* 29, no. 3 (2000): 628–83. Scott Thomas suggests that there are four possible reasons for this state of affairs. First, he argues that with modernization came secularization and the assumption that modern society is secular in orientation. Second is what he terms the "Westphalian presumption," the idea that after 1648 religion became a matter "to be disciplined by the state" and, as a result, could no longer be viewed as "part of international politics." The third factor used to explain the marginalization of religion in the study of international relations is the fact that the dominant paradigms and traditions of thought, according to which the subject is conventionally viewed, have not considered such social forces to be of great importance. Although it is not necessarily incompatible with religious thought—the works of Reinhold Niebuhr stand as testimony to this—realism, the dominant perspective of twentieth-century international relations is, of course, the major culprit in this state of affairs. By focusing on the state and conceiving power primarily in military terms, realism has managed to ignore religion as both a social and an intellectual force. Finally, Thomas also cites the rise of positivism and materialism as a further reason for the marginalization of religion in international relations. By privileging "facts" over "values" and in applying scientific methodologies according to which hypotheses are tested and

"general laws, patterns or regularities" "discovered" religion, and in particular religious belief, is pushed beyond the margins of acceptable scholarship. Scott M. Thomas, *The Global Resurgence of Religion and the Transformation of International Relations: The Struggle for the Soul of the Twenty-First Century* (New York: Palgrave Macmillan, 2005), 54.

37. See the conclusion to my work *Hugo Grotius in International Thought* (New York: Palgrave Macmillan, 2006); Daniel Philpott, "The Religious Roots of Modern International Relations," *World Politics* 52, no. 2 (2000): 206–45.

38. Bernstein, *The Abuse of Evil*, 3.

39. John Kekes, *Facing Evil* (Princeton, NJ: Princeton University Press, 1990), 28.

40. Ibid., 11.

41. Ibid., 11–12.

42. Ibid., 12 and 28.

43. Reinhold Niebuhr, *The Nature and Destiny of Man*, vol. 1 (London: Nisbet, 1941), 18.

44. John Haldane, *An Intelligent Person's Guide to Religion* (London: Duckworth, 2003), 94.

45. Gordon Graham, *Evil and Christian Ethics* (Cambridge: Cambridge University Press, 2001), xiii. See Renée Jeffery and Nicholas Rengger, "Review of Gordon Graham, *Evil and Christian Ethics*," *Conversations in Religion and Theology* 3, no. 1 (May 2005): 24–42.

46. Graham, *Evil and Christian Ethics*, 119.

47. Ibid., 24.

48. The focus is on the Judeo-Christian tradition as the dominant religious tradition of thought about evil in the west. However, this is not to suggest that one singular and continuous tradition of Judeo-Christian thought about evil can be identified in Western thought. For a discussion of what I understand an intellectual tradition to entail, see "Tradition as Invention: The 'Traditions Tradition' and the History of Ideas in International Relations," *Millennium: Journal of International Studies* 34, no. 1 (2005): 57–84. Similarly, it is not to deny that other religious traditions have made important contributions to notions of evil but is rather to simply suggest that Judeo-Christian ideas have dominated Western thought.

49. Most of the modern thinkers whom I do not discuss in detail are covered at length in the works of Susan Neiman and Richard Bernstein. For example, Neiman includes chapters on Hegel and Marx, Nietzsche and Freud in *Evil in Modern Thought*, while Bernstein includes individual chapters on Hegel, Nietzsche, and Freud in *Radical Evil: A Philosophical Interrogation*.

50. R. Douglas Geivett, *Evil and the Evidence for God: The Challenge of John Hick's Theodicy* (Philadelphia: Temple University Press, 1985), 3.

51. C. S. Lewis, *The Problem of Pain* (London: G. Bles, 1940); For a work viewed by many as providing a more honest assessment of pain see C. S. Lewis, *A Grief Observed* (London: Faber, 1961), written after the death of his wife.

52. Philip Yancey, *Where Is God When It Hurts?* (Grand Rapids: Zondervan, 1990). This criticism is a little unfair as Lewis directly addresses the reality of pain as follows: "You would like to know how I behave when I am experiencing pain, not writing books about it. You need not guess, for I will tell you; I am a great coward. . . . But what is the good of telling you about my feelings? You know them already: they are the same as yours. I am not arguing that pain is not painful. Pain hurts. That is what the word means." *The Problem of Pain*, 93.

53. Jennifer L. Geddes, introduction to *Evil After Postmodernism: Histories, Narratives and Ethics*, ed. Jennifer L. Geddes (London: Routledge, 2001), 3.

54. Ibid.

55. Ibid.

56. Ibid., 3–4.

57. Michael Oakeshott, "Present, Future and Past," in *On History and Other Essays*, by Michael Oakeshott (Indianapolis: Liberty Fund, 1999), 18.

58. Michael J. Shapiro, *Language and Political Understanding: The Politics of Discursive Practices* (New Haven: Yale University Press, 1981), 20.

59. Murray Edelman, quoted in Herbert Hirsch, *Genocide and the Politics of Memory: Studying Death to Preserve Life* (Chapel Hill: University of North Carolina Press, 1995), 98.

60. Shapiro, *Language and Political Understanding*, 14.

61. Hans Georg Gadamer, "The Universality of the Hermeneutical Problem," in *Philosophical Hermeneutics*, trans. and ed. David E. Linge, (Berkeley: University of California Press, 1976), 3.

62. Hans Georg Gadamer, "Man and Language," in *Philosophical Hermeneutics*, trans. and ed. David E. Linge, (Berkeley: University of California Press, 1976), 62.

63. Fred Weinstein, quoted in Hirsch, *Genocide and the Politics of Memory*, 98.

Chapter 2

1. Charlotte Delbo, *Auschwitz and After* (New Haven: Yale University Press, 1996), 226.

2. Terrie Waddell, Introduction to *Cultural Expressions of Evil and Wickedness: Wrath, Sex and Crime*, ed. Terrie Waddell (Amsterdam: Rodopi, 2003), ix.

3. Simone Weil, *Gravity and Grace* (London: Routledge, 1952), 62–63. For example, as David Parkin's edited collection *The Anthropology of Evil* makes clear, in the Balinese and Bantu languages, "evil" is related to that which is "physically rotten, misshapen and ugly." Similarly, among the Piaroa

Indians of Venezuela, while "good" is equated with beauty and cleanliness, "evil" is associated with dirt and ugliness. However, of greatest bearing on the Western tradition of thought about evil is its conceptualization in terms of imperfection within ancient Hebrew tradition. David Parkin, ed., Introduction to *The Anthropology of Evil* (Oxford: Basil Blackwell, 1995), 7; Mark Hobart, "Is God Evil?" in *The Anthropology of Evil*, 187; David Parkin, "Entitling Evil: Muslims and non-Muslims in Coastal Kenya," in *The Anthropology of Evil*, 226. As Parkin notes, the relationship between "evil" and physical deformity can be extreme; babies born in the breach position and those who cut their top teeth before the first two that usually appear on the bottom are often deemed "bad" children. Joanna Overing, "There Is No End of Evil: The Guilty Innocents and Their Fallible God," in *The Anthropology of Evil*, 254.

4. Weil, *Gravity and Grace*, 62–63.

5. Raimond Gaita, "Refocusing Genocide: A Philosophical Responsibility," in *Genocide and Human Rights*, by John K. Roth (Basingstoke, UK: Palgrave Macmillan, 2005), 162.

6. Robert Manne, *The Culture of Forgetting: Helen Demidenko and the Holocaust*, (Melbourne: Text Publishing, 1996), 107. Of course there are many thinkers that strongly refute the claim that evil has a mysterious aspect, preferring instead to view evil as "ordinary" and absolutely comprehensible. Their arguments will be discussed in some detail in Chapter 6. See Michael True, "Evil as Mystery: Primal Speech and Contemporary Poetry," in *Destined for Evil? The Twentieth Century Responses*, ed. Predrag Cicovacki, (Rochester, NY: University of Rochester Press, 2005), 241–47.

7. Delbo, quoted in Clendinnen, *Reading the Holocaust*, 62; Charlotte Delbo, *Auschwitz and After* (New Haven: Yale University Press, 1995), 1.

8. W. B. Gallie, "Essentially Contested Concepts," in *Philosophy and Historical Understanding* (New York: Shocken, 1968), 157–91.

9. Frederick Sontag, "How Should Genocide Affect Philosophy?" in *Genocide and Human Rights: A Philosophical Guide*, by John K. Roth (Basingstoke, UK: Palgrave Macmillan, 2005), 29.

10. Neil Forsyth, "The Origin of Evil: Classical or Judeo-Christian?" in *Perspectives on Evil and Human Wickedness* 1, no. 1 (January 2002): 17.

11. David Pocock, "Unruly Evil," in *The Anthropology of Evil*, ed. David Pocock (Oxford: Basil Blackwell, 1985), 57.

12. Alan Macfarlane, "The Root of All Evil," in *The Anthropology of Evil*, ed. David Parkin (Oxford: Basil Blackwell, 1985), 57.

13. Paul Ricoeur, *The Symbolism of Evil*, trans. E. Buchanan, (Boston: Beacon Press, 1967), 155; Hans Morgenthau, "The Evil of Politics and the Politics of Evil," in *Ethics: An International Journal of Social, Political and Legal Philosophy* 56, no. 1 (October 1945): 13.

14. Pocock, "Unruly Evil," 52.
15. Parkin, Introduction to *The Anthropology of Evil*, 23.
16. Susan Neiman, *Evil in Modern Thought: An Alternative History of Philosophy* (Princeton, NJ: Princeton University Press, 2002), 2.
17. Gillian Rose, *Mourning Becomes the Law: Philosophy and Representation* (Cambridge: Cambridge University Press, 1997), 43. Rose seeks to distinguish, as Freud did before her, between mourning, "the sorrowful attitude of those who know the world is cursed by suffering and evil, and that loss must be endured," and melancholia, which is marked by *stasis*, "the refusal to inhabit time, and accept loss, that is a sort of 'bad faith' alternative to mourning." Clearly mourning allows and perhaps even facilitates intelligibility while melancholia does not. Rose in Charles T. Mathewes, *Evil and the Augustinian Tradition* (Cambridge: Cambridge University Press, 2001), 46; Rose, *Mourning Becomes the Law*, 76, 103.
18. Bernstein, *Radical Evil*, 228.
19. Neiman, *Evil in Modern Thought*, 8.
20. Jean-Jacques Rousseau, *The First and Second Discourses Together with the Replies to Critics and Essay on the Origin of Language*, ed. and trans. Victor Gourevitch (New York: Harper & Row, 1986).
21. Susan Neiman, "What's the Problem of Evil?" in *Rethinking Evil: Contemporary Perspectives*, ed. Maria Pia Lara (Berkeley: University of California Press, 2001), 30–31.
22. Neiman, *Evil in Modern Thought*, 8.
23. Theodore W. Adorno, "Cultural Criticism and Society," in *Prisms*, trans. Samuel and Shierry Weber (Cambridge, MA: MIT Press, 1967), 34.
24. Robert B. Pippin, "Hannah Arendt and the Bourgeois Origins of Totalitarian Evil," in *Modernity and the Problem of Evil*, ed. Alan D. Schrift (Bloomington: Indiana University Press, 2005), 149; Theodor Adorno, *Negative Dialectics*, trans. E. B. Ashton (New York: Seabury, 1973).
25. Adorno, quoted in *After the Evil: Christianity and Judaism in the Shadow of the Holocaust*, by Richard Harries (Oxford: Oxford University Press, 2003), 33.
26. Primo Levi, Afterword in *If This Is a Man*, trans. Ruth Feldman, and *The Truce*, trans. Stuart Woolf (London: Abacus, 1987), 390.
27. Elie Wiesel, "Trivializing Memory," in *From the Kingdom of Memory: Reminiscences* (New York: Simon and Schuster, 1990), 166.
28. Elie Wiesel, "Some Questions That Remain Open," in *Comprehending the Holocaust: Historical and Literary Research*, ed. Asher Cohen and Charlotte Wardi (Frankfurt am Main: Verlag Peter Lang, 1988), 12–13.
29. Hannah Arendt, Preface to the first edition of *The Origins of Totalitarianism* (1951), new edition (New York: Brace: Harvourt and Jovanovich, 1973), viii.

NOTES **175**

30. Clendinnen, *Reading the Holocaust*, 26.
31. Susan Sontag, *On Photography*, quoted in *Regarding the Pain of Others* (London: Penguin, 2003), 97.
32. Sontag, *Regarding the Pain of Others*, 7.
33. Ibid.
34. Ibid.
35. Ibid.
36. Ibid., 85.
37. Judith N. Shklar, *Ordinary Vices* (Cambridge, MA: The Belknap Press of Harvard University Press, 1984), 3.
38. Ibid.
39. Pope John Paul II, *Salvifici Doloris: On the Christian Meaning of Human Suffering*, February 11, 1984, 1; V. E. Frankl, quoted in *Life's Meaning in the Face of Suffering: Testimonies of Holocaust Survivors*, by Teria Shantall (Jerusalem: The Hebrew University Magnes Press, 2002), 33.
40. Jamie Mayerfeld, *Suffering and Moral Responsibility* (New York: Oxford University Press, 1999), 11.
41. Ibid., 12.
42. Lewis, *The Problem of Pain*, 78.
43. Mayerfeld, *Suffering and Moral Responsibility*, 24.
44. Ibid., 25.
45. Ibid.
46. R. M. Hare, "Pain and Evil," in *Moral Concepts*, ed. Joel Feinburg (Oxford: Oxford University Press, 1969), 29.
47. Ibid., 32.
48. Ibid., 35.
49. Ophir, *The Order of Evils*, 6.004, 259.
50. Amartya Sen, *Commodities and Capabilities* (Amsterdam: North-Holland, 1985); Martha Nussbaum, "Human Functioning and Social Justice: In Defense of Aristotelian Essentialism," *Political Theory* 20 (1992): 202.
51. Mayerfeld, *Suffering and Moral Responsibility*, 109.
52. Ophir, *The Order of Evils*, 6.023, 261.
53. Emmanuel Levinas, *Time and the Other*, trans. Richard A. Cohen (Pittsburgh: Duquesne University Press, 1987), 69.
54. David Kraemer, *Responses to Suffering in Classical Rabbinic Literature* (New York: Oxford University Press, 1995), 4.
55. Roy F. Baumeister, *Evil: Inside Human Cruelty and Violence* (New York: Freeman, 1997), 18–19.
56. Shklar, *Ordinary Vices*, 18.
57. Ibid.
58. Ibid., 19.
59. Ibid.

60. Ophir, *The Order of Evils*, 6.031, 262.
61. Ibid.
62. Ibid., 6.024, 261.
63. Erich H. Loewy, *Suffering and the Beneficent Community: Beyond Libertarianism* (New York: State University of New York Press, 1991), 4.
64. Ophir, *The Order of Evils*, 6.050, 265; 6.051, 266.
65. Josef Bleicher, *Contemporary Hermeneutics: Hermeneutics as method, philosophy and critique*, (London: Routledge, 1980), 1.
66. James A. Sanders, "Suffering as Divine Discipline in the Old Testament and Post-Biblical Judaism," *Colgate Rochester Divinity School Bulletin* 29 (1955): 1; quoted in Kraemer, 34; see also Oliver Leaman, *Evil and Suffering in Jewish Philosophy* (Cambridge: Cambridge University Press, 1995).
67. Norman Solomon, *Jewish Responses to the Holocaust* (Centre for the Study of Judaism and Jewish-Christian Relations, Birmingham, UK, 1988), 8.
68. Of course different theories of punishment focus on different aspects of punishment. Traditionally, theoretical debates about punishment have taken place between proponents of consequentialism and retributivism. As Matt Matravers writes, "Consequentialist theory defends punishment as a means to secure greater utility, typically through individual and general deterrence. Retributivism, in contrast, justifies punishment through the notion of desert. The criminal is said to deserve to suffer for his past act of wrongdoing." Matt Matravers, Introduction in *Punishment and Political Theory*, ed. Matt Matravers (Oxford: Hart Publishing, 1999), 1.
69. R. A. Dudd and D. Garland, "Introduction: Thinking About Punishment," in *A Reader on Punishment*, ed. Antony Duff and David Garland (Oxford: Oxford University Press, 1994), 7.
70. Jeremy Bentham, quoted in *After Evil: Responding to Wrongdoing*, by Geoffrey Scarre (Aldershot, UK: Ashgate, 2004), 7.
71. Ibid., 34.
72. Marilyn McCord Adams, "Redemptive Suffering: A Christian Solution to the Problem of Evil," in *Rationality, Religious Beliefs and Moral Commitment: New Essays on the Philosophy of Religion*, ed. Robert Audi and William J. Wainwright (Ithaca, NY: Cornell University Press, 1986), 248–67.
73. Weil, "Evil," in *Gravity and Grace*, 65.
74. Ibid.
75. Pope John Paul II, *On the Christian Meaning of Human Suffering*, 1.
76. Harries, *After the Evil*, 49.
77. V. E. Frankl, quoted in *Life's Meaning in the Face of Suffering: Testimonies of Holocaust Survivors*, by Teria Shantall (Jerusalem: The Hebrew University Magnes Press, 2002), 33. See V. E. Frankl, *The Doctor and the Soul: From Psychotherapy to Logotherapy* (New York: Bantam Books, 1969).
78. Arthur Schopenhauer, *On the Suffering of the World*, trans. R. J. Hollingdale (London: Penguin, 1970), 3.

79. C. G. Jung, *Answer to Job*, Vol. 11, *Collected Works* (Princeton, NJ: Princeton University Press, 1973); Carl Gustav Jung, "Searching for Self-Knowledge and Divine Wholeness," in *Destined for Evil? The Twentieth-Century Responses*, ed. Predrag Cicovacki (Rochester, NY: University of Rochester Press, 2005), 171–76.

80. Kraemer, *Responses to Suffering*, 19.

81. Ophir, *The Order of Evils*, 6.333, 286.

82. Ibid., 6.531, 302.

83. Some have attempted to make arguments along these lines and these will be addressed in Chapter 5.

84. Shantall, *Life's Meaning in the Face of Suffering*, 94.

85. R. J. Braham, quoted in Shantall, *Life's Meaning in the Face of Suffering*, 94; see R. J. Braham (ed.), *The Psychological Perspectives of the Holocaust and its Aftermath* (Boston: Kluwer-Nijhoff, 1988).

86. For perhaps the most famous debate on this subject, see Bruno Bettelheim, *Surviving and Other Essays* (London: Thames and Hudson, 1979); and Terence Des Pres, *The Survivor: An Anatomy of Life in the Death Camps* (New York: Oxford University Press, 1976).

87. Friedrich Nietzsche, *On the Genealogy of Morals: A Polemic*, trans. Douglas Smith (Oxford: Oxford University Press, 1996), 49.

88. Ibid., 136.

89. Emmanuel Levinas, "Useless Suffering," in *The Provocation of Levinas: Rethinking the Other*, ed. Robert Bernasconi and David Wood, (London: Routledge, 1988), 157–58.

90. Ibid.

91. Ibid., 159.

92. Ibid.

93. Ibid., 162.

94. Mayerfeld, *Suffering and Moral Responsibility*, 85.

95. Ophir, *The Order of Evils*, 7.014, 331.

96. Mayerfeld, *Suffering and Moral Responsibility*, 85.

97. Lewis, *The Problem of Pain*, 80.

98. Clifford Geertz, "Ethos, World View, and the Analysis of Sacred Symbols," in *The Interpretation of Cultures* (New York: Basic Books, 1973), 130.

99. Clifford Geertz, "Religion as a Cultural System," in *The Interpretation of Cultures*, 107–8.

100. William E. Connolly, *Identity/difference: Democratic Negotiations of Political Paradox* (Ithaca, NY: Cornell University Press, 1991), 2.

Chapter 3

1. Augustine of Hippo, *Enchiridion on Faith, Hope and Love*, trans. J. F. Shaw, available at http://www.newadvent.org/fathers/1302.htm (accessed October

27, 2004), I.11. The *Enchiridion* was composed by Augustine at the request of the little known Roman, Laurentius, who had asked him to write a handbook of Christian doctrine.

2. Epicurus, quoted in Neil Forsyth, "The Origin of 'Evil': Classical or Judeo-Christian?" *Perspectives on Evil and Human Wickedness* 1, no. 1 (January 2002): 20.

3. Graham, *Evil and Christian Ethics*, 98.

4. Kenneth Surin, *Theology and the Problem of Evil* (Oxford: Blackwell, 1986), 27.

5. Marilyn McCord Adams, *Horrendous Evils and the Goodness of God* (Ithaca, NY: Cornell University Press; Melbourne: Melbourne University Press, 1999), 8. Adams also directs the reader to Alvin Plantinga, "Self-Profile," in *Alvin Plantinga*, ed. James E. Tomberlin and Peter Van Inwagen (Dordrecht, Holland: D. Reidel Publishing, 1985), 38.

6. Marilyn McCord Adams and Robert Merrihew Adams, Introduction to *The Problem of Evil*, ed. Marilyn McCord Adams and Robert Merrihew Adams (Oxford: Oxford University Press, 1990), 2.

7. J. L. Mackie, quoted in Adams and Adams, *The Problem of Evil*, 2; J. L. Mackie, "Evil and Omnipotence," *Mind* 64 (1955): 200–12. As Daniel Howard-Snyder remarks, "anyone modestly acquainted with medieval philosophy will tell you that the proposition that evil exists is not an *essential* part of theism. Perhaps Mackie just meant to voice his conviction that it is exceedingly unreasonable for a theist to deny that evil exists, which seems quite right." Daniel Howard-Snyder, Introduction to *The Evidential Argument from Evil*, ed. Daniel Howard-Snyder (Bloomington: Indiana University Press, 1996), xix.

8. Adams and Adams, Introduction, 16.

9. William L. Rowe, "The Problem of Evil and Some Varieties of Atheism," in *The Evidential Argument from Evil*, ed. Daniel Howard-Snyder (Bloomington: Indiana University Press, 1996), 2.

10. Daniel Howard-Snyder, Introduction to *The Evidential Argument from Evil*, xiv.

11. Joseph F. Kelly, *The Problem of Evil in the Western Tradition: From the Book of Job to Modern Genetics* (Collegeville, MN: Liturgical Press, 1989), 121.

12. Gottfried Wilhelm von Leibniz, *Theodicy: Essays on the Goodness of God, the Freedom of Man, and the Origin of Evil*, trans. E. M. Huggard, ed. Austin Farrar, (London: Routledge & Kegan Paul, 1952). As with the so-called "problem of evil" it is also more accurate to speak of "theodicies" in the plural, for different thinkers provide quite divergent, and in some cases, incommensurable, theoretical arguments in answer to the problem of evil.

13. Mathewes, *Evil and the Augustinian Tradition*, 36–37.

14. Ibid., 39.

15. Michael Scott, quoted in Ibid.
16. Rowan Williams quoted in Ibid., 39. See Rowan Williams, "Reply: Redeeming Sorrows," in *Religion and Morality*, ed. D. Z. Phillips (New York: St. Martin's Press, 1996), 132–48.
17. See W. G. Lambert, *Babylonian Wisdom Literature* (Oxford: Oxford University Press, 1960).
18. W. G. Lambert, quoted in Shalom M. Paul, "Psalm XXVII 10 and the Babylonian Theodicy," *Vetus Testamentum* 32, fasc. 4 (October 1982), 489.
19. *The Babylonian Theodicy*, in Thomas D. Winton, "The Babylonian Theodicy," *Documents from Old Testament Times* (New York: Harper, 1961), 97–103.
20. Ibid.
21. *The Babylonian Theodicy*.
22. For example, Hindu philosophers of the Vedanta school include a type of theodicy, albeit with a different structure, in their thought. See J. N. Mohanty, *Classical Indian Philosophy* (Oxford: Rowman and Littlefield, 2000).
23. Donald Taylor, "Theological Thoughts About Evil," in Parkin, *Anthropology of Evil*, 27.
24. See also, Judges 3:7; 3:12; 4:1; 6:1; 10:6; 13:1. In Hebrew, the word *ba'al* means "master," "possessor," or "husband." In the Old Testament, the singular name "Baal" refers to Hadad, the Canaanite storm god. The plural "baals" seems to suggest the existence of multiple deities that were identified as "Baal." D. F. Payne, "Baal," *The Illustrated Bible Dictionary*, vol. 1 (Leicester, UK: Intervarsity Press, 1980), 153.
25. Parkin, Introduction, 4.
26. Kelly, *The Problem of Evil*, 19. It is interesting to note, as Eleonore Stump does, that unlike most contemporary readers who interpret the story of Job as an attempt to reconcile his suffering with the existence of "an omnipotent, omniscient, perfectly good God," Thomas Aquinas "understands the book as an attempt to come to grips with the nature and operations of divine providence." This we will see in more detail when Aquinas is discussed shortly. Eleonore Stump, "Aquinas on the Sufferings of Job," in *The Evidential Argument from Evil*, ed. Daniel Howard-Snyder (Bloomington: Indiana University Press, 1996), 50.
27. Ibid.
28. It is significant that Satan here acts as God's instrument and not, as he is portrayed in the New Testament, as an independent adversary.
29. Kelly, *The Problem of Evil*, 19–20.
30. Arthur S. Peake, *The Problem of Suffering in the Old Testament*, The Hartley Lecture Delivered to the Primitive Methodist Conference in Carr's Lane Chapel, Birmingham, June 8, 1904 (London: Robert Bryant, 1904), 102.
31. Ibid.

32. Kelly, *The Problem of Evil*, 28.
33. Ibid., 21.
34. Forsyth, "The 'Origin' of Evil," 26.
35. Ibid.
36. Kelly, *The Problem of Evil*, 26.
37. Ibid.
38. Ibid., 28. As we will see shortly, dualist theologies proposed the existence of two rival gods, each responsible for either good or evil in the world.
39. Elaine Pagels, *The Origin of Satan* (New York: Random House, 1995), 39.
40. Ibid.
41. Ibid. The Greek word used here is *diabolos*, meaning "one who throws something across one's path." As Jeffrey Burton Russell makes clear, although the "devil" has come to be understood as the "single personification of evil," there is no linguistic connection between "evil" and "devil." Jeffrey Burton Russell, *The Prince of Darkness: Radical Evil and the Power of Good in History* (Ithaca, NY: Cornell University Press, 1988), 5 and 7.
42. Pagels, *The Origin of Satan*, 11.
43. Ibid., 13.
44. Differing accounts date the Gospel of Mark between 50 and 70 CE, thereby situating it well within the period in which Jewish apocalyptic literature remained influential.
45. Russell, *The Prince of Darkness*, 19. Yasna 30, quoted in Kraemer, *Responses to Suffering in Classical Rabbinic Literature*, 5. Translations of the Zoroastrian texts can be found in *Textual Sources for the Study of Zoroastrianism*, ed. and trans. Mary Boyce (Chicago: University of Chicago Press, 1990).
46. Ibid., 19–20.
47. Ibid.
48. Maneckji Nusservanji Dhalla, *History of Zoroastrianism* (New York: Oxford University Press, 1938), 85.
49. Kelly, *The Problem of Evil*, 37.
50. Russell, *The Prince of Darkness*, 57.
51. Ibid., 69.
52. Ibid.
53. Ibid.
54. Tertullian, *Adversus Marcionem*, in *Tertullian: Adversus Marcionem*, ed. Ernest Evans (Oxford: Oxford University Press, 1972), II.5, 98–99.
55. Ibid., II.5, 99.
56. Ibid., II.6, 101
57. Russell, *The Prince of Darkness*, 82.
58. Lucius Caecilius Firmianus Lactantius was, prior to his conversion to Christianity, the head of rhetoric in Nicomedia, appointed by Emperor

Diocletian. After his conversion, he was employed by Constantine to tutor his son. His most important works that discuss the question of evil are his *Divine Institutions*, written between 303 and 311, a work defending Christianity against paganism, and *De Ira Dei*, a supplement to the *Institutions* in which he attacks Epicurus's understanding of suffering.

59. Russell, *The Prince of Darkness*, 82.

60. Lactantius, quoted in Russell, *The Prince of Darkness*, 82.

61. Ibid., 82–83.

62. Ibid., 83.

63. Russell, *The Prince of Darkness*, 83.

64. John Hick, *Evil and the God of Love* (New York: Harper and Row, 1966), 21.

65. Forsyth, "The Origin of 'Evil,'" 22.

66. Alexander of Lycopolis, *Of the Manichaeans* 2, available at http://www.newadvent.org/fathers/0618.htm (accessed October 27, 2004).

67. Forsyth, "The Origin of 'Evil,'" 24–25.

68. Kelly, *The Problem of Evil*, 52.

69. Augustine's disillusionment with the Manichaean system at the time of his conversion to Christianity was multifaceted and saw, in addition to the publication of the works named above, the composition of five other works that explicitly sought to refute the central tenets of Manichaeism: *De Duabus Animabus contra Manichaeos* (*Of Two Souls against Manichaus*) (391 CE), *Contra Epistolam Manichaei quam Vacant Fundamenti* (*Against the Fundamental Epistle of Manichaeus*) (397 CE), *Acta Seu Disputatio contra Fortunatum Manichaeum* (*Acts or Disputation Against Fortunatus the Manichee*) (392 CE), *De Moribus Ecclesiae Catholicae* (*Of the Morals of the Catholic Church*) (388 CE), and *De Moribus Manichaeorum* (*On the Morals of the Manichaeans*) (388 CE). Douglas R. Geivett, *Evil and the Evidence for God: The Challenge of John Hick's Theodicy* (Philadelphia: Temple University Press, 1985), 11.

70. Geivett, *Evil and the Evidence for God*, 11.

71. Augustine, quoted in Geivett, 11–12.

72. Augustine, *Confessions*, trans. Henry Chadwick (Oxford: Oxford University Press, 1991), II.iv(9), 28–29; III.viii(16), 33.

73. Peter Brown, *Augustine of Hippo: A Biography* (London: Faber & Faber, 1967), 59.

74. Augustine, *Against the Fundamental Epistle of Manichaeus, Contra Epistolam Manichaei quam Vacant Fundamenti*, 397 CE, available at http://www.newadvent.org/fathers/1405.htm (accessed October 27, 2004), 34, 24.

75. Jean Bethke Elshtain, *Augustine and the Limits of Politics* (Notre Dame, IN: University of Notre Dame Press, 1995), 20.

76. Augustine, *Confessions*, trans. R. D. Pine-Coffin (London: Penguin, 1961), V.3, 97.

77. Ibid., V.3, 92–93; V.7, 98.
78. Connolly, *Identity/Difference*, 3.
79. Augustine, *Confessions*, IV.1, 71.
80. For a description of Ambrose see *Confessions*, V.13, 107; the conversion, VIII.8–12, 170–79.
81. Augustine, *Against the Fundamental Epistle of Manichaeus*, 35.41; *On the Morals of the Manichaeans, De Moribus Manichaeorum*, 388 CE, available at http://www.newadvent.org/fathers/1402.htm (accessed October 27, 2004), 2.2; *Confessions*, VII.5, 138.
82. Ibid.
83. References to his works and the conversion of his translator, Victorinus, in *Confessions*, VII.20, 154.
84. Plotinus, *Six Enneades*, trans. Stephen Mackenna and B. S. Page, https://ccat.upenn.edu/jod/texts/plotinus, (accessed October 27, 2004), I.8.1.
85. Augustine, *On the Nature of Good*, available at http://www.newadvent .org/fathers/1407.htm (accessed October 27, 2004), 1.
86. Augustine, quoted in Geivett, *Evil and the Evidence for God*, 13.
87. Augustine, *Enchiridion*, I.12.
88. Geivett, *Evil and the Evidence for God*, 14.
89. Augustine, *City of God Against the Pagans*, ed. and trans. R. W. Dyson (Cambridge: Cambridge University Press, 1998), XI.22, 477.
90. Augustine, *Enchiridion*, I.11.
91. David Grumett, "Arendt, Augustine and Evil," *The Heythrop Journal* 41 (2000): 156.
92. Plotinus, *Six Enneades*, I.8.3.
93. Ibid.
94. Ibid., I.8.5.
95. Ibid.
96. Ibid.
97. Hick, *Evil and the God of Love*, 48.
98. Ibid.
99. Augustine, *City of God*, XI.9, 461.
100. Augustine, *Enchiridion*, I.12.
101. Augustine, *On the Nature of Good*, 18.
102. Augustine, *Confessions*, I.12.
103. Augustine, *Against the Fundamental Epistle*, 35, 39.
104. W. S. Babcock, "Sin and Punishment: The Early Augustine on Evil," in *Augustine, Presbyter Factus Sum*, ed. J. T. Leinhard, E. C. Muller, and R. J. Teske (New York: Lang, 1993), 241.
105. Hick, *Evil and the God of Love*, 65.
106. Augustine, *Freedom of the Will*, III.XVII.48.

107. Ibid., II.IX.53.
108. Augustine, *Of Two Souls, De Duabus Animabus Contra Manichaeos*, 391 CE, available at http://www.newadvent.org/fathers/1403.htm (accessed October 27, 2004), 10.14.
109. Hick, *Evil and the God of Love*, 68.
110. Geivett, *Evil and the Evidence for God*, 15.
111. Mathewes, *Evil and the Augustinian Tradition*, 73.
112. Kelly, *The Problem of Evil in the Western Tradition*, 53.
113. Ibid., 54.
114. Stephen Chan, *Out of Evil: New International Politics and Old Doctrines of War* (London: I. B. Tauris, 2005), 10.
115. John Kekes, *The Roots of Evil* (Ithaca, NY: Cornell University Press, 2005), 11.
116. Ibid., 13–14.
117. Saint Thomas Aquinas, *Summa Theologiae*, in *A Shorter Summa: The Essential Philosophical Passages of St. Thomas Aquinas' Summa Theologica*, ed. Peter Kreeft, (San Francisco: Ignatius Press, 1993), I.2.3., 53–54.
118. Ibid., I.2.3., 55–64. Aquinas's five arguments are, in turn: (i) the "argument from motion" that maintains that "whatever is in motion must be put in motion by another" and, as such, something must be responsible for causing the first motion; (ii) the argument "from the nature of efficient cause"; (iii) the argument "from possibility and necessity"; (iv) the argument "from the gradation to be found in things" that "Among beings there are some more and some less good, true, noble and the like. . . . The maximum in any genus is the cause of all in that genus" and, as such, "goodness, and every other perfection" is what "we call God"; and v) the argument "from the governance of the world."
119. Ibid., I.2.3., 64.
120. Ibid.
121. Ibid., I.49.1., 98.
122. Brian Davies, Introduction to *On Evil*, by Thomas Aquinas, trans. Richard Regan (Oxford: Oxford University Press, 2003), 14.
123. Ibid.
124. Aquinas, *On Evil*, 1.1.a.1, 55.
125. Ibid., 1.1.b.1, 57.
126. Ibid., 1.1.Answer, 58.
127. Ibid., 59.
128. Ibid., 1.1.d.20., 62.
129. Hick, *Evil and the God of Love*, 115.
130. Ibid.
131. Ibid., 116.

132. Elmar J. Kremer and Michael J. Latzer, Introduction to *The Problem of Evil in Early Modern Philosophy*, ed. Elmar J. Kremer and Michael J. Latzer (Toronto: University of Toronto Press, 2001), 7.

133. Ibid., 7–8.

134. Ibid., 8.

135. Ibid.

136. Alfred J. Freddoso, "Suarez on God's Causal Involvement in Sinful Acts," in *The Problem of Evil in Early Modern Philosophy*, ed. Elmar J. Kremer and Michael J. Latzer (Toronto: University of Toronto Press, 2001), 10.

137. Ibid., 10–11.

138. Ibid., 11.

139. Suarez, *Disputationes Metaphysicae* 11.2.5., quoted in ibid., 11.

140. Freddoso, "Suarez on God's Causal Involvement in Sinful Acts," 11.

141. Suarez, *Disputationes Metaphysicae* 11.2.5., quoted in ibid.

142. Ibid., 11.3.24, in ibid., 12.

143. Freddoso, "Suarez on God's Causal Involvement in Sinful Acts," 12.

144. Suarez, *Disputationes Metaphysicae* 11.3.24., quoted in Freddoso, ibid.

145. Kremer and Latzer, Introduction, 8.

146. See, for example, Mathewes, *Evil and the Augustinian Tradition*, 77.

Chapter 4

1. Immanuel Kant, *Religion Within the Boundaries of Mere Reason and other essays*, trans. and ed. Allen Wood and George di Giovanni (Cambridge: Cambridge University Press, 1998), 6:44, 65.

2. Hick, *Evil and the God of Love*, 145.

3. William King, *On the Origin of Evil*, trans. Edmund, Lord Bishop of Carlisle (London: Faulder, 1781), ix.

4. Ibid., II.II., 71.

5. Hick, *Evil and the God of Love*, 148.

6. King, *On the Origin of Evil*, II.VII., 76.

7. King, quoted in Hick, *Evil and the God of Love*, 148.

8. Susan Neiman, "Metaphysics, Philosophy: Rousseau on the Problem of Evil," in *Reclaiming the History of Ethics*, ed. Andrews Reath, Barbara Herman, and Christine M. Korsgaard (Cambridge: Cambridge University Press, 1997), 140–41.

9. Hick, *Evil and the God of Love*, 154.

10. Geivett, *Evil and the Evidence for God*, 22.

11. Bayle said the following of Moréri's work: "I share the opinion of Horace on those who lead the way. The first compilers of dictionaries made many errors, but they deserve a glory that their successors ought never to deprive them. Moréri has given himself a great deal of trouble, has been useful to

everybody, and has sufficient information to many." http://www.newadvent
.org/cathen/10567a.htm (accessed March 22, 2007).

12. Leibniz, quoted in Geivett, *Evil and the Evidence for God*, 22.

13. Stuart Brown, "The Seventeenth Century Intellectual Background," in *The Cambridge Companion to Leibniz*, ed. Nicholas Jolley (Cambridge: Cambridge University Press, 1995), 57. As Brown writes in another work, "Leibniz had enjoyed a lengthy and amicable correspondence with Bayle in spite of their being a fundamental disagreement between them on whether faith could be reconciled with reason." Stuart Brown, *Leibniz* (Brighton, UK: The Harvester Press, 1984), 66–67. See Leibniz, *Theodicy*, I.3–4, 124–25.

14. Neiman, *Evil in Modern Thought*, 20.

15. Ibid. What is more, Bayle also argued that "reason cannot buttress faith and that the only plausible way to defend the Church's teaching and doctrines is to adopt a strictly 'fideist' stance." Jonathan I. Israel, *Radical Enlightenment: Philosophy and the Making of Modernity 1650–1750* (Oxford: Oxford University Press, 2001), 332.

16. Bayle, quoted in D. Anthony Lariviére and Thomas M. Lennon, "Bayle on the Problem of Evil," in *The Problem of Evil in Early Modern Philosophy*, ed. Elmar J. Kremer and Michael J. Latzer (Toronto: University of Toronto Press, 2001), 104.

17. Hick, *Evil and the God of Love*, 21.

18. Jonathan I. Israel, *Radical Enlightenment: Philosophy and the Making of Modernity, 1650–1750* (Oxford: Oxford University Press, 2001), 331.

19. Hick, *Evil and the God of Love*, 23.

20. Spinoza, *Ethics*, ed. and trans. G. H. R. Parkinson (Oxford: Oxford University Press, 2000), i, appendix.

21. Ibid., IV. 64. The notion that evil is not real has not been popular in subsequent thought for it seems to deny the reality of human suffering in the world. The most prominent exception to this is found in the 1875 Christian Science work of Mary Baker Eddy, *Science and Health with Key to the Scriptures*, a work John Hick described as a "confused medley of half-digested philosophical themes." In it, Eddy argued that "Evil has no reality. It is neither person, place nor thing, but is simply a belief, an illusion of material sense . . . evil is but an illusion, and it has no real basis." As such, she reasoned that evil along with pain and suffering could be overcome by recognizing that they are nothing. Hick, *Evil and the God of Love*, 24.

22. Leibniz, *Theodicy*, 9, 128–29.

23. Hick, *Evil and the God of Love*, 18–19.

24. Leibniz, *Theodicy*, I.9., 128–29.

25. Alfonso X, quoted in Neiman, "Metaphysics, Philosophy," 142.

26. Ibid.

27. Ibid., 143.
28. Leibniz, *Theodicy*, 194, 248.
29. Ibid., 21, 136.
30. Ibid., 23, 137.
31. Ibid.
32. Neiman, *Evil in Modern Thought*, 22.
33. Jan T. Kozak and Charles D. James, "Historical Depictions of the 1755 Lisbon Earthquake," National Information Service for Earthquake Engineering, University of California, Berkeley. http://nisee.berkeley.edu/lisbon/ (accessed on May 10, 2004).
34. Voltaire, *Candide*, ed. Haydn Mason (London: Bristol Classical Press, 1995), 121.
35. Schopenhauer, *On the Suffering of the World*, 13.
36. As Victor Gourevitch writes, "Optimism" became a much debated topic in subsequent years. In 1755 the Berlin Academy announced as the topic of its Prize competition "a thorough discussion of Pope's thesis, and Kant had considered submitting an essay to it." As we will see shortly, in the end it was Rousseau who emerged as the great defender of Optimism against Voltaire's criticisms. Victor Gourevitch, introduction to Jean-Jacques Rousseau, *The Discourses and other early political writings*, ed. and trans. Victor Gourevitch (Cambridge: Cambridge University Press, 1997), xxvi
37. Voltaire, quoted in Neiman, *Evil in Modern Thought*, 135.
38. Ibid.
39. Schopenhauer, *On the Suffering of the World*, 14.
40. Neiman, "Metaphysics, Philosophy," 145.
41. Jean-Jacques Rousseau, "Observations by Jean-Jacques Rousseau of Geneva: On the Answer Made to His Discourse," in *The Discourses*, 22, 37.
42. Neiman, "Metaphysics, Philosophy," 147.
43. Jean-Jacques Rousseau, "Letter to Voltaire," in *The Discourses*, 1, 232; 37, 246.
44. Ibid., 3, 232.
45. Ibid., 4, 233.
46. Ibid., 4, 5, 233.
47. Neiman, "Metaphysics, Philosophy," 141.
48. Neiman, *Evil in Modern Thought*, 41, emphasis in text.
49. Jean-Jacques Rousseau, *émile*, trans. Barbara Foxley (London: Dent, 1969), 5.
50. Rousseau, "Letter to Voltaire," 8, 234.
51. Neiman, *Evil in Modern Thought*, 39.
52. Rousseau, "Letter to Voltaire," 8, 234.
53. Neiman, *Evil in Modern Thought*, 41.
54. Ibid., 41–42.
55. Rousseau, "Letter to Voltaire," 23, 240.

56. Ibid., 23, 240; 26, 242.
57. Rousseau, "Letter by J. J. Rousseau to M. Philopolis," in *The Discourses*, 10, 225.
58. Ibid.
59. Neiman, *Evil in Modern Thought*, 43.
60. Ibid., 45.
61. Ibid.
62. Kant, quoted in Neiman, "Metaphysics, Philosophy," 140.
63. Gordon E. Michalson, *Fallen Freedom: Kant on Radical Evil and Moral Regeneration* (Cambridge: Cambridge University Press, 1990), 19.
64. Ibid.
65. Michael Despland, *Kant on History and Religion* (Montreal: McGill-Queen's University Press, 1973), 170.
66. Ibid. 171–72.
67. Immanuel Kant, *On the Failure of All Attempted Philosophical Theodicies (1791)*, trans. Michael Despland, in *Kant on History and Religion* (Montreal: McGill-Queen's University Press, 1973), 283.
68. Ibid. 291.
69. Ibid.
70. Kant, quoted in Neiman, "Metaphysics, Philosophy," 149.
71. Kant, *On the Failure of All Attempted Philosophical Theodicies*, 293.
72. Kelly, *The Problem of Evil*, 130.
73. Ibid., 128–29.
74. David Hume, *An Enquiry Concerning Human Understanding*, ed. Tom C. Beauchamp (Oxford: Oxford University Press, 1999), 10.41, 186.
75. David Hume, *Dialogues Concerning Natural Religion in Focus*, ed. Stanley Tweyman (Routledge: London, 1991), 10, 160.
76. Ibid., 157.
77. Bernard M. G. Reardon, *Kant as Philosophical Theologian* (Basingstoke, UK: Macmillan, 1988), 90
78. Ibid., 90, 92.
79. Kant, *Religion Within the Boundaries of Mere Reason*, 6:44, 65.
80. Kant, quoted in Bernstein, *Radical Evil*, 13.
81. Ibid.
82. Ibid.
83. Kant, *Religion Within the Boundaries of Mere Reason*, 6:20, 46.
84. Ibid., 6:26, 50.
85. Ibid., 6:29, 52–53.
86. Ibid., 53.
87. Ibid., 6:23, 55.

88. Henry E. Allison, "Reflections on the Banality of (Radical) Evil: A Kantian Analysis," in *Rethinking Evil*, ed. Maria Pia Lara (Berkeley: University of California Press, 2001), 92.

89. Ibid.

90. Gordon E. Michalson, *Fallen Freedom: Kant on Radical Evil and Moral Regeneration* (Cambridge: Cambridge University Press, 1990), 35. This marks a distinct shift from his earlier *Lectures on Philosophical Theology*, trans. Allen W. Wood and Gertrude M. Clark (Ithaca, NY: Cornell University Press, 1978), 117.

91. Kant, *Religion Within the Boundaries*, 6:32, 56.

92. Bernstein, *Radical Evil*, 20, 27.

93. Ibid., 27.

94. Stephen R. Grimm, "Kant's Argument for Radical Evil," *European Journal of Philosophy* 10, no. 2 (2002): 160–77; Allen Wood, *Kant's Ethical Thought* (New York: Cambridge University Press, 1999).

95. Immanuel Kant, "An Answer to the Question: What is Enlightenment?" [1784], in *Perpetual Peace and Other Essays*, trans. Ted Humphrey (Indianapolis: Hackett Publishing, 1983), 41.

Chapter 5

1. Wiesel, "Some Questions That Remain Open," 16.

2. Primo Levi, *The Drowned and the Saved*, trans. Raymond Rosenthal (London: Michael Joseph, 1988), 169.

3. The intellectual discussion of the Holocaust in this context is mired in controversy, controversy that emanates from a number of different corners of the scholarly, religious, and secular worlds. For example, scholars and theologians alike have disagreed over the very term *Holocaust* itself. For many Jews, the term *Shoah*, signifying catastrophic destruction, is a more appropriate term than *Holocaust*, which is "derived from the Greek *holókauston*, meaning 'burnt whole'" and brings with it connotations of sacrifice. In this vein, Walter Lacquer argues that the term *Holocaust* is "singularly inappropriate" as "it was not the intention of the Nazis to make a sacrifice of this kind, and the position of the Jews was not that of a ritual victim." These arguments aside however, in most scholarship and general discourse, the attempted eradication of the Jewish race at the hands of the Nazis is known as the Holocaust. Richard Rubenstein and John K. Roth, *Approaches to Auschwitz: The Holocaust and its Legacy*, 2nd ed. (Louisville: Westminster John Knox, 2003), 4–5. Walter Lacquer, quoted in Rubenstein and Roth, *Approaches to Auschwitz*, 5; although, as Rubenstein and Roth argue, the term *Shoah* is preferred in Israel, Israeli writers such as Adi Ophir and others still use the term *Holocaust*. Ophir, *The Order of Evils*.

4. Bernstein, *Radical Evil*, 4.
5. Emmanuel Levinas, "The Paradox of Morality: An Interview with Emmanuel Levinas," in *The Provocation of Emmanuel Levinas: Rethinking the Other*, ed. Robert Bernasconi and David Wood (London: Routledge, 1988), 176.
6. Hannah Arendt, "Some Questions of Moral Philosophy," *Social Research* 61, no. 2, (Winter 1994), 742.
7. Berel Lang, *Post-Holocaust: Interpretation, Misinterpretation and the Claims of History* (Bloomington: Indiana University Press, 2005), 35.
8. Bernstein, *Radical Evil*, 214.
9. The exception to this is, of course, Sigmund Freud who argued that alongside overt agency, human action is also directed by impulses that are not apparent to them. He wrote: "Psychological—or, more strictly speaking, psycho-analytic—investigation shows instead that the deepest essence of human nature consists in instinctual impulses which are of an elementary nature, which are similar in all men and which aim at the satisfaction of certain primal needs. These impulses in themselves are neither good nor bad. We classify them and their expressions in that way, according to their relation to the needs and demands of the human community. It must be granted that all the impulses which society condemns as evil—let us take as representative the cruel and selfish ones—are of this primitive kind." Sigmund Freud, *Civilization and Its Discontents: The Standard Edition* (London: Hogarth Press, 1930), 122.
10. Neiman, *Evil in Modern Thought*, 271.
11. The focus in this chapter is on individual moral agency, leaving aside the moral agency of groups. For a discussion of this, see Toni Erskine, ed., *Can Institutions Have Responsibilities? Collective Moral Agency and International Relations* (Basingstoke: Palgrave Macmillan, 2003); and Arne Johan Vetlesen, *Evil and Human Agency: Understanding Evildoing* (Cambridge: Cambridge University Press, 2005).
12. Harries, *After the Evil*, 25.
13. Karl Barth, quoted in Timothy J. Gorringe, *Karl Barth: Against Hegemony* (Oxford: Oxford University Press, 1999), 180.
14. Gorringe, *Karl Barth: Against Hegemony*, 180.
15. Ibid., 181.
16. Ibid.
17. Karl Barth, quoted in Gorringe, 181–82.
18. Elie Wiesel, *Night*, trans. Marion Wiesel (New York: Hill and Wang, 2006), 9.
19. Rubenstein and Roth, *Approaches to Auschwitz*, 321–22.
20. Harries, *After the Evil*, 48.
21. Levinas, "Useless Suffering," 160–61.
22. Ibid., 161.

23. Ibid., 161–62.
24. Ibid., 162.
25. Ibid.
26. Ibid., 163.
27. See, for example, Bruce Reichenbach, "Natural Evils and Natural Laws: A Theodicy for Natural Evils," *International Philosophical Quarterly* 14, no. 2 (June 1976): 179–96; William L. Rowe, "Evil and Theodicy," *Philosophical Topics* 14, no. 2 (Fall 1988): 119–32; John Hick, *Evil and the Love of God* (New York: Harper and Row, 1966); William L. Rowe, "The Problems of Evil and Some Varieties of Atheism," *American Philosophical Quarterly* 16, no. 4 (October 1979), 335–41; Alvin Plantinga, *God, Freedom and Evil* (London: Allen & Unwin, 1975), 29–59; Keith E. Yandell, "The Problem of Evil and the Content of Morality," *International Journal for Philosophy of Religion* 17 (1985): 139–65. What is particularly interesting about this particular discourse about evil is that is revisited a number of themes that had been prominent in early modern literature on the subject, in particular, the claim that this is the "best of all possible worlds" and the "free will defense."
28. Bernstein, *Radical Evil*, 185.
29. Hans Jonas, quoted in Peter Dews, "'Radical Finitude' and the Problem of Evil: Critical Comments on Wellmer's Reading of Jonas," in *Rethinking Evil: Contemporary Perspectives*, ed. Maria Pia Lara (Berkeley: University of California Press, 2001), 48.
30. Hans Jonas, "Mind, Matter and Creation: Cosmological Evidence and Cosmological Speculation," in *Mortality and Morality: A Search for the Good after Auschwitz*, ed. Lawrence Vogel (Evanston, IL: Northwestern University Press, 1996), 189–90.
31. Dews, "Radical Finitude," 48.
32. Rubenstein and Roth, *Approaches to Auschwitz*, 327.
33. Ibid.
34. Ibid.
35. Richard Rubenstein, *Commentary* 1996 symposium on "The Conditions of Jewish Belief," in *After Auschwitz: Radical Theology and Contemporary Judaism* (Indianapolis: Bobbs-Merrill, 1966), 153.
36. Harries, *After the Evil*, 26.
37. Rubenstein, *After Auschwitz*, 151–52.
38. "Toward a Hidden God," *Time*, April 8, 1966, available at http://www.time.com/time/magazine/article10,9171,835309,00.html (accessed March 26, 2007).
39. "The New Ministry: Bringing God Back to Life," *Time*, December 26, 1969, available at http://www.time.com/time/magazine/article/0,9171,9418,16,00.html (accessed March 26, 2007).

40. Paul van Buren, *A Theology of the Jewish Christian Reality*, vol. 1, *Discerning the Way* (New York: Harpercollins, 1987), 116.

41. Rubenstein and Roth, *Approaches to Auschwitz*, 335–36; see Ignaz Maybaum, *The Face of God After Auschwitz* (Amsterdam: Polack & Van Gennep, 1965).

42. Maybaum, quoted in Rubenstein and Roth, *Approaches to Auschwitz*, 336.

43. Harries, *After the Evil*, 49.

44. Ibid.

45. Emil Fackenheim, "Jewish Values in the Post-Holocaust Future," in *The Jewish Return into History: Reflections in the Age of Auschwitz and a New Jerusalem* (New York: Schoken Books, 1989).

46. Yale University, The Cambodian Genocide Program, available at http://www.yale.edu/cgp/ (accessed March 28, 2007).

47. Berel Lang, "The Evil in Genocide," in *Genocide and Human Rights: A Philosophical Guide*, ed. John K. Roth (Basingstoke, UK: Palgrave Macmillan, 2005), 11.

48. Unfortunately, in the aftermath of the tsunami some commentators reverted to the age-old explanation that the people of Southeast Asia somehow deserved to suffer.

49. Bruce Reichenbach, "Natural Evils and Natural Laws: A Theodicy for Natural Evils," *International Philosophical Quarterly* 14, no. 2 (June 1976): 179.

50. Ibid.

51. Nina H. B. Jørgensen, *The Responsibility of States for International Crimes* (Oxford: Oxford University Press, 2000), 73.

52. Toni Erskine, "Making Sense of 'Responsibility,' in International Relations: Key Questions and Concepts," in Erskine, *Can Institutions Have Responsibilities*? 6.

53. Ibid.

54. Ibid.

55. Kekes, *Facing Evil*, 47.

56. Ibid., 46; see also David Marcus, "Famine Crimes in International Law," *American Journal of International Law* 97, no. 2 (April 2003): 245–81.

57. John Kekes, *Moral Wisdom and Good Lives* (Ithaca, NY: Cornell University Press, 1995), 67 and 69.

58. Berel Lang, *Act and Idea in the Nazi Genocide* (Chicago: Chicago University Press, 1990), 23.

59. Ibid., 24.

60. Ibid.

61. William A. Schabas, *An Introduction to the International Criminal Court*, 2nd ed. (Cambridge: Cambridge University Press, 2004), 108.

62. Rome Statute of the International Criminal Court, Article 30, paragraph 2, available at http://www.un.org/law/icc/statute/99_corr/3.htm (accessed March 22, 2007).

63. Ibid.

64. Shapiro, *Language and Political Understanding*, 109.

65. Gaita, "Refocusing Genocide," 160.

66. Justice Robert H. Jackson, quoted in James Owen, *Nuremberg: Evil on Trial* (London: Headline, 2006), 35.

67. Ibid., 39.

68. David Maxwell Fyfe, foreword to G. M. Gilbert *Nuremberg Diary*, (London: Eyre & Spottiswoode, 1948), xi.

69. Charles Dubost in James Owen, *Nuremberg: Evil on Trial*, 109.

70. Hans Frank in G. M. Gilbert, *Nuremberg Diary*, 13.

71. Ibid.

72. Ibid., 53.

73. Ibid., 84.

74. Leon Goldensohn interview with Wilhelm Keitel, May 17, 1946, in Leon Goldensohn, *The Nuremberg Interviews: Conversations with the Defendants and Witnesses*, ed. Robert Gellately (London: Pimlico, 2007), 166.

75. Katz, *Confronting Evil*, 54.

76. Robert Gellately, "Introduction: Nuremberg—Voices from the Past," in *The Nuremberg Interviews*, xxvii.

77. John Kekes, *The Roots of Evil*, (Ithaca, NY: Cornell University Press, 2005), 102.

78. Allen, quoted in Kekes, *Roots of Evil*, 102.

79. Roy F. Baumeister, "The Holocaust and the Four Roots of Evil," in *Understanding Genocide: The Social Psychology of the Holocaust*, ed. Leonard S. Newman and Ralph Erber (Oxford: Oxford University Press, 2002), 254.

80. Tzvetan Todorov, "Ordinary People and Extraordinary Vices," in *Destined for Evil? The Twentieth-Century Responses*, ed. Predrag Cicovacki (Rochester, NY: University of Rochester Press, 2005), 120.

81. Ron Rosenbaum, *Explaining Hitler: The Search for the Origins of his Evil* (New York: Macmillan, 1998), xxi.

82. Ibid., 86.

83. Milton Himmelfarb, "No Hitler, No Holocaust," *Commentary* 76, no. 3 (March 1984): 37–43.

84. Kekes, *Facing Evil*, 84.

85. Ibid.

86. Ibid.

87. Philippa Foot, quoted in Kekes, *Facing Evil*, 84; see Philippa Foot, "Moral Beliefs," in *Virtues and Vices* (Berkeley: University of California Press, 1978), 129.

88. Rudolph Hoess interview with Leon Goldensohn, April 8, 1946, in *The Nuremberg Interviews*, 296.

89. Rudolph Hoess interview with Leon Goldensohn, April 9, 1946, in *The Nuremberg Interviews*, 309.

90. Ibid., 304.

91. Rudolph Hoess interview with Leon Goldensohn, April 11, 1946, in *The Nuremberg Interviews*, 315.

92. Foot, quoted in Kekes, *Facing Evil*, 85.

93. Rudolph Hoess interview with Leon Goldensohn, April 11, 1946, in *The Nuremberg Interviews*, 315.

94. Simon Wiesenthal, quoted in Gitta Sereny, *Into that Darkness: An Examination of Conscience* (London: Picador, 1974), 21.

95. Sereny, *Into that Darkness*, 163–64.

96. Stangl quoted in Sereny, 164.

97. Ibid.

98. Kekes, *Facing Evil*, 66.

99. Kekes, *Roots of Evil*, 56.

100. Rome Statute, Article 30, paragraph 2.

101. Stangl, quoted in Kekes, *Roots of Evil*, 57.

102. Sereny, *Into that Darkness*, 134.

103. Himmler, quoted in Manus I. Midlarsky, *The Killing Trap: Genocide in the Twentieth Century* (Cambridge: Cambridge University Press, 2005), 180–81.

104. Richard Breitman, *The Architect of Genocide: Himmler and the Final Solution* (Hanover, NH: Brandeis University Press and University Press of New England, 1991), 243.

105. Hoess, quoted in Clendinnen, *Reading the Holocaust*, 123. See Rudolph Hoess, *Commandant of Auschwitz: The Autobiography of Rudolph Hoess*, trans. Constantine Fitzgibbon (London: Weidenfeld and Nicholson, 1959), 181.

106. Kekes, *The Roots of Evil*, 101.

107. Kekes, *Moral Wisdom and Good Lives*, 68.

108. Lang, *Act and Idea in the Nazi Genocide*, 24–25.

109. J. R. Lucas, *Responsibility* (Oxford: Clarendon Press, 1993), 5.

110. Michael S. Moore, "Causation and Responsibility," in *Responsibility*, ed. Ellen Frankel Paul, Fred D. Miller, Jr., and Jeffrey Paul (Cambridge: Cambridge University Press, 1999), 4.

111. For more on Moore's distinction between causation and correlation, see Moore, "Causation and Responsibility," 7–8.

112. Lucas, *Responsibility*, 5.

113. Martin Buber, quoted in Daniel Warner, *An Ethic of Responsibility in International Relations* (Boulder, CO: Lynne Rienner, 1991), 20; see Martin

Buber, *Between Man and Man*, trans. Ronald Gregor Smith (New York: Macmillan, 1965), 16.

114. See also Joel Feinburg, "Action and Responsibility," in *Philosophy in America*, ed. Max Black (London: G. Allen and Unwin, 1965), 134–60.

115. Midlarsky, *The Killing Trap*, 11.

Chapter 6

1. C. S. Lewis, preface to the 1961 edition of *The Screwstape Letters* (London: G. Bles, 1961).

2. Primo Levi, Afterword, 214.

3. Hannah Arendt, "The Concentration Camps," *Partisan Review* 15, no. 7 (1948): 745.

4. Hannah Arendt to Karl Jaspers, August 17, 1946, in *Hannah Arendt and Karl Jaspers Correspondence 1920–1969* (New York: Harcourt, Brace and Jovanovich, 1992), 69.

5. Jaspers to Arendt, Ibid., 62.

6. Arendt to Jaspers, Ibid., 69

7. Ibid.

8. Dana Villa, *Politics, Philosophy, Terror: Essays on the Thought of Hannah Arendt* (Princeton, NJ: Princeton University Press, 1999), 32.

9. Henry E. Allison, "Reflections on the Banality of (Radical) Evil: A Kantian Analysis," in *Rethinking Evil: Contemporary Perspectives*, ed. Maria Pia Lara (Berkeley: University of California Press, 2001), 87.

10. See Arendt, *The Human Condition*, for an explanation of the role of spontaneity in the *vita activa*. Hannah Arendt, *The Human Condition*, 2nd ed. (Chicago: University of Chicago Press, 1998).

11. Arendt to Jaspers, March 4, 1951, *Hannah Arendt and Karl Jaspers Correspondence*, 166.

12. This essay appeared in a revised form as the chapter titled "Total Domination," in *The Origins of Totalitarianism* (New York: Brace, Harcourt and Jovanovich, 1973).

13. Arendt, "The Concentration Camps," 751.

14. Ibid.

15. Arendt, *The Origins of Totalitarianism*, 452.

16. Arendt, "The Concentration Camps," 759.

17. Lara, introduction to *Rethinking Evil*, 7.

18. Villa, *Politics, Philosophy Terror*, 32.

19. Arendt quoted in Richard J. Bernstein, "Did Hannah Arendt Change Her Mind? From Radical Evil to the Banality of Evil," in *Hannah Arendt: Twenty Years Later*, ed. Larry May and Jerome Kohn (Cambridge: Massachusetts Institute of Technology Press, 1996), 130.

20. Arendt, *The Origins of Totalitarianism*, 459, emphasis Bernstein's; Ibid.

21. Arendt, "The Concentration Camps," 748.

22. Hannah Arendt, *Eichmann in Jerusalem: A Report on the Banality of Evil* (New York: Penguin, 1964), 5.

23. Ibid., 263, 253.

24. Ibid., 21.

25. During Eichmann's trial, questions were raised about the alleged murder of an individual but this was not pursued in the trial.

26. Arendt, *Eichmann in Jerusalem*, 153.

27. Katz, *Ordinary People and Extraordinary Evil*, 19.

28. Arendt, *Eichmann in Jerusalem*, 276.

29. Ibid., 276.

30. Ibid., 287.

31. Wiesel, "Some Questions that Remain Open," 16.

32. Arendt, *Eichmann in Jerusalem*, 276.

33. Ibid., 21.

34. Ibid., 25.

35. Ibid., 277.

36. Ibid.

37. Ibid., 24.

38. Ibid., 24.

39. Ibid., 135–36.

40. Ibid., 136.

41. Allison, "Reflections on the Banality of (Radical) Evil," 88.

42. Arendt, *Eichmann in Jerusalem*, 136. Frank, quoted in Arendt.

43. Arendt writes: "Eichmann, who never made a decision on his own, who was extremely careful always to be 'covered' by orders, who—as freely given testimony from practically all the people who had worked with him confirmed—did not even like to volunteer suggestions and always required 'directives,' now, 'for the first and last time,' took an initiative contrary to orders: instead of sending these people to Russian territory, Riga or Minsk, where they could have immediately been shot by the *Einsatzgruppen*, he directed the transport to the ghetto of Lódz, where he knew that no preparations for extermination had yet been made—if only because the man in charge of the ghetto, a certain Regierungspräsident Uebelhör, had found ways and means of deriving considerable profit from 'his' Jews." Arendt, *Eichmann in Jerusalem*, 94.

44. Ibid., 114.

45. Ibid.

46. Ibid., 247.

47. Ibid.

48. Ibid., 248.

49. Ibid., 155.
50. Hannah Arendt, "Thinking and Moral Considerations: A Lecture," *Social Research* 38, no. 3 (Fall, 1971): 417.
51. Bernard J. Bergen, *The Banality of Evil: Hannah Arendt and "The Final Solution"* (Lanham: Rowman and Littlefield, 1998), 102.
52. Arendt, *The Life of the Mind*, (London: Seder and Warburg, 1978), 60–61, and 13–14.
53. David Grumett, "Arendt, Augustine, and Evil," *The Heythrop Journal* 41, (2000): 163.
54. Arendt, *The Life of the Mind*, 131.
55. Arendt, quoted in Dana R. Villa, "The Banality of Philosophy: Arendt on Heidegger and Eichmann," in *Hannah Arendt: Twenty Years Later*, ed. Larry May and Jerome Kohn (Cambridge: Massachusetts Institute of Technology Press, 1996), 185.
56. Hannah Arendt, "For Martin Heidegger's Eightieth Birthday," in *Martin Heidegger and National Socialism: Questions and Answers*, ed. Günther Neske and Emil Kettering, trans. Lisa Harries (New York: Paragon House, 1990), 216.
57. Robert Bernasconi, quoted in Villa, "The Banality of Philosophy," 181.
58. Villa, "The Banality of Philosophy," 181.
59. Ibid.
60. Ibid.
61. Arendt, quoted in Villa, "The Banality of Philosophy," 182.
62. Arendt, "Thinking and Moral Considerations: A Lecture," *Social Research* 38, no. 3 (Fall 1971): 24.
63. Ibid.
64. Arendt, quoted in Villa, "The Banality of Philosophy," 185.
65. Arendt, *Eichmann in Jerusalem*, 221.
66. Eichmann, quoted in Arendt, *Eichmann in Jerusalem*, 48.
67. Ibid.
68. Ibid., 252.
69. Arendt, "Thinking and Moral Considerations," 417.
70. Arendt, *Life of the Mind*, 3–4.
71. Hannah Arendt, "Personal Responsibility Under Dictatorship," *Listener* (August 6, 1964): 186.
72. Gershom Scholem to Hannah Arendt, "Eichmann in Jerusalem: An Exchange of Letters between Gershom Scholem and Hannah Arendt," in *Hannah Arendt, The Jew as Pariah: Jewish Identity and Politics in the Modern Age*, ed. Ron H. Feldman (New York: Grove Press, 1978), 245.
73. Hannah Arendt to Gershom Scholem, "Eichmann in Jerusalem: An Exchange of Letters between Gershom Scholem and Hannah Arendt," 251.
74. Ibid.

75. Bernstein, *Radical Evil*, 218.
76. Robert H. Pippen, "Hannah Arendt and the Bourgeois Origins of Totalitarian Evil," in *Modernity and the Problem of Evil*, ed. Alan D. Schrift (Bloomington: Indiana University Press, 2005), 149.
77. Bernstein, *Radical Evil*, 218.
78. See Renée Jeffery and Nicholas Rengger, "Moral Evil and International Relations: Old Concepts, New Challenges?" *SAIS Review of International Affairs* 25 (2005): 3–16.
79. Elshtain, *Augustine and the Limits of Politics*, 73.
80. Bernard J. Bergen, *The Banality of Evil: Hannah Arendt and "The Final Solution"* (Lanham: Rowman and Littlefield, 1998), ix.
81. Ibid.
82. Julia Kristeva, *Hannah Arendt*, trans. Ross Guberman (New York: Columbia University Press, 2001), 145.
83. Arendt, *Eichmann in Jerusalem*, 5.
84. Kristeva, *Hannah Arendt*, 145.
85. Arendt, *Eichmann in Jerusalem*, 117.
86. Ibid., 91.
87. Ibid., 115.
88. Ibid., 91, indeed, as Julia Kristeva notes, Gershom Scholem argued that Arendt lacked *Herzenstakt*, or sympathy. *Hannah Arendt*, 145.
89. Gershom Scholem, "Exchange," in *The Jew as Pariah*, 243.
90. Arendt, quoted in Kristeva, *Hannah Arendt*, 146.
91. Arendt, quoted in Seyla Benhabib, "Arendt's *Eichmann in Jerusalem*," in *The Cambridge Companion to Hannah Arendt*, ed. Dana R. Villa (Cambridge: Cambridge University Press, 2000), 70–71.
92. Kristeva, *Hannah Arendt*, 145.
93. Ibid.
94. Ron H. Feldman, "The Jew as Pariah: The Case of Hannah Arendt (1906–1975)," in Hannah Arendt, *The Jew as Pariah: Jewish Identity in the Modern Age*, ed. Ron H. Feldman, (New York: Grove Press, 1978), 17.
95. Bergen, *The Banality of Evil*, x.
96. Tzvetan Todorov, "Ordinary People and Extraordinary Vices," in Predrag Cicovacki (ed.), *Destined for Evil? The Twentieth-Century Responses*, (Rochester: University of Rochester Press, 2005), 122.
97. Bergen, *The Banality of Evil*, ix.
98. As Arendt made clear at a conference on her work in Toronto some years later: "You say I said there is an Eichmann in each one of us. Oh no! There is none in you and none in me! This doesn't mean that there are not quite a number of Eichmanns. But they look really quite different. I always hated this notion of 'Eichmann in each one of us.' This is simply not true. This would be as untrue as the opposite, that Eichmann is in nobody." "On

Hannah Arendt," in *Hannah Arendt: The Recovery of the Public World*, ed. Melvin A. Hill (New York: St. Martins Press, 1979), 308.

99. Fred E. Katz, *Ordinary People and Extraordinary Evil: A Report on the Beguilings of Evil* (Albany: State University of New York Press, 1993), 7.

100. Ibid.

101. Ibid., 26. See also Katz, *Confronting Evil*, 69–86.

102. Ibid., 37.

103. Ibid.

104. Ibid., 103.

105. *Lieutenant William Calley: His Own Story, as Told to John Sack* (New York: Viking Press, 1971), 225.

106. Katz, *Ordinary People and Extraordinary Evil*, 103.

107. Herbert C. Kelman and V. Lee Hamilton, *Crimes of Obedience: Towards a Social Psychology of Authority and Responsibility* (New Haven, CT: Yale University Press, 1989), 47.

108. Katz, *Ordinary People and Extraordinary Evil*, 16.

109. Christopher Browning, *Ordinary Men: Reserve Police Battalion 101 and the Final Solution in Poland* (London: Penguin, 2001).

110. Staub, *The Roots of Evil*, 134; Clendinnen, *Reading the Holocaust*, 144. This notion of coming to enjoy killing also accords well with Joanna Bourke's *The Intimate History of Killing* that documents the sense of enjoyment many soldiers have reported upon returning from war. Joanna Bourke, *The Intimate History of Killing: Face-to-face Killing in Twentieth Century Warfare* (London: Granta Books, 1999).

111. Milgrim, quoted in Clendinnen, *Reading the Holocaust*, 147; Stanley Milgram, *Obedience to Authority: An Experimental View* (London: Tavistock, 1974); Craig Haney, Curtis Banks, and Philip Zimbardo, "Interpersonal Dynamics in a Simulated Prison," *International Journal of Criminology and Penology* 1 (1983): 69–97.

112. Katz, *Confronting Evil*, 74.

113. Ibid.

114. Ibid.

115. Ibid., 75.

116. Daniel Jonah Goldhagen, *Hitler's Willing Executioners: Ordinary Germans and the Holocaust* (New York: Vintage Books, 1997), 379.

117. Ibid., 597n4.

118. Clendinnen, *Reading the Holocaust*, 136.

119. Quoted in Clendinnen, *Reading the Holocaust*, 136; see Gordon Craig, *New York Review of Books* (May 23, 1996): 52; Raul Hilberg, "The Goldhagen Phenomenon," *Critical Inquiry* 23 (Summer 1997): 721–28.

120. Neiman, *Evil in Modern Thought*, 277.

121. Morton, *On Evil*, 2 and 4.

122. Neiman, *Evil in Modern Thought*, 2.
123. Morton, 7.
124. Ibid., 8.
125. Ibid.
126. Ibid., 55–56.
127. Ibid., 57.
128. Ibid., 69, 71, and 87.
129. Bernstein, *Radical Evil*, 232.
130. Karl Jaspers to Hannah Arendt, *Hannah Arendt and Karl Jaspers Correspondence*, 542.
131. Arendt, quoted in Villa, *Politics, Philosophy, Terror*, 57.
132. Villa, *Politics, Philosophy, Terror*, 57.
133. Arendt, quoted in Kristeva, *Hannah Arendt*, 154.
134. Voegelin, quoted in Kristeva, *Hannah Arendt*, 154.
135. Arendt, quoted in Kristeva, *Hannah Arendt*, 155.

Chapter 7

1. George W. Bush, September 12, 2001, available at http://www.whitehouse.gov/news/releases/2001/09/20010912-4.html (accessed December 15, 2006).
2. George W. Bush, remarks by the President on Arrival, The South Lawn, September 16, 2001, available at http://www.whitehouse.gov/news/releases/2001/09/print/20010916 (accessed December 15, 2006).
3. Bush has also used the term to refer to the massacre at Srebrenica, domestic violence, segregation and human trafficking in recent years. George W. Bush, Presidential Message: 10th Anniversary of the Massacre in Srebrenica, July 11, 2005, available at http://www.whitehouse.gov/news/releases/2005/07/print/20050711 (accessed December 8, 2006); National Domestic Violence Awareness Month, September 30, 2005; President Signs H.R. 4145 to Place Statute of Rosa Parks in U.S. Capitol, Room 350, Dwight D. Eisenhower Executive Office Building, December 1, 2005, available at http://www.whitehouse.gov/news/releases/2005/12/print/20051201 (accessed December 8, 2006); President signs H.R. 972, Trafficking Victims Protection Reauthorization Act, Eisenhower Executive Office Building, January 10, 2006, available at http://www.whitehouse.gov/news/releases/2006/01/20060110-3.html (accessed December 8, 2006).
4. Louis P. Pojman, *Terrorism, Human Rights and the Case for World Government* (Lanham, MD: Rowman and Littlefield, 2006), 4.
5. United States Department of Defense quoted in Bruce Hoffman, *Inside Terrorism* (London: Victor Gollancz, 1998), 38. The definition of terrorism is a particularly contentious issue. For example, in his survey, *Political*

Terrorism: A Research Guide, Alex Schmid identifies 109 different definitions of the term! Alex P. Schmid, *Political Terrorism: A Research Guide* (New Brunswick, NJ: Transaction Books, 1984).

6. Hoffman, *Inside Terrorism*, 15 and 17. Burke famously described the French Revolution as "Thousands of those Hell hounds called Terrorists . . . let loose on the people."

7. Ibid., 26.

8. Ibid., 27.

9. Pojman, *Terrorism, Human Rights*, 2.

10. Hoffman, *Inside Terrorism*, 28.

11. Pojman, *Terrorism, Human Rights*, 2.

12. The "War on Evil" is a phrase devised by Stephen Chan that combines the "War on Terror" with the "Axis of Evil." Stephen Chan, *Out of Evil*, viii.

13. Pojman, *Terrorism, Human Rights*, 2.

14. Cicovacki, ed., *Destined for Evil?*; Arne Johan Vetlesen, *Evil and Human Agency: Understanding Collective Evildoing* (Cambridge: Cambridge University Press, 2005); Fred Emil Katz, *Confronting Evil: Two Journeys* (New York: State University of New York Press, 2004); Morton, *On Evil*.

15. Singer, *The President of Good and Evil*; Scott Kline, "The Culture War Gone Global: 'Family Values' and the Shape of U.S. Foreign Policy," *International Relations* 18, no. 4 (December 2004): 453–66; Catherine Lu, editor's introduction to *International Relations* 18, no. 4 (2004): 403–4; Bernstein, *The Abuse of Evil*; Michael Ignatieff, *The Lesser Evil: Political Ethics in an Age of Terror* (Edinburgh: Edinburgh University Press, 2004); Graham Maddox, "The 'crusade against evil': Bush's Fundamentalism," *Australian Journal of Politics and History* 49, no. 3 (2003): 398–411.

16. Bernstein, *Radical Evil*; Klusmeyer and Suhrke, "Comprehending 'evil'"; Nieman, *Evil and Modern Thought*; Lara, ed., *Rethinking Evil*; Forsyth, "The Origin of Evil: Classical or Judeo-Christian?"; Geddes, ed., *Evil After Postmodernism*; Ophir, *The Order of Evils*; Morton, *On Evil*.

17. Morton, *On Evil*, 87.

18. Although other world leaders, most notably, Tony Blair, have also used the term evil in contemporary rhetoric, George Bush remains the most prominent proponent of the term and is thus the central focus of this chapter.

19. Bush, quoted in Singer, *The President of Good and Evil*, 4.

20. Howard Fineman, "Bush and God," *Newsweek*, March 10, 2003.

21. David Frum, *The Right Man: An Inside Account of the Bush White House* (New York: Random House, 2003), 4.

22. For a critique of this award, see *Christian Century* 119, no. 2 (January 16, 2002): 14–15.

23. Fineman, "Bush and God."

24. Ibid.

25. Greg Thielmann, quoted in Singer, *The President of Good and Evil*, 100.

26. Kevin Phillips, *American Theocracy: The Peril and Politics of Radical Religion, Oil, and Borrowed Money in the 21st Century* (New York: Penguin, 2006), 192.

27. "How God Speaks in Religious Code," *Boston Globe*, September 12, 2004, quoted in Phillips, 207.

28. Phillips, *American Theocracy*, 192.

29. Stephen Mansfield, quoted in Esther Kaplan, *With God on Their Side: How Christian Fundamentalists Trampled Science, Policy, and Democracy in George W. Bush's White House* (New York: The New Press, 2004), 10; Stephen Mansfield, *The Faith of George W. Bush* (New York: Penguin, 2003), 109.

30. Bush, quoted in Phillips, 208.

31. Quoted in Maddox, "The 'Crusade' Against Evil"; see Tony Carnes, "Bush's Defining Moment: The President, Facing a Grief-stricken Nation Under Attack, Finds His Woice and His Mission," *Christianity Today* 45, no. 14 (November 12, 2001): 38–43.

32. Ivo Daalder and James M. Lindsay, *America Unbound: The Bush Revolution in Foreign Policy* (Hoboken: John Wiley & Sons, 2003), 87.

33. Bush, quoted in Daalder and Lindsay, *America Unbound*, 87.

34. Singer, *The President of Good and Evil*, 2.

35. George W. Bush, quoted in Daalder and Lindsay, *America Unbound*, 86. See George W. Bush, "A Distinctly American Internationalism," Ronald Reagan Library, Simi Valley, California, November 19, 1999, www.mtholyoke.edu/acad/intrel/bush/wspeech.htm (accessed December 15, 2006).

36. George W. Bush, "Remarks by the President at Dedication of Oklahoma City National Memorial," Oklahoma City, Oklahoma, February 19, 2001, available at http://www.whitehouse.gov/news/releases/2001/02/print/20010219.html (accessed December 15, 2006).

37. Daalder and Lindsay, *America Unbound*, 86.

38. George W. Bush, "Statement by the President in His Address to the Nation," September 11, 2001, http://www.whitehouse.gov/news/releases/2001/09/print/20010911.html (accessed December 15, 2006).

39. Frum, *The Right Man*, 132–33. The President's detractors thought that he should have given a far stronger, war-type speech rather than "a hastily revised compassionate conservatism speech." Frum, *The Right Man*, 128.

40. George W. Bush, "President Discusses Nation's Critical Infrastructure," Oak Park High School, Kansas City, Missouri, June 11, 2002, available at http://www.whitehouse.gov/news/releases/2002/06/print/20020611 (accessed December 8, 2006).

41. Frum, *The Right Man*, 240.

42. George W. Bush, State of the Union Address, United States Capitol, Washington, D.C., January 29, 2002, http://www.whitehouse.gov/news/releases/2002/01/20020129-11.html (accessed December 15, 2006).

43. Ibid.

44. Frum, *The Right Man*, 234.

45. Ibid., 236.

46. Ibid., 237.

47. Ibid., 238.

48. Ibid.

49. Ibid., 238 and 240.

50. George W. Bush, "Remarks to First-Responders in Greenville," March 27, 2002, available at http://frwebgate2.access.gpo.gov/cgi-bin/waisgate.cgi?WAISdocID (accessed February 22, 2007).

51. Bush, "President Discusses Nation's Critical Infrastructure," June 11, 2002.

52. Bush, "Statement by the President in His Address to the Nation," September 11, 2001.

53. George W. Bush, "President Asks Seniors to Get Involved in USA Freedom Corps," Daytona Beach International Airport, Daytona Beach, Florida, January 30, 2002, http://www.whitehouse.gov/news/releases/2002/01/print/20020131.htm (accessed December 15, 2006).

54. George W. Bush, "President Unveils Back to Work Plan," Department of Labor, Washington, D.C., October 4, 2001, available at http://www.whitehouse.gov/news/releases/2001/10/print/20011004 (accessed December 15, 2006).

55. George W. Bush, "Remarks by the President Upon Arrival," September 16, 2001.

56. George W. Bush, "President Meets with Muslim Leaders," The Roosevelt Room, September 26, 2001, available at http://www.whitehouse.gov/news/releases/2001/09/print/20010926 (accessed December 15, 2006).

57. George W. Bush, "Nigerian President Offers Solidarity to U.S.," remarks by President Bush and President Obasanjo of Nigeria in Photo Opportunity, The Rose Garden, November 2, 2001, available at http://www.whitehouse.gov/news/releases/2001/11/print/20011102 (accessed December 15, 2006).

58. George W. Bush, "SOTU Excerpts on Defending Peace & Security at Home," January 28, 2003 available at http://www.whitehouse.gov/new/releases/2003/01/print/20030128 (accessed December 8, 2006).

59. George W. Bush, "President Honors Fallen Peace Officers at Memorial Service," remarks by the President at Annual Peace Officers Memorial Service, Peace Officers Memorial, Washington, D.C., May 15, 2003, available at http://www.whitehouse.gov/news/releases/2003/05/20030515 (accessed December 8, 2006).

60. George W. Bush, "President Pays Tribute at Pentagon Memorial," remarks by the President at the Department of Defense Service of Remembrance, The Pentagon, Arlington, Virginia, October 11, 2001, available at http://www.whitehouse.gov/news/releases/2001/10/print/20011011 (accessed December 15, 2006). See also, "President Rallies Troops at Travis Air Force Base," remarks by the President to Military Personnel, Travis Air Base, California, October 17, 2001, at which he said: "The victims of September 11th were innocent, and this nation will never forget them. The men and women who murdered them were instruments of evil, and they have died in vain," available at http://www.whitehouse.gov/news/releases/2001/01/print/20011017 (accessed December 15, 2006).
61. Ibid.
62. George W. Bush, "No Nation Can Be Neutral in this Conflict," remarks by the President to the Warsaw Conference on Combating Terrorism, November 6, 2001, available at http://www.whitehouse.gov/news/releases/2001/11/print/20011106 (accessed November 15, 2006); "President Discusses Stronger Economy and Homeland Defense," Dixie Printing Company, Glen Burnie, Maryland, October 24, 2001, available at http://www.whitehouse.gov/news/releases/2001/10/print/20011024 (accessed December 15, 2006).
63. Phillips, *American Theocracy*, 250.
64. George W. Bush, "National Day of Prayer and Remembrance for the Victims of the Terrorist Attacks on September 11, 2001," September 13, 2001, available at http://www.whitehouse.gov/news/releases/2001/09/print/20010913 (accessed December 15, 2006).
65. Bush, "Remarks by the President Upon Arrival," September 16, 2001.
66. Bush, "Statement by the President in His Address to the Nation," September 11, 2001.
67. Bush, "Remarks by the President Upon Arrival," September 16, 2001.
68. Maddox, "The 'Crusade Against Evil,'" 401.
69. Ibid.
70. See for example, "'Islam is Peace' Says President," remarks by the President at Islamic Center of Washington, D.C., September 17, 2001, available at http://www.whitehouse.gov/news/releases/2001/09/print/20010917 (accessed December 15, 2006); "President Meets with Muslim Leaders," September 26, 2001; "King of Jordan: 'We will stand behind you,'" remarks by President Bush and His Majesty King Abdullah of Jordan in a Photo Opportunity, The Oval Office, September 28, 2001; "America's Youth Respond to Afghan Children's Fund," October 16, 2001, available at http://www.whitehouse.gov/news/releases/2001/09/print/20010928 (accessed December 15, 2006).

71. George W. Bush, "National Character Counts Week Proclamation," October 23, 2001, available at http://www.whitehouse.gov/news/releases/2001/10/print/20011023 (accessed December 15, 2006).

72. As we will see shortly, the demonization of Islam has, nonetheless, been a persistent theme in late twentieth and early twenty-first century American evangelical Christianity.

73. George W. Bush, President Bush Delivers Graduation Speech at West Point, United States Military Academy, West Point, June 1, 2002, available at http://www.whitehouse.gov/news/releases/2002/06/20020601-3.html (accessed December 15, 2006).

74. George W. Bush, President Promotes Compassionate Conservatism, Parkside Hall, San Jose, California, April 30, 2002, available at http://whitehouse.gov/news/releases/2002/04/20020430-5.html (accessed December 15, 2006).

75. George W. Bush, "President Directs Humanitarian Aid to Afghanistan," remarks by the President to State Department Employees, U.S. Department of State, Washington, D.C., October 4, 2001, available at http://www.whitehouse.gov/news/releases/2001/10/print/20011004.html (accessed December 15, 2006).

76. Samantha Power, "Hannah Arendt's Lesson," *New York Review of Books* 51, no. 7 (April 29, 2004): 37.

77. Chan, *Out of Evil*, 129.

78. George W. Bush, "President's Easter Message," March 27, 2002, available at http://www.whitehouse.gov/news/releases/2002/03/print/20020327 (accessed December 8, 2006).

79. George W. Bush, "Radio Address by the President to the Nation," August 31, 2002, available at http://www.whitehouse.gov/news/releases/2002/08/print/20020831.html (accessed December 8, 2006).

80. George W. Bush, "President Shares Thanksgiving Meal with Troops," remarks by the President to Troops and Families at Fort Campbell, Fort Campbell, Kentucky, November 21, 2001, available at http://www.whitehouse.gov/news/releases/2001/11/print/20011121.html (accessed December 15, 2001).

81. George W. Bush, "President Calls for Crime Victims' Rights Amendment," Robert F. Kennedy Department of Justice, Washington, D.C., April 16, 2002, available at http://www.whitehouse.gov/news/releases/2002/04/print/20020416.html (accessed December 8, 2006).

82. George W. Bush, "President Calls on Congress to Pass Economic Security Package," Cecil I. Walker Machinery Company, Charleston, West Virginia, January 22, 2002, available at http://www.whitehouse.gov/news/releases/2002/01/print/20020122 (accessed December 15, 2006).

83. George W. Bush, "President Urges Responsibility in Speech Congratulating Lakers," remarks by the President in Welcome of the NBA Champion Los Angeles Lakers, The East Room, January 28, 2002, available at http://www.whitehouse.gov/news/releases/2002/01/print/20020128 (accessed December 15, 2006); "President Asks Seniors to Get Involved in USA Freedom Corps," January 30, 2002.

84. Bush, "Remarks to First-Responders in Greenville," March 27, 2002.

85. Ibid.

86. Bush, President Discusses Critical Infrastructure, June 11, 2002.

87. Singer, *The President of Good and Evil*, 209

88. Ibid.

89. Richard Hofstadter, "The Paranoid Style in American Politics," in *The Paranoid Style in American Politics and Other Essays* (London: Jonathan Cape, 1966), 29.

90. Ibid., 31.

91. Bernstein, *The Abuse of Evil*, 48.

92. Ibid., 118.

93. Maddox, "The 'crusade against evil,'" 411.

94. Bernstein, *The Abuse of Evil*, 83.

95. Chan, *Out of Evil*; Farid Abdel-Nour, "An International Ethics of Evil?" *International Relations* 18, no. 4 (2004): 425–39.

96. Abdel-Nour, "An International Ethics of Evil?" 431.

97. Michael Ignatieff, *The Lesser Evil*, 8.

98. Harry S. Truman, "Radio Address to the American People After the Signing of the Terms of Unconditional Surrender by Japan," September 1, 1945, available at http://www.trumanlibrary.org/calendar/viewpapers.php?pid=129 (accessed February 22, 2007).

99. Harry S. Truman, "Broadcast to the American People Announcing the Surrender of Germany," May 8, 1945, available at http://www.truman library.org/publicpapers/index/ (accessed February 22, 2007).

100. Scott Kline, "The Culture War Gone Global: 'Family Values' and the Shape of U.S. Foreign Policy," *International Relations* 18, no. 4 (December 2004): 454.

101. Harry S. Truman, "Address in Harlem, New York, Upon Receiving the Franklin Roosevelt Award," October 29, 1948, available at http://www.trumanlibrary.org/publicpapers/index.php?pid=2016 (accessed February 22, 2007); "Annual Message to the Congress on the State of the Union, January 8, 1951, available at http://www.trumanlibrary.org/whistlestop/tap/1815 .htm (accessed February 22, 2007).

102. Lyndon B. Johnson, "Address Before a Joint Session of the Congress," November 27, 1963 available at http://www.presidency.ucsb.edu/ws/index .php?pid=25988&st=evil (accessed February 22, 2007).

103. Ronald Reagan, "Remarks at the Annual Convention of the National Association of Evangelicals in Orlando, Florida," March 8, 1983, available at http://www.reagan.utexas.edu/archives/speeches/1983/30883.htm (accessed, February 22, 2007).

104. Ronald Reagan, "Address to Members of the British Parliament," June 8, 1982, http://www.reagan.utexas.edu/archives/speeches/1982/60882.htm (accessed February 22, 2007).

105. George Bush, Open Letter to College Students on the Persian Gulf Crisis, January 9, 1991, available at http://frwebgate1.access.gpo.gov/cgi-bin/waisgate.cgi?WAISdocID (accessed February 22, 2007).

106. George Bush, Radio Address to the Nation on National Day of Prayer, February 2, 1991, available at http://frwebgate1.access.gpo.gov/cgi-bin/waisgate.cgi?WAISdocID (accessed February 22, 2007).

107. William J. Clinton, Statement on the Terrorist Bombing in Israel, January 22, 1995, available at http://frwebgate4.access.gpo.gov/cgi-bin/waisgate.cgi?WAISdocID (accessed February 22, 2007).

108. William J. Clinton, The President's Radio Address, October 15, 1994, available at http://frwebgate4.access.gpo.gov/cgi-bin/waisgate.cgi?WAISdocID (accessed February 22, 2007).

109. William J. Clinton, remarks at a Memorial Service for the Bombing Victims in Oklahoma City, April 23, 1995, available at http://frwebgate4.access.gpo.gov/cgi-bin/waisgate.cgi?WAISdocID (accessed February 22, 2007); The President's Radio Address, April 6, 1996, available at http://frwebgate4.access.gpo.gov/cgi-bin/waisgate.cgi?WAISdocID (accessed February 22, 2007).

110. William J. Clinton, The President's Radio Address and an Exchange with Reporters, July 27, 1996, available at http://frwebgate4.access.gpo.gov/cgi-bin/waisgate.cgi?WAISdocID (accessed February 22, 2007).

111. William J. Clinton, "Statement on the Anniversary of the Bombing of Pan American Flight 103, December 21, 1996, available at http://frwebgate4.access.gpo.gov/cgi-bin/waisgate.cgi?WAISdocID (accessed February 22, 2007).

112. William J. Clinton, remarks at the National Prayer Breakfast, February 2, 1995, available at http://frwebgate4.access.gpo.gov/cgi-bin/waisgate.cgi?WAISdocID (accessed February 22, 2007); remarks at the National Prayer Breakfast, February 6, 1997 available at http://frwebgate4.access.gpo.gov/cgi-bin/waisgate.cgi?WAISdocID (accessed February 22, 2007).

113. Clinton, remarks at a Memorial Service for the Bombing Victims in Oklahoma City, April 23, 1995.

114. Phillips, *American Theocracy*, 103.

115. Ibid., 100 and 125.

116. Ibid., 100.

117. Ibid., 405n14.

118. Ibid., 118.

119. Mark Noll, *The Old Religion in a New World* (Grand Rapids: Eerdmans, 2002), 78.

120. Ed Dobson and Ed Hindson, *The Fundamentalist Phenomenon: The Resurgence of Conservative Christianity*, ed. Jerry Falwell (New York: Doubleday, 1981), 4, 3.

121. Charles B. Strozier, *Apocalypse: On the Psychology of Fundamentalism in America* (Boston: Beacon Press, 1994), 189.

122. Dobson and Hindson, *The Fundamentalist Phenomenon*, 7.

123. David S. Domke, *God Willing? Political Fundamentalism in the White House* (Ann Arbor, MI: Pluto Press, 2004), 2.

124. A CNN/*Time* magazine survey conducted in 2002 revealed that 71 percent of evangelical Christians believe that the world will end in an Armageddon battle between Jesus Christ and the Antichrist. Cited in Phillips, 102.

125. Phillips, *American Theocracy*, 185.

126. Clyde Wilcox, *God's Warriors: The Christian Right in Twentieth-Century America* (Baltimore: Johns Hopkins University Press, 1992), 12.

127. Ronald Reagan, "Remarks at the Annual Convention of the National Association of Evangelicals in Orlando, Florida," March 8, 1983, http://www.reagan.utexas.edu/archives/speeches/1983/30883.htm (accessed February 22, 2007).

128. Phillips, *American Theocracy*, 251.

129. Richard Cizik, vice president of the National Association of Evangelicals, quoted in Phillips, 251.

130. Phillips, *American Theocracy*, 251.

131. Paul Boyer, "When U.S. Foreign Policy Meets Biblical Prophecy," *Alternet*, February 20, 2003, http://www.alternet.org/story/15221, 3.

132. In Phillips, *American Theocracy*, 254.

133. Boyer, "When U.S. Foreign Policy Meets Biblical Prophecy."

134. Barbara R. Rossing, *The Rapture Exposed: The Message of Hope in the Book of Revelation* (Boulder, CO: Westview Press, 2004), 99.

135. Voter News Service Exit Polls, 2000, in Phillips, *American Theocracy*, 191.

136. Tony Blair, "International Terrorism and Attacks in the USA," House of Commons, The United Kingdom Parliament, September 14, 2001, available at http://www.publications/parliament.uk (accessed February 28, 2007).

137. Tony Blair, "Coalition against International Terrorism," House of Commons, The United Kingdom Parliament, October 4, 2001, available at http://www.publications/parliament.uk (accessed February 28, 2007).

138. Tony Blair, "Coalition against International Terrorism," House of Commons, The United Kingdom Parliament, October 8, 2001, available at http://www.publications/parliament.uk (accessed February 28, 2007);

"International Coalition against International Terrorism," House of Commons, The United Kingdom Parliament, November 14, 2001, available at http://www.publications/parliament.uk (accessed February 28, 2007).

139. Tony Blair, House of Commons Hansard Debates, The United Kingdom Parliament, October 29, 2003, available at http://www.publications/parliament.uk (accessed February 28, 2007); Tony Blair, House of Commons Hansard Debates, The United Kingdom Parliament, December 17, 2001, available at http://www.publications/parliament.uk (accessed February 28, 2007).

140. Michael White, Alan Travis, and Duncan Campbell, "Blair: Uproot this Ideology of Evil," *The Guardian*, July 14, 2005, available at http://www.guardian.co.uk/attackonlondon/story/0,,1528086,00.html (accessed February 28, 2007).

141. Tony Blair, quoted in Mark Oliver, "Blair Calls for Task Force to Combat 'Evil Ideology,'" *The Guardian*, July 19, 2005, available at http://www.guardian.co.uk/attackonlondon/story/0,16132,1531798.html (accessed February 28, 2007).

Conclusion

1. Hannah Arendt, "Nightmare and Flight," in *Hannah Arendt: Essays in Understanding, 1930–1954*, ed. Jerome Kohn (New York: Harcourt, Brace, 1994), 134.

2. Richard J. Bernstein, *Hannah Arendt and the Jewish Question* (Cambridge, MA: Massachusetts Institute of Technology Press, 1996), 137.

3. Arendt, *Eichmann in Jerusalem*; Paul Ricoeur, *The Symbolism of Evil* (Boston: Beacon Press, 1967).

4. Susan Sontag, "In Plato's Cave," in *On Photography* (London: Allen Lane, 1977), 19.

5. "The Falling Man" was taken by Richard Drew on September 11, 2001, for Associated Press.

6. Sontag, "In Plato's Cave," 19.

7. Bush, "Statement by the President in His Address to the Nation," September 11, 2001.

8. Thomas, *The Global Resurgence of Religion*, 51.

9. Ibid., 51–52.

10. Ibid., 52.

11. Ibid.

12. Ibid., 53.

Bibliography

Adams, Marilyn McCord. "Redemptive Suffering: A Christian Solution to the Problem of Evil." In *Rationality, Religious Beliefs and Moral Commitment: New Essays on the Philosophy of Religion*, edited by Robert Audi and William J. Wainwright. Ithaca, NY: Cornell University Press, 1986, 248–67.

Adams, Marilyn McCord and Robert Merrihew Adams. Introduction to *The Problem of Evil*, edited by Marilyn McCord Adams and Robert Merrihew Adams. Oxford: Oxford University Press, 1990.

————, eds. *The Problem of Evil*. Oxford: Oxford University Press, 1990.

Adams, Marilyn McCord. *Horrendous Evils and the Goodness of God*. Ithaca, NY: Cornell University Press, 1999.

Adorno, Theodor W. "Cultural Criticism and Society." In *Prisms*, translated by Samuel and Shierry Weber, 17–34. Cambridge, MA: Massachusetts Institute of Technology Press, 1967.

Adorno, Theodor. *Negative Dialectics*. Translated by E. B. Ashton. New York: Seabury, 1973.

Abdel-Nour, Farid. "An International Ethics of Evil?" *International Relations* 18, no. 4 (2004): 425–39.

Alexander of Lycopolis. *Of the Manichaeans* http://www.newadvent.org/fathers/0618.htm (accessed October 27, 2004).

Allison, Henry E. "Reflections on the Banality of (Radical) Evil: A Kantian Analysis." In *Rethinking Evil: Contemporary Perspectives*, edited by Maria Pia Lara. Berkeley: University of California Press, 2001.

Aquinas, Thomas. *On Evil*. Translated by Richard Regan. Edited by Brian Davies. Oxford: Oxford University Press, 2003.

————. *Summa Theologiae*. In *A Shorter Summa: The Most Essential Philosophical Passages of St. Thomas Aquinas's Summa Theologica*, edited by Peter Kreeft. San Francisco: Ignatius Press, 1993.

Arendt, Hannah. "The Concentration Camps." *Partisan Review* 15, no. 7 (1948): 743–63.

————. *Eichmann in Jerusalem: A Report on the Banality of Evil*. New York: Viking Press, 1963; Harmondsworth, UK: Penguin, 1994.

————. "For Martin Heidegger's Eightieth Birthday." In *Martin Heidegger and National Socialism: Questions and Answers*, translated by Lisa Harries, edited by Günther Neske and Emil Kettering, 207–17. New York: Paragon House, 1990.

————. *Hannah Arendt and Karl Jaspers Correspondence 1920–1969*. New York: Harcourt, Brace and Jovanovich, 1992.

————. *The Human Condition*. 2nd ed. Chicago: University of Chicago Press, 1998.

————. *The Life of the Mind*. New York: Harcourt, Brace and Jovanovich, 1978.

————. *The Origins of Totalitarianism*. New York: Harcourt, Brace and Jovanovich, 1973

————. "Nightmare and Flight." In *Hannah Arendt: Essays in Understanding, 1930–1954*, edited by Jerome Kohn, 134–57. New York: Harcourt, Brace, 1994.

————. "Personal Responsibility Under Dictatorship." *The Listener*, August 6, 1964, 186–87.

————. "Some Questions of Moral Philosophy." *Social Research* 61, no. 2 (Winter 1994): 739–64.

————. "Thinking and Moral Considerations: A Lecture." *Social Research* 38, no. 3 (Fall 1971): 417–46.

Audi, Robert, and William J. Wainwright, eds. *Rationality, Religious Beliefs, and Moral Commitment: New Essays on the Philosophy of Religion*. Ithaca, NY: Cornell University Press, 1986.

Augustine of Hippo. *Against the Fundamental Epistle of Manichaeus* [*Contra Epistolam Manichaei Quam Vacant Fundamenti*]. http://www.newadvent .org/fathers/1405.htm (accessed October 27, 2004).

————. *City of God Against the Pagans*. Translated by R. W. Dyson. Cambridge: Cambridge University Press, 1998.

————. *Confessions*. Translated by R. D. Pine-Coffin. London: Penguin, 1961.

————. *Enchiridion on Faith, Hope, and Love*. Translated by J. F. Shaw. http:// www.newadvent.org/fathers/1302.htm (accessed October 27, 2004).

————. *Of Two Souls* [*De Duabus Animabus contra Manichaeos*]. http://www .newadvent.org/fathers/1403.htm (accessed October 27, 2004).

————. *On the Morals of the Manichaeans* [*De Moribus Manichaeorum*]. http://www.newadvent.org/fathers/1402.htm (accessed October 27, 2004).

————. *On the Nature of Good* [*De Natura Boni contra Manichaeos*]. http://www .newadvent.org/fathers/1407.htm (accessed October 27, 2004).

Babcock, W. S. "Sin and Punishment: The Early Augustine on Evil." In *Augustine, Presbyter Factus Sum*, edited by J. T. Leinhard, E. C. Muller, and R. J. Teske. New York: Lang, 1993.

Bailie, Gil. "Two Thousand Years and No New God" In *Destined for Evil? The Twentieth-Century Responses*, edited by Predrag Cicovacki, 19–43. Rochester, NY: University of Rochester Press, 2005.

Baumeister, Roy F. *Evil: Inside Human Cruelty and Violence*. New York: Freeman, 1997.

———. "The Holocaust and the Four Roots of Evil." In *Understanding Genocide: The Social Psychology of the Holocaust*, edited by Leonard S. Newman and Ralph Erber, 241–58. Oxford: Oxford University Press, 2002.

Bergen, Bernard J. *The Banality of Evil: Hannah Arendt and "The Final Solution."* Lanham, MD: Rowman and Littlefield, 1998.

Berkeley, Bill. *The Graves Are Not Yet Full: Tribe and Power in the Heart of Africa.* New York: Basic Books, 2001.

Bernasconi, Robert and David Wood, eds. *The Provocation of Levinas: Rethinking the Other*. London: Routledge, 1988.

Bernstein, Richard. *Hannah Arendt and the Jewish Question*. Cambridge, MA: Massachusetts Institute of Technology Press, 1996.

———. "Did Hannah Arendt Change Her Mind? From Radical Evil to the Banality of Evil." In *Hannah Arendt: Twenty Years Later*, edited by Larry May and Jerome Kohn, 127–46. Cambridge, MA: Massachusetts Institute of Technology Press, 1996.

———. *Radical Evil: A Philosophical Interrogation*. Cambridge: Polity, 2002.

———. *The Abuse of Evil: The Corruption of Politics and Religion since 9/11.* Cambridge: Polity, 2005.

Bettelheim, Bruno. *Surviving and Other Essays*, London: Thames and Hudson, 1979.

Blair, Tony. Statement from Gleneagles, July 7, 2005. https://news.bbc.co.uk/1/hi/uk/4659953.stm (accessed July 15, 2005).

Blair, Tony. "Blair Speech on Terror." Labor Party National Conference, July 16, 2005, https://news.bbc.co.uk/2/hi/uk_news/4689363.stm (accessed July 20, 2005).

Bleicher, Josef. *Contemporary Hermeneutics: Hermeneutics as Method, Philosophy, and Critique*. London: Routledge, 1980.

Boyce, Mary, ed. and trans. *Textual Sources for the Study of Zoroastrianism.* Chicago: University of Chicago Press, 1990.

Boyer, Paul. "When U.S. Foreign Policy Meets Biblical Prophecy." *Alternet*, February 20, 2003. http://www.alternet.org/story/15221 (accessed March 22, 2007).

Breitman, Richard. *The Architect of Genocide: Himmler and the Final Solution*. Hanover, NH: Brandeis University Press and the University Press of New England, 1991.

Brown, Peter. *Augustine of Hippo: A Biography*. London: Faber and Faber, 1967.

Brown, Stuart. *Leibniz*. Brighton, UK: The Harvester Press, 1984.

Brown, Stuart. "The Seventeenth Century Intellectual background." In *The Cambridge Companion to Leibniz*, edited by Nicholas Jolley, 43–66. Cambridge: Cambridge University Press, 1995.

Browning, Christopher. *Ordinary Men: Reserve Police Battalion 101 and the Final Solution in Poland*. London: Penguin, 2001.

Brunée, Jutta and Stephen J. Toope. "Slouching Towards New 'Just' Wars: The Hegemon After September 11th." *International Relations* 18, no. 4 (2004): 405–23.

Bush, George. "Open Letter to College Students on the Persian Gulf Crisis," January 9, 1991. http://frwebgate1.access.gpo.gov/cgi-bin/waisgate.cgi? WAISdocID (accessed February 22, 2007).

———. Radio Address to the Nation on National Day of Prayer, February 2, 1991. http://frwebgate1.access.gpo.gov/cgi-bin/waisgate.cgi?WAISdocID (accessed February 22, 2007).

Bush, George W. "Remarks by the President at Dedication of Oklahoma City National Memorial," Oklahoma City, Oklahoma, February 19, 2001. http://www.whitehouse.gov/news/releases/2001/02/print/20010219.html (accessed December 15, 2006).

———. "A Distinctly American Internationalism," Ronald Reagan Library, Simi Valley, California, November 19, 1999. http://www.mtholyoke.edu/ acad/ intrel/bush/wspeech.htm (accessed December 15, 2006).

———. "Statement by the President in Address to the Nation," September 11, 2001. http://www.whitehouse.gov.news/releases/2001/09/print/20010911 (accessed December 15, 2006).

———. Speech, September 12, 2001. http://www.whitehouse.gov/news/ releases/2001/09/20010912-4.html (accessed December 15, 2006).

———. "National Day of Prayer and Remembrance for the Victims of the Terrorist Attacks on September 11, 2001," September 13, 2001. http://www.whitehouse.gov/news/releases/2001/09/print/20010913 (accessed December 15, 2006).

———. "President's Remarks at National Day of Prayer and Remembrance," September 14, 2001. http://www.whitehouse.gov/news/releases/2001/09/ 20010913-2html (accessed December 15, 2006).

———. Remarks by the President on Arrival, The South Lawn, September 16, 2001. http://www.whitehouse.gov/news/releases/2001/09/print/20010916 (accessed December 15, 2006).

———. "'Islam is Peace' Says President," Remarks by the President at Islamic Center of Washington, D.C., September 17, 2001. http://www.whitehouse .gov/news/releases/2001/09/print/20010917 (accessed December 15, 2006).

———. "President Meets with Muslim Leaders." The Roosevelt Room, September 26, 2001. http://www.whitehouse.gov/news/releases/ 2001/09/ print/20010926 (accessed December 15, 2006).

————. "President Unveils Back to Work Plan." Department of Labor, Washington, D.C., October 4, 2001. http://www.whitehouse.gov/news/ releases/2001/10/print/20011004 (accessed December 15, 2006).

————. "President Directs Humanitarian Aid to Afghanistan." Remarks by the President to State Department Employees, U.S. Department of State, Washington, D.C., October 4, 2001. http://www.whitehouse.gov/news/ releases/2001/10/print/20011004.html (December 15, 2006).

————. "President Pays Tribute at Pentagon Memorial." Remarks by the President at the Department of Defense Service of Remembrance, The Pentagon, Arlington, Virginia, October 11, 2001. http://www.whitehouse .gov/news/releases/2001/10/print/20011011 (accessed December 15, 2006).

————. "America's Youth Respond to Afghan Children's Fund." October 16, 2001. http://www.whitehouse.gov/news/releases/2001/09/print/20010928, (accessed December 15, 2006.

————. "President Rallies Troops at Travis Air Force Base." Remarks by the President to Military Personnel, Travis Air Base, California, October 17, 2001. http://www.whitehouse.gov/news/releases/2001/01/print/20011017 (accessed December 15, 2006).

————. "National Character Counts Week Proclamation." October 23, 2001. http://www.whitehouse.gov/news/releases/2001/10/print/20011023 (accessed 15 December 2006).

————. "President Discusses Stronger Economy and Homeland Defense." Dixie Printing Company, Glen Burnie, Maryland, October 24, 2001. http://www.whitehouse.gov/news/releases/2001/10/print/20011024 (accessed December 15, 2006).

————. "Nigerian President Offers Solidarity to US." Remarks by President Bush and President Obasanjo of Nigeria in Photo Opportunity, The Rose Garden, November 2, 2001. http://www.whitehouse.gov/news/releases/ 2001/11/print/20011102 (accessed December 15, 2006).

————. "No Nation Can Be Neutral in this Conflict." Remarks by the President to the Warsaw Conference on Combating Terrorism, November 6, 2001. http://www.whitehouse.gov/news/releases/2001/11/print/20011106 (accessed November 15, 2006).

————. "President Shares Thanksgiving Meal with Troops." Remarks by the President to Troops and Families at Fort Campbell, Fort Campbell, Kentucky, November 21, 2001. http://www.whitehouse.gov/news/releases/ 2001/11/print/20011121.html (access December 15, 2001).

————. "President Calls on Congress to Pass Economic Security Package." Cecil I. Walker Machinery Company, Charleston, West Virginia, January 22, 2002. http://www.whitehouse.gov/news/releases/2002/01/print/20020122 (accessed December 15, 2006).

————. "President Urges Responsibility in Speech Congratulating Lakers." Remarks by the President in Welcome of the NBA Champion Los Angeles Lakers, The East Room, January 28, 2002. http://www.whitehouse.gov/news/releases/2002/01/print/20020128 (accessed December 15, 2006).

————. "State of the Union Address." January 29, 2002. http://www/whitehouse.gov/news/releases/2002/01/20020219-11.html (accessed December 15, 2006).

————. "President Asks Seniors to Get Involved in USA Freedom Corps." Daytona Beach International Airport, Daytona Beach, Florida, January 30, 2002. http://www.whitehouse.gov/news/releases/2002/01/print/20020131.htm (accessed December 15, 2006).

————. "President's Easter Message," March 27, 2002. http://www.whitehouse.gov/news/releases/2002/03/print/20020327 (accessed December 8, 2006).

————. "Remarks to First-Responders in Greenville." March 27, 2002. http://frwebgate2.access.gpo.gov/cgi-bin/waisgate.cgi?WAISdocID (accessed February 22, 2007).

————. "President Calls for Crime Victims' Rights Amendment." Robert F. Kennedy Department of Justice, Washington, D.C., April 16, 2002. http://www.whitehouse.gov/news/releases/2002/04/print/20020416.html (accessed December 8, 2006).

————. President Bush Delivers Graduation Speech at West Point United States Military Academy, West Point, June 1, 2002. http://www.whitehouse.gov/news/releases/2002/06/20020601-3.html (accessed December 15, 2006).

————. "President Discusses Nation's Critical Infrastructure." Oak Park High School, Kansas City, Missouri, June 11, 2002. http://www.whitehouse.gov/news/releases/2002/06/print/20020611 (accessed December 8, 2006).

————. "Radio Address by the President to the Nation." August 31, 2002. http://www.whitehouse.gov/news/releases/2002/08/print/20020831.html (accessed December 8, 2006).

————. "SOTU Excerpts on Defending Peace & Security at Home." January 28, 2003. http://www.whitehouse.gov/new/releases/2003/01/print/20030128 (accessed 8 December, 2006).

————. "President Honors Fallen Peace Officers at Memorial Service." Remarks by the President at Annual Peace Officers Memorial Service, Peace Officers Memorial, Washington, D.C., May 15, 2003. http://www.whitehouse.gov/news/releases/2003/05/20030515 (accessed December 8, 2006).

————. Speech from Gleneagles, July 7, 2005. https://www.cba.ca/news/background/london_bombing/bush_speech.html (accessed July 8, 2005).

————. Presidential Message: 10th Anniversary of the Massacre in Srebrenica, July 11, 2005. http://www.whitehouse.gov/news/releases/2005/07/print/20050711 (accessed December 8, 2006).

————. "President Signs H.R. 4145 to Place Statute of Rosa Parks in U.S. Capitol." Room 350, Dwight D. Eisenhower Executive Office Building, December 1, 2005. http://www.whitehouse.gov/news/releases/2005/12/print/20051201 (accessed December 8, 2006).

————. "President Signs H.R. 972, Trafficking Victims Protection Reauthorization Act." Eisenhower Executive Office Building, January 10, 2006. http://www.whitehouse.gov/news/releases/2006/01/20060110-3.html (accessed December 8, 2006).

Chalk, Frank and Kurt Jonassohn. *The History and Sociology of Genocide: Analyses and Case Studies.* New Haven, CT: Yale University Press, 1990.

Chan, Stephen. *Out of Evil: New International Politics and Old Doctrines of War.* London: I. B. Tauris, 2005.

Cicovacki, Predrag, ed. *Destined for Evil? The Twentieth-Century Responses.* Rochester, NY: University of Rochester Press, 2005.

Clendinnen, Inga. *Reading the Holocaust.* Melbourne: Text Publishing, 1998.

Clinton, William J. "The President's Radio Address." October 15, 1994. http://frwebgate4.access.gpo.gov/cgi-bin/waisgate.cgi?WAISdocID (accessed February 22, 2007).

————. "Statement on the Terrorist Bombing in Israel." January 22, 1995. http://frwebgate4.access.gpo.gov/cgi-bin/waisgate.cgi?WAISdocID (accessed February 22, 2007).

————. "Remarks at a Memorial Service for the Bombing Victims in Oklahoma City." April 23, 1995. http://frwebgate4.access.gpo.gov/cgi-bin/waisgate.cgi?WAISdocID (accessed February 22, 2007).

————. "Remarks at the National Prayer Breakfast." February 2, 1995. http://frwebgate4.access.gpo.gov/cgi-bin/waisgate.cgi?WAISdocID (accessed February 22, 2007).

————. "The President's Radio Address." April 6, 1996. http://frwebgate4.access.gpo.gov/cgi-bin/waisgate.cgi?WAISdocID (accessed February 22, 2007).

————. "The President's Radio Address and an Exchange with Reporters." July 27, 1996. http://frwebgate4.access.gpo.gov/cgi-bin/waisgate.cgi?WAISdocID (accessed February 22, 2007).

————. "Statement on the Anniversary of the Bombing of Pan American Flight 103." December 21, 1996. http://frwebgate4.access.gpo.gov/cgi-bin/waisgate.cgi?WAISdocID (accessed February 22, 2007).

————. "Remarks at the National Prayer Breakfast." February 6, 1997. http://frwebgate4.access.gpo.gov/cgi-bin/waisgate.cgi?WAISdocID (accessed February 22, 2007).

Cohen, Asher and Charlotte Wardi, eds. *Comprehending the Holocaust: Historical and Literary Research.* Frankfurt am Main: Verlag Peter Lang, 1988.

Connolly, William E. *Identity/Difference: Democratic Negotiations of Politicle Paradox.* Ithaca, NY: Cornell University Press, 1991.

Connolly, William E. "Faith, Territory and Evil." In *Modernity and the Problem of Evil*, edited by Alan D. Schrift, 132–47. Bloomington: Indiana University Press, 2005.

Daalder, Ivo and James M. Lindsay. *America Unbound: The Bush Revolution in Foreign Policy*. Hoboken, NJ: John Wiley and Sons, 2003.

Davies, Brian. Introduction to *On Evil*, by Thomas Aquinas. Translated by Richard Regan. Oxford: Oxford University Press, 2003.

Delbanco, Andrew. *The Death of Satan*. New York: Farrar Straus and Giroux, 1995.

Delbo, Charlotte. *Auschwitz and After*. New Haven, CT: Yale University Press, 1995.

Despland, Michael. *Kant on History and Religion*. Montreal: McGill-Queen's University Press, 1973.

Des Pres, Terence. *The Survivor: An Anatomy of Life in the Death Camps*. New York: Oxford University Press, 1976.

Dews, Peter. "Disenchantment and the Persistence of Evil: Habermas, Jonas, Badiou." In *Modernity and the Problem of Evil*, edited by Alan D. Schrift, 51–65. Bloomington: Indiana University Press, 2005.

Dews, Peter. "'Radical Finitude' and the Problem of Evil: Critical Comments on Wellmer's Reading of Jonas." In *Rethinking Evil: Contemporary Perspectives*, edited by Maria Pia Lara, 46–52. Berkeley: University of California Press, 2001.

Dhalla, Maneckji Nusservanji. *History of Zoroastrianism*. New York: Oxford University Press, 1938.

Dobson, Ed, and Ed Hindson. *The Fundamentalist Phenomenon: The Resurgence of Conservative Christianity*. Edited by Jerry Falwell. New York: Doubleday, 1981.

Domke, David S. *God Willing? Political Fundamentalism in the White House*. Ann Arbor, MI: Pluto Press, 2004.

Elshtain, Jean Bethke. *Augustine and the Limits of Politics*. Notre Dame, IL: Notre Dame University Press, 1995.

Erskine, Toni, ed. *Can Institutions Have Responsibilities? Collective Moral Agency and International Relations*. Basingstoke, UK: Palgrave Macmillan, 2003.

———. "Making Sense of 'Responsibility' in International Relations: Key Questions and Concepts." In *Can Institutions Have Responsibilities? Collective Moral Agency and International Relations*, edited by Toni Erskine, 1–18. Basingstoke, UK: Palgrave Macmillan, 2003.

Everett, Charles. *Jeremy Bentham*. London: Wiedenfeld and Nicholson, 1966.

Fackenheim, Emil. "Jewish Values in the Post-Holocaust Future." In *The Jewish Return into History: Reflections in the Age of Auschwitz and a New Jerusalem*. New York: Schoken Books, 1989.

Feinburg, Joel. *Problems at the Roots of Law*. Oxford: Oxford University Press, 2003.

Feldman, Ron H., ed. *Hannah Arendt, The Jew as Pariah: Jewish Identity and Politics in the Modern Age*. New York: Grove Press, 1978.

Forsyth, Neil. "The Origin of Evil: Classical or Judeo-Christian?" *Perspectives on Evil and Human Wickedness* 1, no. 1 (January 2002): 17–50.

Freddoso, Alfred J. "Suarez on God's Casual Involvement in Sinful Acts." In *The Problem of Evil in Early Modern Philosophy*, edited by Elmar J. Kremer, and Michael J. Latzer, 10–34. Toronto: University of Toronto Press, 2001.

Freud, Sigmund. *Civilization and Its Discontents: The Standard Edition*. London: Hogarth Press, 1930.

Frum, David. *The Right Man: An Inside Account of the Bush White House*. New York: Random House, 2003.

Gadamer, Hans Georg. "Man and Language." In *Philosophical Hermeneutics*, translated and edited by David E. Linge, 59–68. Berkeley: University of California Press, 1976.

———. "The Universality of the Hermeneutical Problem." In *Philosophical Hermeneutics*, translated and edited by David E. Linge, 3–17. Berkeley: University of California Press, 1976.

Gaita, Raimond. "Refocusing Genocide: A Philosophical Responsibility." In *Genocide and Human Rights: A Philosophical Guide*, by John K. Roth, 153–66. Basingstoke, UK: Palgrave Macmillan, 2005.

Gallie, W. B. "Essentially Contested Concepts." In *Philosophy and Historical Understanding*, 157–91. New York: Shocken, 1968.

Geddes. Jennifer L., ed. *Evil After Postmodernism: Histories, Narratives, and Ethics*. London: Routledge, 2001.

———. Introduction to *Evil After Postmodernism: Histories, Narratives and Ethics*, edited by Jennifer L. Geddes, 1–23. London: Routledge, 2001.

Geertz, Clifford. "Ethos, World View, and the Analysis of Sacred Symbols." In *The Interpretation of Cultures*, 126–41. New York: Basic Books, 1973.

———. "Religion as a Cultural System." In *The Interpretation of Cultures*, 87–125. New York: Basic Books, 1973.

Geivett, R. Douglas. *Evil and the Evidence for God: The Challenge of John Hick's Theodicy*. Philadelphia: Temple University Press, 1985.

Gilbert, G. M. *Nuremberg Diary*. London: Eyre and Spottiswoode, 1948.

Goldensohn, Leon. *The Nuremberg Interviews: Conversations with Defendants and Witnesses*, edited by Robert Gellately. London: Pimlico, 2007.

Gorringe, Timothy J. *Karl Barth: Against Hegemony*. Oxford: Oxford University Press, 1999.

Gourevitch, Philip. *We Wish to Inform You that Tomorrow We Will be Killed With Our Families*. London: Picador, 2000.

Gourevitch, Victor. Introduction to *The Discourses and Other Early Political Writings*, by Jean-Jacques Rousseau. Edited and translated by Victor Gourevitch, ix–xxxi. Cambridge: Cambridge University Press, 1997.

Graham, Gordon. *Evil and Christian Ethics*. Cambridge: Cambridge University Press, 2001.

Grimm, Stephen R. "Kant's Argument for Radical Evil." *European Journal of Philosophy* 10, no. 2 (2002): 160–77.

Grumett, David. "Arendt, Augustine and Evil." *The Heythrop Journal* 41 (2000): 154–69.

Haldane, John. *An Intelligent Person's Guide to Religion*. London: Duckworth, 2003.

Hare, R. M. "Pain and Evil." In *Moral Concepts*, edited by Joel Feinburg, 29–42. Oxford: Oxford University Press, 1969.

Harries, Richard. *After the Evil: Christianity and Judaism in the Shadow of the Holocaust*. Oxford: Oxford University Press, 2003.

Hegel, G. F. von. *Lecture on the Philosophy of Religion*, edited by Peter C. Hodgson, translated by R. F Brown and P. C. Hodson. Berkeley: University of California Press, 1988.

Hick, John. *Evil and the God of Love*. New York: Harper and Row, 1966.

Himmelfarb, Milton. "No Hitler, No Holocaust." *Commentary* 76, no. 3 (March 1984): 37–43.

Hirsch, Herbert. *Genocide and the Politics of Memory: Studying Death to Preserve Life*. Chapel Hill: University of North Carolina Press, 1995.

Hobart, Mark, "Is God Evil?" In *The Anthropology of Evil*, edited by David Parkin, 165–93. Oxford: Basil Blackwell, 1985.

Hoess, Rudolph. *Commandant of Auschwitz: The Autobiography of Rudolph Hoess*, translated by Constantine Fitzgibbon. London: Wiesenfeld and Nicholson, 1959.

Hoffman, Bruce. *Inside Terrorism*. London: Victor Gollancz, 1998.

Hofstadter, Albert. *Reflections on Evil*. The Lindley Lecture, University of Kansas, 1971.

Hofstadter, Richard. "The Paranoid Style in American Politics." In *The Paranoid Style in American Politics and Other Essays*. London: Jonathan Cape, 1966.

Howard, Michael. Speech, July 11, 2005. http://uk/news/yahoo/com/050711/143/fn3yb/html (accessed July 15, 2005).

Howard-Snyder, Daniel, ed. *The Evidential Argument from Evil*. Bloomington: Indiana University Press, 1996.

Hume, David. *Dialogues Concerning Natural Religion in Focus*, edited by Stanley Tweyman. London: Rouledge, 1991.

Hume, David. *An Enquiry Concerning Human Understanding*, edited by Tom C. Beauchamp. Oxford: Oxford University Press, 1999.

Irwin, Jones. "The Cruelty Beyond Cruelty: Deleuze and the Concept of Masochism." *Perspectives on Evil and Human Wickedness* 1, no. 1 (January 2002): 51–60.

Israel, Jonathan I. *Radical Enlightenment: Philosophy and the Making of Modernity 1650–1750*. Oxford: Oxford University Press, 2001.

Jeffery, Renée. "Beyond Banality? Ethical Responses to Evil in Post-September 11 International Relations." *International Affairs* 81, no. 4 (2005): 175–86.

———. *Hugo Grotius in International Thought*. New York: Palgrave Macmillan, 2006.

———. "Tradition as Invention: The 'Traditions Tradition' and the History of Ideas in International Relations." *Millennium: Journal of International Studies* 34, no. 1 (2005): 57–84.

Jeffery, Renée, and Nicholas Rengger. "Moral Evil and International Relations: Old Concepts, New Challenges?" *SAIS Review of International Affairs* 25 (2005): 3–16.

———. "Review of Gordon Graham, *Evil and Christian Ethics*." *Conversations in Religion and Theology* 3, no. 1 (May 2005): 24–42.

Johnson, Lyndon B. "Address Before a Joint Session of the Congress." November 27, 1963. http://www.presidency.ucsb.edu/ws/index.php?pid=25988&st=evil (accessed February 22, 2007).

Jonas, Hans. "Mind, Matter, and Creation: Cosmological Evidence and Cosmological Speculation." In *Mortality and Morality: A Search for the Good after Auschwitz*, edited by Lawrence Vogel. Evanston, IL: Northwestern University Press, 1996.

Jørgensen, Nina, H. B. *The Responsibility of States for International Crimes*. Oxford: Oxford University Press, 2000.

Kabalkova, Vendulka. "Towards an International Political Theology." *Millennium: Journal of International Studies* 29, no. 3 (2000): 628–83.

Kant, Immanuel. *On the Failure of All Attempted Philosophical Theodicies (1791)*. In *Kant on History and Religion*, translated by Michael Despland. Montreal: McGill-Queen's University Press, 1973.

———. *Lectures on Philosophical Theology*. Translated by Allen W. Wood and Gertrude M. Clark. Ithaca, NY: Cornell University Press, 1978.

———. "An Answer to the Question: What is Enlightenment?" (1784). In *Perpetual Peace and Other Essays*, translated by Ted Humphrey. Indianapolis, IN: Hackett Publishing, 1983.

———. *Religion Within the Boundaries of Mere Reason*. Translated and edited by Allen Wood and George di Giovanni. Cambridge: Cambridge University Press, 1998.

Kaplan, Esther. *With God on Their Side: How Christian Fundamentalists Trampled Science, Policy, and Democracy in George W. Bush's White House*. New York: The New Press, 2004.

Katz, Fred E. *Ordinary People and Extraordinary Evil: A Report on the Beguilings of Evil*. Albany: State University of New York Press, 1993.

Katz, Fred Emil. *Confronting Evil: Two Journeys*. New York: State University of New York Press, 2004.

Kekes, John. *Facing Evil*. Princeton, NJ: Princeton University Press, 1990.

———. *Moral Wisdom and Good Lives*. Ithaca, NY: Cornell University Press, 1995.

———. "The Reflexivity of Evil." *Social Philosophy and Policy* 15, no. 1 (1998): 216–32.

———. *The Roots of Evil*. Ithaca, NY: Cornell University Press, 2005.

Kelly, Joseph F. *The Problem of Evil in the Western Tradition: From the Book of Job to Modern Genetics*, Collegeville, MN: Liturgical Press, 1989.

King, William. *On the Origin of Evil*. Translated by Edmund, Lord Bishop of Carlisle. London: Faulder, 1781.

Kline, Scott. "The Culture War Gone Global: 'Family Values' and the Shape of U.S. Foreign Policy." *International Relations* 18, no. 4 (December 2004): 453–66.

Klusmeyer, Douglas and Astri Suhrke. "Comprehending 'Evil': Challenges for Law and Policy." *Ethics and International Affairs* 16, no. 1 (2002): 27–42.

Kohn, Jerome, ed. *Hannah Arendt: Essays in Understanding, 1930–1954*. New York: Harcourt, Brace, 1994.

Kohn, Jerome. "Evil and Plurality: Hannah Arendt's Way to *The Life of the Mind*." In *Hannah Arendt: Twenty Years Later*, edited by Larry May and Jerome Kohn, 147–78. Cambridge, MA: Massachusetts Institute of Technology Press, 1996.

Kraemer, David. *Responses to Suffering in Classical Rabbinic Literature*. New York: Oxford University Press, 1995.

Kremer, Elmar J., and Michael J. Latzer, eds. *The Problem of Evil in Early Modern Philosophy*. Toronto: University of Toronto Press, 2001.

Kremer, Elmar J. and Michael J. Latzer. Introduction to *The Problem of Evil in Early Modern Philosophy*, edited by Elmar J. Kremer and Michael J. Latzer, 3–9. Toronto: University of Toronto Press, 2001.

Kristeva, Julia. *Hannah Arendt*. Translated by Ross Guberman. New York: Columbia University Press, 2001.

Lambert, W. G. *Babylonian Wisdom Literature*. Oxford: Oxford University Press, 1960.

Lang, Berel. *Act and Idea in the Nazi Genocide*. Chicago: Chicago University Press, 1990.

———. "The Evil in Genocide." In *Genocide and Human Rights: A Philosophical Guide*, edited by John K. Roth, 5–17. Basingstoke, UK: Palgrave Macmillan, 2005.

Lara, Maria Pia, ed. *Rethinking Evil: Contemporary Perspectives*. Berkeley: University of California Press, 2001.

Larivière, Anthony D., and Thomas M. Lennon. "Bayle on the Moral Problem of Evil." In *The Problem of Evil in Early Modern Philosophy*, edited by Elmar J. Kremer and Michael J. Latzer, 101–18. Toronto: University of Toronto Press, 2001.

Leaman, Oliver. *Evil and Suffering in Jewish Philosophy*. Cambridge: Cambridge University Press, 1995.

Leibniz, Wilhelm Gottfried. *Theodicy: Essays on the Goodness of God, the Freedom of Man, and the Origin of Evil*. Translated by E. M. Huggard, edited by Austin Farrar. London: Routledge and Kegan Paul, 1952.

Levi, Primo. *If This Is a Man*, translated by Stuart Woolf. London: Abacus, 1987.

———. Afterword to *If This Is a Man*, translated by Ruth Feldman, and *The Truce*, translated by Stuart Woolf. London: Abacus, 1987, 381–98.

———.*The Drowned and the Saved*, translated by Raymond Rosenthal. London: Michael Joseph, 1988.

Levinas, Emmanuel. *Time and the Other*. Translated by Richard A. Cohen. Pittsburgh: Duquesne University Press, 1987.

———. "Useless Suffering." In *The Provocation of Levinas: Rethinking the Other*, edited by Robert Bernasconi and David Wood, 156–67. London: Routledge, 1988.

———. "The Paradox of Morality: An Interview with Emmanuel Levinas." In *The Provocation of Levinas: Rethinking the Other*, edited by Robert Bernasconi and David Wood, 168–80. London: Routledge, 1988.

Lewis, C. S. *A Grief Observed*. London: Faber, 1961.

———. *The Problem of Pain*. London: G. Bles, 1940.

———. *The Screwtape Letters*. London: G. Bles, 1961.

Loewy, Erich H. *Suffering and the Beneficent Community: Beyond Libertarianism*. New York: State University of New York Press, 1991.

Lu, Catherine. Editor's Introduction to *International Relations* 18, no. 4 (2004): 403–4.

Lucas, J. R. *Responsibility*. Oxford: Clarendon Press, 1993.

Macfarlane, Alan. "The Root of All Evil." In *The Anthropology of Evil*, edited by David Parkin, 57–76. Oxford: Basil Blackwell, 1985.

Mackie, J. L. "Evil and Omnipotence." *Mind* 64 (1955): 200–12.

Manne, Robert. *The Culture of Forgetting: Helen Demidenko and the Holocaust*. Melbourne: Text Publishing, 1996.

Mansfield, Stephen. *The Faith of George W. Bush*. New York: Penguin, 2003.

Mathewes, Charles T. *Evil and the Augustinian Tradition*. Cambridge: Cambridge University Press, 2001.

Matravers, Matt, ed. *Punishment and Political Theory*. Oxford: Hart Publishing, 1999.

May, Larry, and Jerome Kohn, eds. *Hannah Arendt: Twenty Years Later*. Cambridge, MA: Massachusetts Institute of Technology Press, 1996.

Maybaum, Ignaz. *The Face of God After Auschwitz.* Amsterdam: Polack and Van Gennep, 1965.

Mayerfeld, Jamie. *Suffering and Moral Responsibility.* New York: Oxford University Press, 1999.

Michalson, Gordon E. *Fallen Freedom: Kant on Radical Evil and Moral Regeneration.* Cambridge: Cambridge University Press, 1990.

Midlarsky, Manus I. *The Killing Trap: Genocide in the Twentieth Century.* Cambridge: Cambridge University Press, 2005.

Milgram, Stanley. *Obedience to Authority: An Experimental View.* London: Tavistock, 1974.

Minnow, Martha. *Between Vengeance and Forgiveness: Facing History After Genocide and Mass Violence.* Boston: Beacon Press, 1998.

Morgenthau, Hans. "The Evil of Politics and the Ethics of Evil." *Ethics: An International Journal of Social, Political and Legal Philosophy* 61, no. 1 (October 1945): 1–18.

Morton, Adam. *On Evil.* New York: Routledge, 2004.

Neiman, Susan. *Evil in Modern Thought: An Alternative History of Philosophy.* Melbourne: Scribe, 2003.

———. "Metaphysics, Philosophy: Rousseau on the Problem of Evil." In *Reclaiming the History of Ethics*, edited by Andrews Reath, Barbara Herman, and Christine M. Korsgaard, 140–69. Cambridge: Cambridge University Press, 1997.

———. "What's the Problem of Evil?" In *Rethinking Evil: Contemporary Perspectives*, edited by Maria Pia Lara, 27–45. Berkeley: University of California Press, 2001.

Newman, Leonard S., and Ralph Erber, eds. *Understanding Genocide: The Social Psychology of the Holocaust.* Oxford: Oxford University Press, 2002.

Niebuhr, Reinhold. *The Nature and Destiny of Man.* Vol. 1. London: Nisbet, 1941.

Nietzsche, Friedrich. *Beyond Good and Evil: Prelude to a Philosophy for the Future.* Translated by R. J. Hollingdale. Harmondsworth, UK: Penguin, 1990.

Nietzsche, Friedrich. *On the Genealogy of Morals: A Polemic.* Translated by Douglas Smith. Oxford: Oxford University Press, 1996.

Nino, Carlos Santiago. *Radical Evil on Trial: Reflecting on the Rwandan Genocide.* New Haven, CT: Yale University Press, 1996.

Noll, Mark. *The Old Religion in a New World.* Grand Rapids, MI: Eerdmans, 2002.

Ophir, Adi. *The Order of Evils: Toward an Ontology of Morals.* Translated by Rela Mazali and Havi Carel. New York: Zone Books, 2005.

Overing, Joanna, "There is No End of Evil: The Guilty Innocents and Their Fallible God." In *The Anthropology of Evil*, edited by David Parkin, 244–78. Oxford: Basil Blackwell, 1985.

Owen, James. *Nuremberg: Evil on Trial.* London: Headline, 2006.

Pagels, Elaine. *The Origin of Satan.* New York: Random House, 1995.

Parkin, David, ed. *The Anthropology of Evil*. Oxford: Basil Blackwell, 1985.

———. "Entitling Evil: Muslims and non-Muslims in coastal Kenya." In *The Anthropology of Evil*, edited by David Parkin, 224–43. Oxford: Basil Blackwell, 1985.

———. Introduction to *The Anthropology of Evil*, edited by David Parkin, 1–25. Oxford: Basil Blackwell, 1985.

Paul, Shalom M. "Psalm XXVII 10 and the Babylonian Theodicy." *Vetus Testamentum* 32, fasc. 4 (October 1982): 489–92.

Peake, Arthur S. *The Problem of Suffering in the Old Testament*. The Hartley Lecture Delivered to the Primitive Methodist Conference in Carr's Lane Chapel, Birmingham, June 8, 1904. London: Robert Bryant, 1904.

Phillips, Kevin. *American Theocracy: The Peril and Politics of Radical Religion, Oil, and Borrowed Money in the 21st Century*. New York: Penguin, 2006.

Philpott, Daniel. "The Religious Roots of Modern International Relations." *World Politics* 52, no. 2 (2000): 206–45.

Pippen, Robert B. "Hannah Arendt and the Bourgeois Origins of Totalitarian Evil." In *Modernity and the Problem of Evil*, edited by Alan D. Schrift, 148–66. Bloomington: Indiana University Press, 2005.

Plantinga, Alvin. *God, Freedom, and Evil*. London: Allen and Unwin, 1975.

Plantinga, Alvin. "Self-Profile." In *Alvin Plantinga*, edited by James E. Tomberlin and Peter Van Inwagen. Dordrecht: D. Reidel Publishing, 1985.

Plotinus, *Six Enneades*. Translated Stephen Mackenna and B. S. Page. https://ccat.upenn.edu/jod/texts/plotinus (accessed October 27, 2004).

Pocock, David. "Unruly Evil." In *The Anthropology of Evil*, edited by David Parkin, 42–56. Oxford: Basil Blackwell, 1985.

Pojman, Louis P. *Terrorism, Human Rights, and the Case for World Government*. Lanham: Rowman and Littlefield, 2006.

Pope John Paul II. Apostolic Letter, *Salvifici Doloris, "On the Christian Meaning of Suffering."* February 11, 1984.

Power, Samantha. "Hannah Arendt's Lesson." *New York Review of Books* 51, no. 7 (April 29, 2004).

Reagan, Ronald. "Address to Members of the British Parliament," June 8, 1982. http://www.reagan.utexas.edu/archives/speeches/1982/60882.htm (accessed February 22, 2007).

———. "Remarks at the Annual Convention of the National Association of Evangelicals in Orlando, Florida." March 8, 1983. http://www.reagan.utexas.edu/archives/speeches/1983/30883.htm (accessed February 22, 2007).

Reardon, Bernard M. G. *Kant as Philosophical Theologian*. Basingstoke, UK: Macmillan, 1988.

Reichenbach, Bruce. "Natural Evils and Natural Laws: A Theodicy for Natural Evils." *International Philosophical Quarterly* 14, no. 2 (June 1976): 179–96.

Ricoeur, Paul. *The Symbolism of Evil*, translated by E. Buchanan. Boston: Beacon Press, 1967.

Rome Statute of the International Criminal Court. http://www.un.org/law/icc/statute/99_corr/3.htm (accessed March 22, 2007).

Rose, Gillian. *Mourning Becomes the Law: Philosophy and Representation.* Cambridge: Cambridge University Press, 1997.

Rosenbaum, Ron. *Explaining Hitler: The Search for the Origins of his Evil.* New York: Macmillan, 1998.

Roth, John K. *Genocide and Human Rights: A Philosophical Guide.* Basingstoke, UK: Palgrave Macmillan, 2005.

Rousseau, Jean-Jacques. *The Discourses and Other Early Political Writings.* Edited and translated by Victor Gourevitch. Cambridge: Cambridge University Press, 1997.

———. *Émile.* Translated by Barbara Foxley. London: Dent, 1955.

———. *The First and Second Discourses Together with the Replies to Critics and Essay on the Origin of Language.* Edited and translated by Victor Gourevitch. New York: Harper and Row, 1986.

———. "Letter from J. J. Rousseau to M. de Voltaire, 18 August 1756." In *The Discourses and Other Early Political Writings*, edited and translated by Victor Gourevitch, 223–28. Cambridge: Cambridge University Press, 1997.

———. "Observations by Jean-Jacques Rousseau of Geneva: On the Answer made to his Discourse." In *The Discourses and other early political writings*, edited and translated by Victor Gourevitch, 32–51. Cambridge: Cambridge University Press, 1997.

Rowe, William L. "Evil and Theodicy." *Philosophical Topics* 16, no. 2 (Fall 1988): 119–32.

———. "The Problems of Evil and Some Varieties of Atheism." *American Philosophical Quarterly* 16, no. 4 (October 1979): 335–41.

Rubenstein, Richard L. *After Auschwitz: Radical Theology and Contemporary Judaism.* Indianapolis: Bobbs-Merrill, 1966.

Rubenstein, Richard L. and John K. Roth. *Approaches to Auschwitz: The Holocaust and Its Legacy.* Louisville, KY: Westminster John Knox Press, 2003.

Russell, Jeffrey Burton. *The Prince of Darkness.* Ithaca, NY: Cornell University Press, 1988.

Sanders, James A. "Suffering as Divine Discipline in the Old Testament and Post-Biblical Judaism." *Colgate Rochester Divinity School Bulletin* 29 (1955).

Scarre, Geoffrey. *After Evil: Responding to Wrongdoing.* Aldershot, UK: Ashgate, 2004.

Schabas, William A. *An Introduction to the International Criminal Court.* 2nd ed. Cambridge: Cambridge University Press, 2004.

Schelling, F. W. J. *Schelling on Human Freedom.* Translated by James Gutmann. Chicago: Open Court, 1936.

Schmid, Alex P. *Political Terrorism: A Research Guide*. New Brunswick, NJ: Transaction Books, 1984.

Schopenhauer, Arthur. *On the Suffering of the World*. Translated by R. J. Hollingworth. London: Penguin, 1970.

———. "On the Vanity and Suffering of Life." In *The World as Will and Idea*, translated by R. B. Haldane and J. Kemp. London: Kegan Paul, 1909.

Schrift, Alan D., ed. *Modernity and the Problem of Evil*. Bloomington: Indiana University Press, 2005.

Sereny, Gitta. *Into That Darkness: An Examination of Conscience*. London: Picador, 1974.

Shantall, Teria. *Life's Meaning in the Face of Suffering: Testimonies of Holocaust Survivors*. Jerusalem: The Hebrew University Magnes Press, 2002.

Shapiro, Michael J. *Language and Political Understanding: The Politics of Discursive Practices*. New Haven, CT: Yale University Press, 1981.

Shklar, Judith N. *Ordinary Vices*. Cambridge, MA: The Belknap Press of Harvard University Press, 1984.

Singer, Peter. *The President of Good and Evil: The Ethics of George W. Bush*. New York: Dutton, 2004.

Simon, Thomas W. "Genocide, Evil, and Injustice: Competing Hells." In *Genocide and Human Rights: A Philosophical Guide*, by John K. Roth, 65–77. Basingstoke, UK: Palgrave Macmillan, 2005.

Sontag, Frederick. "How Should Genocide Affect Philosophy?" In *Genocide and Human Rights: A Philosophical Guide*, by John K. Roth, 29–34. Basingstoke: Palgrave Macmillan, 2005.

Sontag, Susan. *On Photography*. London: Allen Lane, 1977.

———. *Regarding the Pain of Others*. London: Penguin, 2003.

Spinoza, Benedict. *Ethics*, edited and translated by G. H. R. Parkinson. Oxford: Oxford University Press, 2000.

Staub, Ervin. *The Roots of Evil: The Origins of Genocide and Other Group Violence*. Cambridge: Cambridge University Press, 1989.

Strozier, Charles B. *Apocalypse: On the Psychology of Fundamentalism in America*. Boston: Beacon Press, 1994.

Stump, Eleonore. "Aquinas on the Sufferings of Job." In *The Evidential Argument from Evil*, edited by Daniel Howard-Snyder. Bloomington: Indiana University Press, 1996.

Surin, Kenneth. *Theology and the Problem of Evil*. Oxford: Blackwell, 1986.

Tertullian. *Adversus Marcionem*. Edited by Ernest Evans. Oxford: Oxford University Press, 1972.

Thomas, Scott M. "Faith, History, and Martin Wight: The Role of Religion in the Historical Sociology of the English School of International Relations." *International Affairs* 77, no. 4 (October 2001): 905–29.

————. *The Global Resurgence of Religion and the Transformation of International Relations: The Struggle for the Soul of the Twenty-First Century.* New York: Palgrave Macmillan, 2005.

Todorov, Tzvetan. "Ordinary People and Extraordinary Vices." In *Destined for Evil? The Twentieth Century Responses*, edited by Predrag Cicovacki, 119–31. Rochester, NY: University of Rochester Press, 2005.

Toope, Stephen, and Jutta Brunnée. "Slouching Towards New 'Just' Wars: The Hegemon after September 11th." *International Relations* 18, no. 4 (2004): 405–23.

True, Michael. "Evil as Mystery: Primal Speech and Contemporary Poetry." In *Destined for Evil? The Twentieth Century Responses*, edited by Predrag Cicovacki, 241–47. Rochester, NY: University of Rochester Press, 2005.

Truman, Harry S. "Broadcast to the American People Announcing the Surrender of Germany." May 8, 1945. http://www.trumanlibrary.org/calendar/viewpapers .php?pid=34 (accessed December 15, 2006).

Truman, Harry S. "Radio Address to the American People After the Signing of the Terms of Unconditional Surrender by Japan." September 1, 1945. http:// www.trumanlibrary.org/calendar/viewpapers.php?pid=129, (accessed February 22, 2007).

————. "Address in Harlem, New York, Upon Receiving the Franklin Roosevelt Award." October 29, 1948. http://www.trumanlibrary.org/publicpapers/ index.php?pid=2016 (accessed February 22, 2007).

————. "Annual Message to the Congress on the State of the Union." January 8, 1951. http://www.trumanlibrary.org/whistlestop/tap/1815.htm, (accessed February 22, 2007).

United Nations, Report of the Panel on United Nations Peacekeeping Operations, A.55.305, S/2000/809, August 21, 2000, paragraph 50. http://www.un.org/ peace/reports/peace_operations (accessed March 22, 2007).

Villa, Dana R. "The Banality of Philosophy: Arendt on Heidegger and Eichmann." In *Hannah Arendt: Twenty Years Later*, edited by Larry May and Jerome Kohn, 179–96. Cambridge, MA: Massachusetts Institute of Technology Press, 1996.

————. *Politics, Philosophy, Terror: Essays on the Thought of Hannah Arendt.* Princeton, NJ: Princeton University Press, 1999.

Vogel, Lawrence, ed. *Mortality and Morality: A Search for the Good after Auschwitz.* Evanston, IL: Northwestern University Press, 1996

Voltaire. *Candide.* Edited by Haydn Mason. London: Bristol Classical Press, 1995.

Waddell, Terrie. Introduction to *Cultural Expressions of Evil and Wickedness: Wrath, Sex and Crime*, edited by Terrie Waddell. Amsterdam: Rodopi, 2003.

Weil, Simone. *Gravity and Grace.* London: Routledge, 1952.

Wiesel, Elie. "Some Questions That Remain Open." In *Comprehending the Holocaust: Historical and Literary Research*, edited by Asher Cohen and Charlotte Wardi, 9–20. Frankfurt am Main: Verlag Peter Lang, 1988.

———. "Trivializing Memory." In *From the Kingdom of Memory: Reminiscences.* New York: Simon and Schuster, 1990.

———. *Night.* Translated by Marion Wiesel. New York: Hill and Wang, 2006.

Wilcox, Clyde. *God's Warriors: The Christian Right in Twentieth-Century America.* Baltimore: Johns Hopkins University Press, 1992.

Winton, Thomas D. "The Babylonian Theodicy." *Documents from Old Testament Times*, 97–103. New York: Harper, 1961.

Wood, Allen. *Kant's Ethical Thought.* New York: Cambridge University Press, 1999.

Yancey, Philip. *Where Is God When It Hurts?* Grand Rapids, MI: Zondervan, 1997.

Yandell, Keith E. "The Problem of Evil and the Content of Morality." *International Journal for Philosophy of Religion* 17 (1985): 139–65.

Young, James E. *Writing and Representing the Holocaust: Narrative and the Consequences of Interpretation.* Bloomington: Indiana University Press, 1988.

Index

Bold numbers indicate a detailed discussion of the topic.